Writes of Passage: Writing Through the Seasons of Your Life
https://www.amazon.com/dp/B08M8HF97H

My copy of *Writes of Passage* is full of annotations and highlighting. I found something new to think about each time I read a section or worked on one of the writing or art exercises. In the margins, I ask questions of myself, "Who am I as a writer?" and I ask questions of the author, e.g., "Is there another way to look at it?" While reading the myths and stories, I recorded my "Aha!" moments: on one page, "...a reclaiming of one's own skin, claiming a new life and place in the world" and on another, "on a journey, the dragons *are* the lessons!" To read, think, and write about life's passages using Marjorie St. Clair's text as a workbook is to open a door of self-discovery.

...Andi Penner

Everyone has a story to tell. If you want to write your memoir or simply leave your life story for your children and grandchildren, this book will get you started and take you places you hadn't thought of or barely imagined! You'll get to dive into some great art projects besides developing your writing skills.

... Gina T. Ogorzaly

A SOUTHERN BELLE IN PARIS

Bikinis, Bombs, de Beauvoir & Billy Bob

Marjorie B. St. Clair

ISBN: 979-8-218-05012-2

Earth Muse Press
2000 Aina Mahi'ai St.
Lahaina, Maui, 96761

OTHER BOOKS
BY MARJORIE ST. CLAIR

Wild Women Write: Re-Connecting with the Wild Feminine
https://www.amazon.com/dp/1080022953

Wild Women Write, is a spiraling gyre of masterfully arranged excursions into a uniquely beneficial constellation of writing exercises inspired by first visiting one of our many psychologically powerful archetypes. Coupled in this manner, the creative lessons serve to draw you closer to your own source of pure creativity, which is so necessary in a writer's quest to obtain clarity of message, without the pretense of intent. This fine work is a marvelous tool for diving into the archetypal depths of the self, disguised as the great author's assistant that it is!

...Sonya Blaydes

Wild Women Write is a necessary resource for women or anyone for that matter who wants to explore a deeper understanding of the feminine and how it relates to you. As an artist, this book helped to boost my creativity and self-knowledge. The exercises made me question, connect, and expand on ideas in a completely different way. While I may have written about angry characters in my past creative projects, this book helped me to explore them in a more personal way. As artists when we are writing or creating a work of art, we are very present in each aspect of the work we create. Our work represents our psyche. While I learned something from each chapter—chapter 7 *Wild Flesh and The Myth of Feminine Evil* and chapter 8 *Sacred Sexuality: Reverence for All Life* are my favorites. I found myself reflecting on these chapters often when working on my current story. Thank you, Ms. St Clair, your book is amazing.

... Dunya Moss

WITH GRATITUDE

To all women who have risked taking a bite of the forbidden apple and dared to live free...

And to all men who followed them in love and with awe

"One of the best things that ever happened to me is that I'm a woman. That is the way all females should feel."

...Marilyn Monroe

"Life is short. Break the Rules. Forgive quickly. Kiss slowly. Love truly. Laugh uncontrollably. And never regret ANYTHING that makes you smile."

...Mark Twain

"What is the knowledge of freedom?" Thomas Merton asked a Buddhist abbot, to which the abbot replied, "One must ascend all the steps, but then when there are no more steps, one must make the leap. Knowledge of freedom is the knowledge, the experience, of this leap."

...Thomas Merton, From Merton, A Biography by Monica Furlong

"Upon such sacrifices, my Cordelia,
The Gods themselves throw incense."

...Shakespeare, King Lear

"To Discover who she is, a woman must descend to her own depths. She must leave the safe role of remaining a faithful daughter of the collectives around her and descend to her individual feeling values ... a woman must trust the places of darkness where she can meet her own deepest nature and give it voice."

...Judith Duerk, Circle of Stones: Woman's Journey to Herself

AUTHOR'S NOTE

For writing this book, I relied on my journals, letters, and researched facts as well as my own memory and recollection of events. I changed the names for most of the people in the book to protect their privacy except those belonging to public figures or well-known persons.

FORWARD

It takes courage and emotional stamina to look back on your life. Beating myself up over mistakes, and there were many, is not what I was after in this book. Nor did I wish to place blame on anyone else or any circumstance for choices I made. Rather, I came to the page in writing this story with a curiosity about my younger self in an earlier time. What was she up to and why? What helped her when she fell down and who urged her to stand up again? How did being raised in the South and being a Southern Belle influence her early choices? What was it like to be a young sensitive, idealist girl raised inside an impenetrable belief system of fundamentalist Christianity and a culture rooted in racism?

What did it take to break free and learn to see life and others in the world from a more inclusive perspective, one that not only accepted differences but came to see their beauty as an integral part of an unfathomable creation orchestrated by a Divine Intelligence?

For me, looking back and remembering how slow I was in recognizing my flaws and taking actions to self-correct them has been a humbling and sometimes painful journey. The reward has been in the honoring of the magnitude of the journey undertaken and forms the book's narrative.

May everyone who reads this beginning part of my life's journey be blessed in the recognition and appreciation of their own journey. May we all move forward to a greater consciousness that love is all there is.

TABLE OF CONTENTS

PART THREE

A SOUTHERN BELLE IN PARIS

Bikinis, Bombs, de Beauvoir & Billy Bob

Marjorie B. St. Clair

PART ONE

PART ONE

RADIOACTIVE FALLOUT

"She's not breathing!" Saren said with alarm, picking up our infant daughter struggling to get her breath.

"Should we take her to the hospital again?" I frantically asked.

At four months old, our newborn had begun to suffer shortness of breath and was having difficulty nursing. These terrifying episodes were increasing and she was losing weight.

It was a short drive, only a few blocks to the small island clinic where we had rushed baby Marie numerous times over the past several months. We knew the routine at the clinic; knew that they would place her inside an oxygen tent to regulate and stabilize her breathing; knew that the one doctor on the island would again have no idea what the problem was; knew that we would continue to be frightened to be thousands of miles away from any substantial medical care and most frightening of all, knew that our daughter's condition was worsening.

"I'm afraid we're going to have to air-evacuate your baby to Tripler Army Hospital in Honolulu as soon as we can arrange passage on a military air transport plane. I've done all I can here at the clinic," said a concerned Dr. Jenkins, who had delivered our baby. "We just don't have the equipment to do the extensive testing she needs to determine the cause of her continued breathing difficulties."

Within a few days my baby and I were aboard a huge C-47 military transport plane designed to transport large equipment, cargo and military troops on an emergency evacuation flight of 2,400 miles from the island of Kwajalein in the Marshall Islands to the Army Hospital on Oahu, Hawaii. The roar inside the huge aircraft was deafening and instead of individual seats, the few other passengers and myself were buckled into metal seating that wrapped around the hull of the aircraft. An Army ambulance met us at the military airport and several enlisted men gathered baby, luggage and me, rushing us to Tripler Army Hospital where a medical team of specialists and pediatricians were waiting to see Marie. "She'll be placed in isolation until we can find out what's wrong," a brusque young pediatrician informed me as the team began their examination.

"We've arranged for you to have a room on the floor near the children's ward so you can visit and have time with your daughter while we do a battery of tests to find out what she may be allergic to," he continued.

As he took Marie from my arms, now crying and frantically struggling for each breath, his arms brushed against my breasts and as I caught his glance, I saw that his mouth was curled into a grin. Startled, I pulled back in disbelief but wasn't sure how to respond to his disrespectful, inappropriate behavior and flirtatious stares that continued throughout the examination. My Southern Belle upbringing had prepared me to smile and be nice no matter the situation. But how was I supposed to be nice to a man who should be focusing on my baby, not flirting with me? A woman standing up for herself, speaking out, defending herself whether justified or not, didn't exist in the world I'd been raised in. That was the man's job ... to protect the woman.

Here in this hospital, I knew no one. I felt alone. Who was going to protect me now? In time I would learn that all military wives experience being alone, sometimes for years at a time when their husbands left for wars and tours of duty in far-away countries. Although newly married, I had already spent six months alone with our newborn son Alex before joining my soldier husband on his assignment to the island of Kwajalein in the South Pacific.

"My baby needs all the attention you can give her doctor," I said sternly, my face flushed with anger.

Fatigued but relieved when the initial medical exam was completed, I left baby Marie with the medical staff and followed one of the enlisted men who showed me to my room. He'd driven the ambulance that had picked us up at the airport and was about my age, early twenties, friendly and kind, something I needed very badly since communication with Kwajalein Island was only possible by ham-radio. No phones and of course no Internet. I fretted about not being able to share what was going on with my husband Saren and felt alone in the scary situation with our baby daughter. I knew I needed to keep it together for her sake, but I was terrified. She was so sick and no one knew why. The young soldier seemed to sense my terror, maybe he'd seen combat, he never said, but he made it a point to check in on me regularly throughout my hospital stay and I was very grateful for his friendship.

Built on a ridge overlooking Honolulu, the pink-colored Tripler Army Hospital was the largest treatment facility in the Pacific Rim and was situated only a short distance from the beautiful Waikiki Beach. One of the empty hospital clinics near my room had a lanai with a view of the beach in the distance. I'd often go and sit in one of the chaise lounge chairs, trying my best to relax in between visits with baby Marie who within a few days was gradually improving since the doctors had stopped her nursing and put her on a soy-based formula.

I closed my eyes to enjoy the cool tropical breeze, which felt so good on my face, eyes red and puffy from crying, but my breasts ached from having stopped nursing so suddenly even though I was taking several hot showers a day for relief. How was it possible that my baby was allergic to my milk? It just didn't make any sense.

As I looked out to the beautiful Waikiki beach in the distance, I remembered how I had desperately wanted to leave home my entire four years of high school, had wanted to be grown up and be out on my own, making my own decisions, but now I had been married for two years, had birthed two babies, and life at age twenty-one was coming at me fast and furious and I was struggling to keep up. I was so happy I had married an older man; someone mature who knew so much about the world, and someone I could lean on. Remembering how we'd met and overcome all the drama resulting from our cultural and religious differences was reassuring. But meeting and marrying Saren seemed like decades ago.

Suddenly, I was startled when the offending pediatrician walked through the door to the lanai. How had he discovered my secret retreat space?

"What are you doing here?" I demanded.

"I work here as you may know," he answered sarcastically. "Seriously, I just wanted to check on you."

"Well, as you can see, I'm fine. Now you can go, please."

"Why are you being so unfriendly to me," he asked defensively, as though I had wronged him.

"Look, I think you know you behaved inappropriately during my baby's first check-up and you've been flirting with me ever since then. You should be apologizing to me." I said, getting up and walking over to the railing along the lanai to put some distance between us. He followed and stood next to me.

"Yes. You're right and I apologize. Now can we be friends?"

"Friends? I don't even know you. My only concern is that you take care of my baby." He moved his body closer until it was touching mine.

"Please don't stand so close. You're making me nervous," I pleaded in my most pleasant lady-like manner, while moving away again. Though I imagined myself to be an adult possessing a certain amount of maturity and sophistication; in truth I embodied the archetype of a bona fide Southern Belle, someone thoroughly trained in the feminine arts of "make nice" and be pleasant in your demeanor and conversation, whatever the situation. Nothing in this training helped a young girl respect herself, or consider her own needs or give her any confidence to function successfully in the world without a man at her side. Like the young heroine Scarlet O'Hara in the classic novel *Gone With the Wind*, had advised, a Southern young lady would have to learn to become a manipulator to get what she wanted or she would forever be a passive spectator to her life, never daring to challenge the rules for fear of the consequences.

"I find you extremely attractive," he said, ignoring my request to move away from me.

I couldn't believe his lack of respect and arrogance. "I'm leaving now."

As I turned to go, he grabbed me and kissed me directly on the mouth. I pulled away and slapped him, stunning him and myself. I quickly ran from the lanai and down the corridor to my room.

Shaking, I locked the door behind me and threw myself on the bed, dissolving into tears. I wanted so desperately to talk to Saren, to have him reassure me that everything was going to be all right. I knew I had done nothing to encourage the doctor's predatory behavior towards me. All I could think about was my baby regaining her health and getting back home.

After the episode on the lanai of the kiss followed by the slap, the doctor kept his distance and was very cool and professional anytime he and the team of doctors met with me to discuss baby Marie's condition. After more than two weeks of care, her breathing had returned to normal and I was given the okay to leave the hospital. Her final diagnosis: *severe allergies to mother's milk and numerous other allergies including possibly, to the island's coral dust.* The doctors had advised that she stay permanently on the soybean milk formula and that I discontinue any future nursing.

Once we were back on Kwajalein, I never mentioned the pediatrician's inappropriate behavior to Saren because baby Marie was okay now and that's all that mattered. Sadly, I had no sense of having been the victim of sexual misconduct.

Had my mother been right in worrying about our health and access to good medical care in so remote a region or was there more to it than our remote location? I would soon come face to face with the dire consequences of the U.S. military's past actions in the Marshall Islands that would help me to not only understand why my daughter was allergic to my mother's milk, but also why babies born to native islanders exposed to radioactive fallout were born deformed.

How was being a Southern Belle from a small town in Georgia coloring my experience in the remote region of Micronesia? What exactly was a Southern Belle and did such an identity with its strict rules and instructions, give me the skills and understanding necessary to live my best life?

"I FEEL PRETTY"

...from musical *West Side Story*

Is there anything to the notion of a Southern Belle or is it simply an archetype popularized by such female characters as Scarlett O'Hara and Melanie Wilkes in the novel of the Ante-bellum South, *Gone with the Wind*?

One could say that the creation of a Southern Belle archetype emerged fairly recently in historical times. For a girl growing up in the South, being pretty and catering to men had roots as far back as the 1800s, decades before the Civil War. In the period known as the Ante-Bellum South, respectable women from the wealthy class began to present themselves with a particular look. "The look" for the Belle, a French word meaning beautiful, meant she would always walk underneath a parasol to ensure not a ray of sun would darken her fair skin; a hoop skirt, hat and gloves and a whale-bone corset to slim her waist to under 20 inches. A Southern Belle became the epitome of a genteel woman. She would have received classes in proper locution, meaning how to speak in a pleasing manner; how to write in a beautiful handwriting style for all those proper invitations to balls and receptions she'd be writing in her own delicate hand. She'd also possess a reasonably good singing voice or the ability to play a few religious hymns on the piano ... these were the minimum qualifications to insure her being a desirable candidate for marriage to someone of good-standing and with good prospects of acquiring more wealth.

Of course, a Southern Belle had to be from a monied family and would be expected to marry someone of her own social standing. That's what the debutante balls all Southern Belles attended were all about. It was at such gala events where girls would be paraded out, or presented, as prized objects, desirable and ready for marriage to a suitable suitor. Surprisingly, or not, these debutante balls, or Cotillions, are still practiced in the South today. Although the contemporary focus is to give to or support a charity dear to the hearts of the girls, the quintessential Southern Belle and being a "deb" has survived. Today, there are even ways that young women who aren't from money can be invited to these societal affairs of the wealthy, giving the appearance of equality.

******

In the 50s and 60s when I was growing up, the only vestiges remaining of debutantes and social balls were in the older pre-Civil War towns such as Macon, Savannah and Atlanta. My hometown wasn't even a town until after WWII when the Air Force built an air base and the town grew up around it. It was a town of working class and middle-class folks. None of us girls called ourselves, or were referred to by others, as Southern Belles. There were no debutante balls or cotillions; rather, we were just girls wanting to wear lipstick, get our ears pierced and own a record player so we could play our 45 rpm records of our favorite pop singers.

As quaint or ridiculous as these ideas might seem now about women and Southern Belles and the whole rigamarole around getting a good man to marry you, I want to be clear: to a good number of Southern folks, these still carry a lot of sway and the popular debutante balls of the past are still a "thing." Being a pretty, sweet girl mattered a long time ago and to some, it still does. In the year of our Lord, nineteen hundred and sixty, it mattered a lot to me.

By the time I was a senior in high school in 1960, I had entered and been a finalist in several local beauty contests, setting me firmly onto one of only several paths that pretty, white Southern girls were allowed to follow: wife, mother, or teacher.

The path for me to become an even more widely recognizable beauty queen began one day when the phone rang and it was Mr. Baker, owner of the largest local bank and real estate business in our small town. "Miss Beene, I'm calling to ask if you would consider running as a contestant in the Miss Warner Robins Beauty Pageant coming up soon. If you're a winner," he said with a hint of excitement, "it means you'll be a participant in the Miss Georgia Pageant, and if you win there, then you'll go on to the Miss America Beauty Pageant!"

After a short pause, he cleared his throat and continued, "We'll be your sponsors and pay all your expenses. If this sounds like anything you'd be interested in, drop by the bank and let's talk about it."

"Why, this is a big surprise Mr. Baker," I said hardly breathing. "I'll have to ask my parents but I'm sure they'll think it's all right," I said in the rather cheery conciliatory tone required of a well-mannered young Southern girl. The moment I placed the phone receiver down, I was so excited I ran to the den and hugged mother, something completely out of the ordinary since we were a family that didn't give hugs and took pride in not giving hugs. It was considered vulgar behavior.

******

Once I had agreed to be a contestant in the Chamber of Commerce's sponsored *Miss Warner Robins Beauty Pageant* and signed on with the Bank of Warner Robins as my sponsor, the real work began. Gowns, swimsuits, choosing a talent, getting a chaperon, hair, make-up, rehearsals ... it was an all-consuming effort, especially since I was also a high school senior with all its many related activities and commitments. All of this activity practically insured I would break out in hives, fulfilling mother's ongoing critical observation that I was too sensitive about everything.

When the night of the beauty pageant finally arrived, I sang my heart out for my talent, answered ubiquitous questions from the judges, modeled evening gown and swimsuit and competed with twelve other pretty young girls, some in college or careers, and was declared the winner of the *Miss Warner Robins Beauty Pageant* to the acclaim of everyone; everyone but my mother, that is. When asked by my chaperon after the contest, "What do you think of your daughter winning *Miss Warner Robins*, Mrs. Beene?" had replied, "Frankly, I was surprised she won. I thought Sarah Nelson would win."

Although my chaperon had fallen into a stunned silence at mother's answer, I wasn't surprised at her response since she'd always been very forthright with her critical assessments of me. But her critical remark didn't lessen the feeling of bliss I'd had when the judges announced me the winner, when the crown was placed on my head by the former *Miss Warner Robins*, when the massive bouquet of flowers was placed in my arms, and when I took the winner's walk down the runway to greet the audience as the new *Miss Warner Robins*. Truthfully, it was as amazing to me as it had been to my mother that I had been named the winner.

Still, mother was my mother and I kind of thought she'd root for me and say some supporting, encouraging things, but that wasn't who she was. She felt it was her duty to be critical of me so that I wouldn't think too highly of myself ... at least that's what she told me decades later when we began to see and respect each other as two individuals who had made different life choices. In spite of mother being my worst critic and a "here let me rain on your parade" kind of person, she had washed and ironed my clothes, shined my shoes and generally helped keep my wardrobe together for the pageant. Did she do all those things to insure I would be a flawless reflection of her and our respectable family? Maybe. I was pretty sure it wasn't because she was proud of me; although years later after she died, her friends told me she had always been over-the-moon proud of me. Eventually, I came to think that what it came down to was that she'd been living her life vicariously through mine, seeing me as having a life of opportunities she'd never had, the story of so many women of her era who literally had no life choices beyond wife and mother.

I'd won quite a number of prizes in the *Miss Warner Robins Pageant*, including money that would go towards funding college. I was now the "face" of the city and I "belonged" to them, which most of the time I thought was utterly wonderful; however, it was becoming obvious that I did have a few kinks in my Southern Belle wiring that might interfere with my performing well long-term.

One problem besides my too vivid imagination, so I was told, was my too inquisitive mind that led to my asking too many questions. For a Southern Belle, asking too many questions was a gigantic flaw that would need correcting. There was one exception. When going out on a date, girls were told they should write down a few questions to ask their date about things he liked because that would keep him interested in you because you were interested in everything about him; you were to keep the paper in your compact, which a girl always carried in her purse and could pull out at a moment's notice when she needed to ask him more things about himself; and very importantly, a girl should never be better than her date at anything or know more things about things than he did! Those were the rules. It was all about being pleasing to the boy and making him feel important.

Another troubling revelation in my Southern Belle persona was discovering that I really didn't like the limelight all that much. I didn't like being looked at; at least not in the way that was required when you were competing in a beauty contest. Who in their right mind would want to parade around in their swimsuit, or an evening gown for that matter, and have people, mostly males, judge you and your looks? It was a shocking revelation for a beauty queen to make, especially when she was getting ready to compete in the *Miss Georgia Beauty Pageant* and possibly leading to participating in the *Miss American Beauty Contest*!

When Natalie, my chaperon, and I sat out for Columbus, Georgia where the pageant was being held, we had several suitcases of clothes and shoes, plus, three evening gowns covered in plastic and laid out flat in the back seat so they wouldn't wrinkle. I just hoped I wouldn't break out in hives from all the nervousness I was feeling, something that I'd already done a few weeks earlier.

During the weeklong *Miss Georgia Beauty Pageant* in Columbus, the thirty or more contestants from throughout Georgia ate every meal with different judges. We dressed up or dressed down to fit the occasion, and of course, all the while tried to impress a variety of people we'd never met before and would probably never meet again, that we were wonderful and deserved to be chosen as the next *Miss Georgia*. Through it all I told the same contrived but well-meaning, sincere stories about wanting to help others and smiled until my jaws literally hurt. But I was genuinely thrilled to be there and considered myself one of the luckiest girls in the world. Most of all, I wanted my family, friends and hometown to be proud of me.

Several days into the contest, rumors began to fly that the pageant was "fixed." One day while waiting backstage to go on for an evening gown competition, I innocently protested to one of the media photographers in the only way a Southern Belle could protest, with sweet words dripping like honey from her bright red lips.

"Some of us have been wondering," I cooed, "why y'all are only taking photos of certain girls? I mean, well, what I mean is, why don't y'all take some pictures of the rest of us girls so we can get our photos in the newspapers, too. It would mean so much to us. It really would!"

Spontaneously, I grabbed a single rose from a vase sitting on a nearby table, stuck it between my teeth, flung my arm behind my head and, *voila,* a provocative Carmen, posed and ready for her photo to be taken. Snap went the flash bulb! The next day, on the front page of the *Atlanta Journal*, there I was, front and center in a large photograph, rose clinched between my smiling teeth, with a caption underneath claiming, *Miss Warner Robins, Marjorie Beene, chided photographers to take her photo while alleging they were only taking photos of certain girls in the contest.*

Truth or not, there would certainly be no *Miss Georgia* title for me. I had broken rule number one, two and three: *Always Do as You're Told, Make Nice,* and *Thou Shalt Not Ask Questions.* I was disappointed that the PR I'd gotten wasn't the kind I'd wanted and worried I'd let a lot of people down who had worked hard to help me do well in the pageant. True, cards and telegrams from fellow classmates and others from the community had poured in the entire week I was in Columbus competing for the title of Miss Georgia and had helped me to get through the grueling, non-stop performances of talent, swimsuit and evening dress events as well as dinners and other public and televised appearances for which we were being judged every moment.

After the pageant was over and *Miss Atlanta*, whom the rumors had said would win, was crowned *Miss Georgia*, all we contestants were packing to go home when one of the judges, a professional musician in the Atlanta Symphony, still dressed in his stylish suit and tie, approached me.

"*Miss Warner Robins.* I want to apologize," he said with a pained look on his face.

"Apologize for what, sir?" I asked, puzzled as to his meaning.

"All the judges and I thought you'd be voted *Miss Congeniality* by the other contestants and since we wanted to spread the awards among as many girls as possible to dissolve any rumors that the pageant might have been fixed," he said delicately, "we deliberately didn't vote you as number one in the talent segment of the contest."

I stared at him in disbelief, tears welling up in my eyes. "I don't know what to say," I mumbled. "You thought I was the most talented?"

"I just wanted you to know how sorry I am, how sorry we all are," he said, lightly touching his hand to my shoulder. "Your oboe solo was absolutely outstanding," he added.

I watched as he walked away, too exhausted to cry. I just wanted to find my chaperon and go home. I had learned so much by putting myself out there: self-confidence, perseverance, humility, and had become absolutely convinced that I was cursed for asking too many questions. There had to be other ways for a girl to succeed in life and be all she could be, even if she did ask a lot of questions. I guess I can get married and be a wife to someone; or, maybe at least, I could be a music teacher, I thought, consoling myself.

When I returned to high school after the pageant, I was cheered and welcomed back with genuine enthusiasm by teachers and fellow students alike. Becoming a beauty queen, I soon learned had its dark side, however: jealousy, bullying and stalking.

******

"Hi!" I answered the phone with excitement, expecting a friend's call. The voice on the other end of the line answered back with a gruff "Hello, Miss Warner Robins."

"Who's this?" I asked, still friendly.

"I'm a big fan of yours and that's not all that's big. I've got nine inches I want to give you," the voice growled.

"What... what did you say?" I asked, not sure what the man on the other end of the line was talking about but sensing something was really wrong with him and this phone call.

"I'm saying, *Miss Warner Robins*, that I saw your lovely picture in the newspaper yesterday and I got something to give you that's gonna make you very happy; very happy. I want to give it to you till you yell for more."

"Who are you?" I asked again, beginning to shake.

"I'm a soldier on the Air Force Base. I've been watching you through your bedroom window at night. Bet you didn't know that, did you?"

"Whoever you are," I responded in a calm voice belying my actual terrified state, something I was always able to do, "I want to ask you if you know Jesus. Do you know Jesus?"

"What? What did you say? Jesus? I'm talking about poking you really good, girl. This ain't got nothin' to do with Jesus."

"Oh, but it's got everything to do with Jesus," I insisted. "If you knew Jesus as your personal savior you wouldn't be calling me and threatening me like this. Jesus loves you and will forgive you all your sins. You should go to chapel on the base and talk to someone and ask them how you can be saved."

"What the hell? What are you talking about?" he asked, angrily.

"I'm talking about your calling me and talking to me like this is a cry for help. You need to give your life to Jesus, let him help you give up trying to scare people, scare me."

"Oh, you're scared, are you?" he asked, delight returning to his voice.

"Jesus will help you turn your life around. I'm hanging up now. Goodbye," I said, hanging up the receiver and immediately going to daddy who was resting in his room.

"Daddy," I said, shaking horribly, "something awful just happened."

"What is it, honey? What's happened?" he asked, concerned once he saw how terrified I was.

I told him about the phone conversation, even the part about "nine inches" which I actually didn't know what it meant because there was no such thing as sex education and there was no way to know anything about the body or sexual intercourse, but I intuitively knew it wasn't anything good the man had said to me. Daddy immediately went to the upper top shelf in his closet and pulled out a rifle wrapped in a blanket, something I didn't even know he had.

"I'll check outside the house and make sure the maniac isn't stalking around here. You stay inside with your mama, you hear. I'll take care of this."

When he found no one outside, he told me to "go on back to sleep, you hear?" No one got any sleep that night and for many nights to come. When the obscene phone caller continued to call, daddy called the police who came to the house to talk with me.

"Look," the two officers said, "we've come up with a plan to capture this guy and put an end to these calls. Next time he calls, you arrange a time to meet and when you go to meet him, we'll be following you and will arrest him."

I was petrified! Was this part of what being a Beauty Queen meant? I was simply too afraid to talk to the obscene caller and set up a meeting with him and mother and daddy agreed. I'd already decided that when I graduated high school in a few months I was going to live with my relatives and work at the Redstone Army Arsenal in Huntsville, Alabama to save money for college. I figured I'd never hear from the anonymous caller again once I'd moved, but

I was wrong. He tracked down the phone number belonging to my cousin's residence in Alabama, but fortunately soon stopped calling because she or her husband always answered the phone, never me. But after this incident, I became extremely nervous and jumpy and rarely went out at night anymore.

******

Unexpectedly, being a beauty queen also invited jealously and bullying. After the *Miss Georgia Beauty Pageant*, when I'd returned to high school and was finishing senior year, three girls, prior good friends since elementary school, began calling me by a new name: Beauty. "Hello Beauty," they'd say when they passed me in the hall. At first, I thought they were just joking with me but when they began to draw grotesque cartoons of me, labeling them Beauty, passing them around in class, laughing and making derisive remarks, I knew it was more than a little teasing. The cartoons were soon followed by their creation of an imaginary fan club for *Beauty*. They drew images of Beauty on large posters and tacked them up in the girl's bathroom with negative comments written underneath.

I was being bullied and had no idea how to handle it. What had I done to them? I was crushed by their hatefulness and cruelty but I wasn't brave enough to directly confront them and it never occurred to me to seek a teacher or other adult's help. Being a Christian, I prayed about it and ignored them as best I could.

The secret ally that got me through almost everything from the bullying, the obscene phone calls, the betrayal of my former boyfriend who'd started seeing another girl behind my back once he'd gone off to college; to my self-imposed hectic schedule of activities was music. I was no Beauty with aspirations for becoming a model or movie star. At heart, I was a serious young girl who loved music as much as she loved God; a girl who loved to study and learn new things; who asked a lot of questions and just happened to have a pleasing-enough looking face.

A SOUTHERN BELLE LEARNS WHO MATTERS

An audible gasp went up when she walked into the classroom. None of us had ever seen anyone like her ... tall, with beautiful shoulder length wavy blonde hair, bright blue eyes and SHE WORE MAKE-UP! None of our other female teachers wore make-up except maybe a smidge of lipstick! Wearing make-up was still questionable behavior for women, a bit too edgy for most good Baptist folk while those of other religious persuasions were even more conservative, forbidding women in their congregation to wear any make-up or cut their hair, these things being temptations from the devil causing men to think evil thoughts by focusing on women instead of God.

We were mesmerized as she stood before us like a movie star who had just dropped in from Hollywood to tell us about all the wonderful things we were going to learn in choir. She cast a spell over us and we adored her from that day forward. Here was someone, a true Southern Belle for sure, who was pretty and wore beautiful clothes, who dressed and acted like a sophisticated lady, and who loved music as much as we did.

I instantly wanted to be like her. She took a special interest in me and several other girls who were serious about music, giving us private voice lessons and grooming us to be solo performers. Through her mentorship and encouragement, I developed the skill and confidence to appear in starring roles in school musicals and perform in choral ensembles in statewide singing competitions and was selected numerous times to sing in Georgia's All-State Choir. She taught us girls to be excellent in everything we did, to be caring and considerate of others and to take seriously our talent as musicians.

Even though I adored Mrs. Caulfield and she was my mentor throughout my high school years, in the Q & A segment of the *Miss Warner Robins Beauty Pageant* I'd named my high school history teacher Mr. Howard as being the most influential person in my life. Why was that?

Because everyone knew that it was men who were important and in control of the world. After all, our Lord and Savior was a man. It was the man who mattered more than the woman.

Even the biblical creation story seemed to support the notion that man was superior to woman. The Father God created the first man, Adam; then, like an afterthought, He decided that man might get lonesome, and took one of Adam's ribs and created Eve. It was no time at all before an inferior and tricky Eve had messed up the whole of paradise and gotten herself and Adam kicked out. Incredibly, she had listened to what a cunning snake told her to do. "Eat the apple!" the snake said. In an act of untenable evil and gross ignorance, that's exactly what Eve did.

One might think it was just an apple after all, but unfortunately it was the one food strictly forbidden for consumption by the Father God. Maybe if He'd forbidden broccoli or kale there would have been no problems. But no, it was the apple that He declared as the forbidden food.

"Take a bite of this delicious apple," Eve had said to Adam, enticing him as women will do with men to get them to do the wrong thing. No wonder Eve's overt rebellious acts of disobedience fell on the heads of women. According to scripture, Eve's sin was the reason that women would forever have to give birth in pain and even more horrible, it was through Eve that all evil had entered the world!

Since there was little doubt that it was men who were important in the world, then what could a Southern Belle, a nice, sweet accommodating girl indoctrinated in patriarchal values and fundamentalist Christianity do with her life? Sunday school teachers encouraged us girls to take as our role models the strong and obliging women of the Bible like Ruth and Naomi, two women, daughter and mother-in-law from the Old Testament who were humble, obedient and true to their faith in God; or Queen Esther who was in service to her people and tricked an enemy to save them.

What about the wicked women of the bible like Mary Magdalene and temptresses like Bathsheba and Eve; those harlots, like any of us girls in the late 50s even knew what a "harlot" was. I must admit that we young church-going girls rather liked all the renditions artists made of Bathsheba, scantily clothed and direct from her bath when King David had looked upon her with desire. All us young girls knew something was amiss between those two, but exactly what, we had no idea other than it, whatever "it" was, was to be avoided. Certain words never entered a Southern Belle's vocabulary; words like sex or intercourse. "They "knew one another" was the acceptable biblical phrase for having sexual intercourse, but for us youth who had had no sex education whatsoever, we were left guessing as to what "knowing one another" meant. We figured it had something to do with "girls who went all the way"... but unless you'd "gone all the way," you still didn't know the details.

Obviously, none of these wicked women were acceptable role models and their stories were examples of what not to do or to be like.

There was one story in the New Testament about two sisters Mary and Martha who were followers of Jesus that had a hint of a woman having authority to make a choice about what she wanted to do rather than follow a strict protocol for a woman's behavior. Jesus was visiting the two women, so the story goes, and they were sitting in rapt attention to his words. Martha got up to go to the kitchen to prepare some food, but Mary stayed behind to listen to Jesus. Martha chastised her sister for not doing her kitchen duty, but Jesus, in a surprise response, defended Mary's action, saying that it was okay for her to stay behind and listen to his words instead of preparing the meal.

Every woman who ever heard that story in a Sunday morning sermon smiled to themselves, however, knowing that when they got home from church, she would be the one to cook the dinner while the man rested, having worked all week, poor thing, feet up and reading the Sunday newspaper until dinner was served. Nevertheless, it was a nice story showing how loving and kind Jesus was to women.

There was another big idea that we church-going girls had to reckon with and absorb. Preachers always praised Jesus for his loving attitude towards women but extending this respect towards women in their everyday contemporary lives only went so far. Love and respect for women had it limits. Enter the Apostle Paul and his vast influence on Christianity and treatment of women since the early days of the followers of Jesus. Paul's misogynistic message, unlike that of Jesus, was that women should be silent in the house of the Lord because only men had the right to speak. And even more amazing ... men being the heads of the household, were the ones to decide what happened at home too, and it was women's duty to obey them; rules still endorsed by the Southern Baptist Association today.

Regardless of what Paul had said about what women should or should not do, the women in the Bible didn't inspire me as role models, anyway, because they had little to no power over their lives unless they were the Queen and, to my young mind, they were all dead anyway.

But it was obvious from these biblical stories and the prevailing attitudes towards women, that the important people in the world were men. No doubt about it. They were the movers and shakers; they had the power to say things, outrageous things, and people would listen and do what they said. So, of course, I'd named history teacher Mr. Howard as the most influential person in my life!

I understood that a girl was supposed to marry and her husband would support her so she didn't really need to go to college; still, it was my heart's desire to go and since my parents had told me any money they had would have to go towards my brother's college expenses, I knew I was going to need financial assistance. With this understanding, I began to plan trips to check out colleges that had offered me full four-year scholarships based on my grade point average or music scholarships.

My first trip was to the nearby all-women's Baptist school, Bessie Tift College that my mentor, music teacher Mrs. Caulfield had attended. I arranged to stay in the dormitory with several girls who were music majors. The campus was beautiful, with elegant colonial-styled buildings and ivy tendrils cascading down their brick walls, like many of the Ante-bellum homes in the Deep South before the Civil War.

The girls toured me through the new music department, assuring me that "all the professors are amazin' and they'll just luv to have you as a student!"

Later that evening as we sat around the dorm rooms, talking more about music and college life, I shared that I had just performed the starring role as

Nellie in the musical production of *South Pacific*. "The music is some of the most melodic I've ever sung. I loved singing 'I'm Gonna Wash That Man Right Outta My Hair.' We actually had a bucket of water on stage that one of the actors poured over my head!"

"Your school allowed you to put on *South Pacific*?" one girl asked in a shocked voice.

"Really?" another pretty, soft-spoken girl asked. "Tift wouldn't let us do that musical because of the offensive lyrics of one of the songs."

"Which song was that?" I asked, puzzled.

"The one about loving Negroes."

"Negroes? I don't remember any song about Negroes in *South Pacific*. Are you talking about *Porgy and Bess*?"

No! It's right there in the one where they say 'you've got to be taught before it's too late, before you are six or seven or eight; to hate all the people your relatives hate; you've got to be carefully taught!" All the girls had chimed in, repeating the lyrics together.

"What's that got to do with Negroes?" I asked, still not understanding what was offensive.

"Silly," one hostess replied. "It's got everything to do with Negroes. They're talking about how people down here in the South hate the Negroes and that we teach our children to hate them, too!"

"Oh. I guess I never thought about it that way," I answered slowly, still trying to comprehend what the girls were saying.

"Well," the pretty blond with sky-blue eyes replied, flipping back her long golden blonde tresses, "you have to think about those things. We're college students now."

******

I finally decided to accept a four-year honor's scholarship, full tuition paid, to Mercer University, a private co-ed Baptist University in nearby Macon, Georgia. Although I'd decided against attending Tift College, I did give thought to what the pretty girls in the dorm had said to me. Did parents, teachers and institutions teach us in the South to hate black people while we were children? I thought about what Mr. Howard, our high school history teacher had told us about integration and equal rights for black people. He was the only teacher who ever mentioned the word integration, explaining that Negroes wanted the same rights as white people, that some Negroes wanted to go to school with us because our schools were better; they wanted to be allowed to sit in the movies and eat in the restaurants, same as white people did. They also wanted the right to vote but were often not allowed, a situation only thinly masked as improper registration.

Everybody in class was shocked to hear such things. Why, we wondered, did Negroes want to hang out with us? Didn't they have their own schools and churches? Didn't they have the same rights as us? What rights didn't they have? It was all very puzzling and disturbing.

Although no one I knew encouraged or talked about hating black people, I began to notice things I'd never noticed before, like at the movies when I saw that black people had to use a separate entrance at the theater marked "coloreds" and sat upstairs while we white folks sat below.

Many students and teachers didn't like Mr. Howard for talking about such things as racial discrimination and integration. One day a group of boys tricked him into going into the boy's bathroom where they had rigged firecrackers to go off when he opened the bathroom door. The explosion caused him to go deaf in one ear and sent a clear message to all of us: it was just plain dangerous to challenge the way things were done in the South.

No mention of the Ku Klux Klan was ever made in school or in church and it remained in the shadows much as the fact that there were hangings of black people, rape and torture still occurring in the South. Even Mr. Howard, who had brought our attention to the problem of segregation, when he taught us about the Civil War, had focused almost exclusively on military strategies and battles between the Blue and Grey with elaborate diagrams he'd draw on the blackboard. Little if any mention was made of the Negroes' plight before or during the Civil War or what happened to them during all the years since that time.

Black people in the South that I grew up in were not even on the radar. They were invisible. Except for their music, soul food they called it, which had begun to fill the very air that every Southerner breathed, eventually helping to reshape the entire world in the most profound ways that only music can do: by bringing people together by touching their hearts and bypassing their heads. I began to observe, however, that many Southerners genuinely believed, if they thought about it at all, that Negroes were happy living the way they did, mostly in poverty and in shantytowns. "It was better than being a slave, wasn't it?" was the attitude of many whites. As good Christian folks, we'd dutifully take food baskets at Christmas time to black families who lived in a shantytown across the railroad tracks. That showed we cared. What else were we supposed to do?

And so it was, I learned through the inculcation of the values adhered to and rooted in the Deep South that everyone had their "proper place in society" and it was critical that everyone know their place so as not to upset the "apple cart" of long-held beliefs and traditions. We girls learned that women should turn to men as mentors, friends and ultimate authorities when puzzled about the right thing to do or for getting something accomplished in the world. Even though I'd never heard of the Greek gods and goddesses and their myths, I grew up a devoted "daughter of the patriarchy," just like the Greek Goddess Athena had done in the Greek tragedy *The Eumenides* by Aeschylus, when she proclaimed "there is no mother anywhere who gave me birth, and but for marriage, I am always for the male with all my heart and strongly on my father's side."

DAMN YANKEE

"What? How old is he?" cousin Betty shrieked when I told her the Lieutenant had asked me out on a date.

"I don't know. I didn't ask him how old he is. He's just older, that's all I know. What does that even matter?"

"It matters. I heard he's going to make Captain soon, which means he's much too old for you," Betty's husband Hank, who worked near Saren's office, chimed in.

I bit my tongue so as not to remind Betty that she'd married a military man right out of high school and gotten a divorce a few years later, and that she and Hank had begun dating while both of them were still married! They weren't exactly the paragon of relationship success to offer advice. But they did have my back by warding off a stalker's phone calls that had begun in Georgia after a Beauty Pageant win and had continued once I'd moved to Alabama. I figured I owed them for that and for letting me stay with them for the summer.

"You can't do anything until I talk with your mother and get her okay," Betty said, wringing her hands that her young charge for the summer had already begun to be a problem.

Everyone balked at the idea of the dark, handsome man, officer or not, and I seeing one another. Wasn't he a Damn Yankee after all? That was no proper match for a young, recently graduated from high school and soon to be college student, a Southern Belle, devoted Christian and Beauty Queen! What would people say?

After many phone conversations to convince mother that I wasn't too young, that I was a good judge of character and that "Damn Yankees" were a thing belonging to the past, she reluctantly gave her consent. "But you be careful and do whatever cousin Betty tells you."

The Damn Yankee's office was directly across from my desk where we both worked at Redstone Arsenal in Huntsville, Alabama. I tried not to let him see me staring at him, which would have been so embarrassing, but who wouldn't stare at someone that handsome, with pearly white teeth and dimpled chin like the movie star Kirk Douglas? We flirted for weeks before he finally asked me out.

Once mother gave her consent, the Yankee and I began dating, spending lots of time taking his boat out water skiing on Guntersville Lake where I lived with cousin Betty and Hank. "Where did you get such an interesting name... Saren Canto?" I asked him one day after we'd gotten closer, having made out on several occasions which I figured made it natural that I'd want to know more about this man whom I was falling in love with. I didn't want to insult him but it was the strangest name I'd ever heard.

"My family's from Romania. They originally immigrated to Canada where I was born and then we moved to Cleveland, Ohio where we had lots of Romanian relatives. I grew up there and went to Ohio State University for college."

"You're Romanian? Where is Romania?"

"It's in eastern Europe ... a very beautiful country. Maybe I'll take you to see it one day," he laughed, taking my hand and kissing it. I loved his good manners and that he always wanted to introduce me to new things.

We continued to see each other on weekends when I returned to Georgia for my freshman year at Mercer University. He met my parents and they thought him weird, with his foreign name and of course the Damn Yankee thing, but we kept seeing one another because we had fallen in love. Shortly before Christmas, he proposed and I accepted.

******

All the obvious differences in our cultural upbringing didn't surface until, during college Christmas break, along with my mother, Aunt Ellie and several other relatives, we headed off to Cleveland to attend an engagement party in our honor at the Orthodox Romanian Community Hall.

Once we crossed the Mason-Dixon line into Ohio, home to Yankees... meaning those people living in states that fought against the South during the Civil War, there seemed to be a palpable difference in the air. Maybe just our imagination but to those of us born and bred in the South, the Civil War between the North and the South was much more than something we read about in history books. We had been born and raised on the very land where most of the bloody battles between the Blue and the Grey had been fought, and at its destructive end, had left the South decimated and in shambles, and was still in major economic recovery.

On the night of the engagement party, excited and all decked out in our finery, my family and I entered the Romanian Community Hall with great anticipation. But nothing had prepared us for meeting a hall full of strangers... let's be honest ... we viewed them as foreigners... Romanians, they were, whatever that meant. Who even knew where Romania was anyway? But they'd also come for an engagement party for one of their own who, in their minds, had unfortunately stepped outside their community and was going to marry an outsider.

As we Southerners seated ourselves in one corner of the large hall, the sights, sounds and pungent smells emanating from the kitchen assaulted our nostrils with their unfamiliar aromas. Our senses now on high alert, we cautiously eased into the festivities ... equal parts terrified and downright enthralled with the spectacle.

"You won't find anything like this at the First Baptist Church, Susie," Aunt Ellie said, poking my mother in the side with her elbow and grinning ear to ear. Southern ladies loved a good show and the more outrageous the better.

"I should hope not," mother shot back in a stern voice meant to show disapproval but she, too, was enjoying all the new sights and smells.

Suddenly, exotic, unfamiliar sounding music being played by clarinets, clavicles and a variety of stringed instruments began to fill the hall as we Southern folk gazed, mouths agape as women, many wearing babushkas or head scarves, danced with other women, men danced with men, children danced with grandmas and grandpas and alcohol flowed freely. Aromas from the spicy, strange-looking food continued to pour out from the kitchen, all prepared by robust, full-bodied cousins, aunts and other Romanian women who had cooked for days in preparation for the celebration of one of their own.

Saren's extended Romanian family who had settled in Ohio after a brief time in Canada, were as horrified as my own relations about this unholy alliance. "But we're pure bloods," his mother had proudly declared on the occasion of first meeting my mother. "No one in our family has ever married anyone who wasn't a Romanian."

Mother, much too Southern and polite to challenge anyone directly, later complained bitterly to me in private. "Who does she think she is? Pure bloods, my be-hind! For her information, we never had anyone in our family marry a Damn Yankee either and a foreigner to boot. If anybody's pure bloodied, it's us!"

Meantime at the party, I was being whisked around the dance floor by one of Saren's full-bodied uncles. "You're too skinny," he declared without the least hesitation as to whether or not it was an appropriate thing to say to a newly engaged young woman whom he'd only met less than five minutes ago. "Romanians like their women to have some meat on their bones. You like to cook? You'll have to learn how to cook Romanian food for Saren. It's what he expects from a wife," he said, twirling me around like a ballerina whose feet only occasionally touch the floor.

"Uncle Canto," I said laughing, "I promise you I'm going to learn how to cook all the Romanian dishes that Saren is accustomed to."

After everyone was seated at long tables groaning under the weight of enormous amounts of unfamiliar-looking food, the numerous toasts to the engaged couple began. I, a shining girl of eighteen dressed in a flaming red chiffon dress and he, a proud and beaming groom-to-be of thirty-one, watched as baskets on the tables were passed among the attendees who placed envelopes stuffed with various amounts of money inside intended to help the couple get a good start in life.

"Haven't they ever heard of a bridal registry?" mother commented under her breath. She and my other relatives were stunned at the lack of customary bridal and pre-wedding etiquette they were witnessing.

"And giving a couple money? Why, that's just down right vulgar. Were they just too lazy to go out and buy them something?"

******

The following day after we'd picked out a gorgeous ring from a jeweler whom Saren knew offered good discounts, I told him I wanted to formally accept it inside a Baptist church. I'd reached this decision after we'd attended his Romanian Orthodox Church earlier where I'd been dumbstruck by what I'd seen ... priests adorned in theatrical like costumes of red and purple satin, wearing large, pointy hats like Merlin the magician, chanting as they walked down the aisle, waving containers filled with incense sending thick smoke rippling out over the worshippers; not to mention the idolatry present in the many gilded statues. All of this led me to the conclusion that the only way I could ever marry someone who for all intents and purposes was unsaved in the sight of Jesus Christ, would be for him to convert to the Baptist faith and be baptized.

Once we'd found a Baptist church and had gone inside, I told Saren, "You've got to join the Baptist church, promise to never take another drink and we can't have any alcohol in the house and you have to get baptized."

Saren, seemingly unruffled by these requests, wrapped his arms around me. "If those things are important to you, then I agree to them. But I also have something I want. I may be called up to the Korean war next year if it's still going on and I want to be married before I go."

"But what about my college? I don't want to stop my education after I've only just started. Can't we just be engaged for a while?"

"If we don't get married before I get my new assignment, which might be Korea, the engagement is off."

I was stunned by what was more an ultimatum than a request. Tearfully, I agreed and accepted his engagement ring and with it, his terms to get married within the year.

That next fall we were married in the First Baptist Church in Warner Robins, Georgia, attended by several hundred people. It was a military wedding, thought by many to be very romantic, with groom and groom's military attendants dressed in full military officer dress blues, gold cummerbunds at their waists, decorations and medals pinned to coats and shining sabers hanging by their sides. The stunning bride in a beautiful wedding dress with lace, tiny pearls and lots of tulle surrounded by her lovely bridesmaids dressed in bright turquoise dresses with a church full of candelabras and baskets of flowers. After exchanging vows, the fairy-tale-looking couple walked out the front steps of the church under a canopy of crossed sabers while well-wishing guests tossed rice and the happy couple drove away to a two-week honeymoon in Nassau, Bahamas, paid for by the vulgar money stuffed into baskets at an Ohio engagement party.

ISLAND OF THE LONE PALM TREE

"I'll be waiting for you at the Honolulu airport when you arrive from San Francisco," Saren had promised in a ham-operator, patched phone call from the Marshall Islands to Georgia where I'd been living with our 6-month-old son Alex at my parent's home until housing became available at our new duty post. "We'll spend a few days relaxing in Oahu and then we'll fly to Kwajalein just in time for Christmas!"

Come December, I boarded an airplane in Atlanta for a 6,800-mile journey that took baby Alex and myself halfway around the world to join Saren in the Marshall Islands, a place that bore little reality beyond a red dot on a map he'd sent to show where we'd be living. This being my first airplane trip, I calmed myself by hugging my precious baby son and imagining how happy we'd be once we were reunited as a family. It had been an exhausting twelve-hour trip from Atlanta to Oahu due to bad weather and flight delays, but it was worth it all when I spotted my handsome husband Saren waiting on the tarmac in Honolulu just as he had said he would be. Alex, with his blond curly hair, dark brown eyes and dimpled chin like his dad, was our handsome little prince from the moment he was born. Even though he'd only known Saren a few months before he'd left for Kwajalein, baby Alex didn't hesitate to leap into his dad's outstretched arms. Saren and I hugged and kissed and cried and laughed and spent the next three days making love in our accommodations at the Army Officer's Club at Schofield Barracks in Fort Shafter, nestled at the foot of the beautiful Waianae Mountain range on Oahu, and headquarters of the US Army Pacific Command. When we boarded the plane from Honolulu a few days later for Micronesia, I was pregnant with another baby.

******

After hours of flying over vast expanses of nothing but ocean below us, it was thrilling to hear the pilot announce, "Ladies and gentlemen, we are approaching our destination, Kwajalein Island." Looking out the window below at what was to be our new home, all I could see was a small speck on the expanse of blue. Kwajalein, an island shaped like a banana, measured a meager one-mile wide by one and a half miles long, which wasn't exactly reassuring for a second-time-ever airplane passenger like myself. I gulped hard; my little bit of bravery having quickly evaporated as the airplane dropped low for its approach to the island's landing strip that extended down one entire side of the island. Luckily, it was only later that I learned the garbage dump at the end of the runway was always brimming with sharks feasting on the debris. No airplane could afford to miss the approach.

Saren took my hand, squeezing it hard. "Big jets are always challenged with a landing here if the trade winds are blowing too hard, but nothing to worry about today," he said, "because the winds are calm." Saren was an avid airplane buff and had wanted to join the Air Force to be a pilot but couldn't because he was colorblind. I trusted his assessment of the situation, something that was to be a mainstay of our relationship for many years. Saren's older and more experienced in worldly things, I'd always remind myself if I had any doubts about his decisions being the right ones. Besides, my upbringing had taught me that men were the authorities on things of the world and the final decision-makers in a family.

The plane landed safely, coming to a full stop directly in front of the island's air terminal, not much larger than an oversized living room. Waiting outside to greet us were the island's commanding officer along with a few other officers and their wives. "Aloha, and welcome to Kwajalein!" they beamed, placing colorful flower leis around our necks.

Saren loaded us and our baggage into a car, a luxury since there were few personal vehicles on the island, and off we went to our new home, a deluxe brand-new double-wide mobile home parked at the very end of the island directly in front of the ocean in an area allocated for family housing. Before we'd finished unpacking our few belongings, Saren eagerly loaded baby Alex into a basket he'd rigged onto the front of his bicycle, and with me jumping onto another rusty one like all bikes became within a few months due to the salt air, off we went, cycling around the island for the short but grand tour.

"There's the Officer's Club. Everyone calls it *YukWeYuk*. That's Marshallese for fun gathering place. You'll like it. Good food and we can go dancing, too," Saren beamed enthusiastically, pointing to a hut-like structure with thatched roof and lots of bamboo. While it looked more like a movie set from Bob Hope's movie *Road to Bali* made in the 40s, it made me deeply happy to see how much Saren wanted me to like this dot in the middle of the South Pacific. We were both so relieved when the possibility of his being assigned to Korea was replaced instead by a tour of duty in the South Pacific. His position as *Aide de Camp* for the Commanding General of the Redstone Arsenal Army Base in Huntsville had played a big role in making that happen. "It's all about who you know," older Army wives had dutifully instructed me while we were stationed for a short time after we first married, at the Army's Aberdeen Proving Grounds in Maryland where baby Alex had been born.

"There's the medical clinic," Saren pointed out, as we pedaled past a two-story small structure that looked more like a large barrack. "It's not very big but a doctor from the mainland just arrived a few months ago, so now there's a few nurses and a second doctor." That fact became important when the new GP Dr. Jenkins confirmed a short time later that indeed I was pregnant with our second child and would be giving birth in that clinic.

We pedaled by the island chapel, built in the shape of a cross, with a roof that sloped down into wide eaves a few feet above the ground, leaving the sides entirely open to the trade winds, which kept worshippers cool. Inside were long wooden benches for seating, a simple lectern at the front where the minister gave his sermons. Next-door to the chapel was the commissary, a large rectangular concrete structure holding all the supplies and food available to the islanders, regularly shipped in on large cargo vessels, and supplemented by an airplane that flew in bi-monthly with fresh produce.

"There's the school, K-12," Saren said, pointing to a small building a few blocks upwind from the commissary and chapel.

"This area is off limits unless you work here," Saren said, stopping his bike a short distance further on where we gazed through a tall chain link fence that enclosed almost one-fourth of the entire island behind it. It was the military-industrial complex consisting of three massive missile tracking radars, several long concrete buildings housing huge computers, and numerous missile silos storing missiles to be fired in monthly anti-ballistic-missile testing exercises done in coordination with Vandenberg Air Force Base in California.

Near the small boat docks on the lagoon side of the island, we paused to catch our breath and look out at the vast expanse of the crystal-clear turquoise-blue ocean stretching to the edges of the far horizon. What a beautiful part of the world this dot is, I thought, hugging Saren and baby Alex, who by this time was nodding off. Throughout the entire 6,800-mile grueling trip from Georgia to California to Hawaii with delay after delay, he never cried or made a fuss. He was like an Angel that had incarnated to help me make the very scary journey to the other side of the world.

"Look at this," Saren called as we turned our bikes and headed back to our new home. He had stopped his bike in front of a solitary palm tree. The rather ordinary looking palm tree bore a plaque commemorating the bloody battle with the Japanese that was fought on Kwajalein during World War II for control of this strategically important island. The plaque said that the battle to win Kwajalein was so fierce that nothing, no trees or buildings, remained except this lone palm tree.

In the weeks and months to come I would often ride my bike around the island past the lone palm tree and wonder what the history of the island had been after WWII. The answers I eventually uncovered were disturbing and horrifying.

******

Like most military and civilian wives, I went to work right away as a secretary with Bell Telephone Laboratories, BTL, a contractor that along with Raytheon Corporation were the two main civilian agencies under contract from the government to administer the ballistic missile systems testing program on Kwajalein. A small booklet giving a brief history of Kwajalein was handed out to newcomers by BTL. It explained that the area known as the Marshall Islands was composed of 29 atolls, which included Bikini Atoll and five other islands scattered across a distance of 357,000 square miles in an area of the South Pacific known as Micronesia.

The Marshall Islands had been "discovered" the booklet said, by a succession of dominator cultures beginning in the early 1600s, first by the Spanish and later by the Germans, and was used primarily for high quality production of copra oil from coconuts. In the early 1900s the Japanese arrived and took control, and in anticipation of WWII, recognizing the strategic importance of the remote coral atolls, Tokyo being only several thousand miles away, had set up their military headquarters on Kwajalein Atoll with a watchtower on Bikini Island to guard against a possible American invasion. After a bloody battle for Kwajalein, similar to the one on Midway Island, the Japanese were defeated in December 1945, the booklet said, with American losses being 142 dead and 845 wounded while the Japanese losses numbered 4938 dead and 206 taken as prisoners. The war came to an end, with Micronesia becoming a Trust Territory of the Pacific Islands administered by the United States government. The booklet ended with various facts about post war United States administration, socio-political facts about the Marshallese and how good the shelling was on the reef.

The booklet made no mention of other critical historical facts such as the extensive atomic and thermonuclear weapons tests that had been done in Micronesia and, more importantly, it contained no warning of any possible adverse health effects of exposure to radioactive fallout still present in the coral dust and water from the nuclear testing. At the time, 1962, I'd never heard of toxic radiation and regarded the booklet as nothing more than an interesting short synopsis of the remote part of the world called Micronesia where we lived.

"IT AIN'T NECESSARILY SO, THE THINGS THAT YOU'RE LIABLE TO READ IN THE BIBLE..."

... from *Porgy & Bess* by George Gershwin

Being from an ultra-conservative religious background had in no way prepared me for the many challenges of living in a diverse culture like that of the Polynesians who worshipped strange gods like stones and even sharks. This new culture thoroughly challenged my values and beliefs, heralding the beginning of a crisis in faith that would culminate years later in my leaving the church altogether. At the time, however, I was full of confusion and questions regarding Christianity and its message of Christ and His plan of salvation according to Baptist doctrine.

I sought out the Chaplin of the small island chapel for advice. Chaplin Simon Tinker, a Navy officer and former Baptist pastor from Atlanta, Georgia listened quietly and respectfully during our first of many talks as I poured out my religious concerns regarding the Marshallese.

The Chaplin was one of the island's most distinguishable characters, short and wearing overly large glasses, he dressed in the same outfit every day, including Sundays, heavy combat boots, knee-high socks, and khaki-colored Bermuda shorts emphasizing his severely knobby legs, causing him to look more like a comic book character than a minister of the Lord. He could regularly be spotted out on the shallow waters of the reef, not fishing but surveying the many natural wonders of the coral reef below through the lens of his glass-bottom boat. He could identify all the fish species by name and possessed a wealth of knowledge about the ocean's coral reef ecosystem. He respected the Marshallese people and was held in high regard by them, something that also made him a unique character since most Kwajalein residents considered the

Marshallese to be the hired help and to some, they possessed no discernable culture of any value.

"Unless they become Christians," I said sorrowfully to Chaplin Tinker during an early talk in his Chapel office, "our Baptist faith and the Bible teaches us they're living in sin and will go to hell."

Chaplin Tinker only nodded and made a slight grunting noise every so often as I continued my sincere, narrow and white-superiority-induced concerns, which of course, I didn't see in that way. "What is my proper role with the Marshallese, Chaplin? As a Christian and a Baptist, we're taught we have a responsibility to witness to the unsaved, but I'm not sure how to go about that." Rather than being a source of joy and comfort, my religious beliefs were becoming a heavy burden.

It was as though I was looking at the world through Chaplin Tinker's glass bottom boat that only allowed a very limited perspective of the otherwise vast and extensive ocean that lay beneath. Religious and cultural fundamentalism was indeed a narrow lens to look at the world and its inhabitants because, among its many shortcomings, it only gave a person solace in conformity and regiment. It was a worldview of limited thinking and perspective. I had no notion that what I saw as religious beliefs based on teachings in the Bible might be extreme to others who didn't see Christianity as the one and only path to God.

"Why don't you direct our adult choir?" Chaplin Tinker asked one day during one of my visits. "Our tenor, a Navy Captain, has been directing the choir and he's being re-assigned. I know you have a background in music and if you'd take on that role, it would be a big help to me and our small community."

Motivated in part by a desire to make a difference in the world, and taking no notice that I had one child, was pregnant and worked a six-day week, I accepted the position of choir director, slipping into the role of Super Woman as easily as if I'd been born to it.

Even though my questions around faith raised doubts in my mind and caused some slight fraying at the edges of my tightly held religious beliefs, my indoctrination to the cause of bringing the word of God to the unsaved remained impenetrable and strong.

******

Life for everyone on the entire island was structured around monthly missile-testing exercises, always done at night, and in coordination with Vandenberg Air Force Base in California. During a missile test operation, California would fire a missile armed with a "dummy" warhead in an arc or trajectory aimed at Kwajalein's lagoon while the military-civilian group located on Kwajalein would fire their anti-ballistic missile intended to intercept and blow-up Vandenberg's missile before it could hit the water and go off course; if it did go off course, it could possibly impact somewhere on the island itself. Because of this possibility, civilians were ordered to evacuate their homes and go to cement shelters for the night. Sirens placed strategically around the island sounded incessantly one hour prior to the appointed launch time, warning everyone to begin evacuation while military police patrolled the sandy roads running between the mobile homes to make sure no one remained behind during the firing mission.

"I don't want to go to the bomb shelter," I complained to Saren. "I know lots of other wives who don't go. It's too much for me with Alex. Is it okay if I stay behind?" I was pregnant with our second child and evacuating to a concrete shelter for the night was exhausting.

To my relief Saren was in agreement. "Look," he said, "it's okay with me if you stay in the trailer. I know you'll be absolutely safe. There's never been a misfiring. You can trust the military. They know what they're doing. Just make sure you turn off all the lights and lay low until the military police leave the area. You and Alex will be fine."

******

Large flat-bottomed motorized boats made the daily twenty-minute trek from the nearby island of Ebeye, bringing many Marshallese to Kwajalein where they worked as maids, nannies and manual laborers for the Americans who were the most recent occupiers of their islands. We hired a beautiful, brown-skinned young woman named Jai to clean our three-bedroom trailer and watch baby Alex everyday while we both worked. Jai was short and small, unlike many of the island women who were large-boned and heavier set. I would sometimes see her near the commissary on her days off, talking and laughing with friends, none of whom ever carried umbrellas or wore raincoats despite the frequent downpours of rain; all of the women greased their hair with coconut oil until it was shiny and hung in long oily tassels down their backs. Jai had a penchant for nail polish and fancy underwear as I soon discovered when those items kept disappearing from my dresser drawers.

"Does your maid ever take anything from your house, like any of your personal things?" I asked my best friend Cindy one day.

"Yeah, a few times I've had hair clips and shampoo go missing, but not much else."

"Did you ever say anything to her about it?"

"No. Didn't figure it was worth it. They don't make much money and I hear they live in poverty and don't have much."

I was soon to find out to what extent the native islanders lived in poverty but for the time being, I decided to do what Cindy and other white women who lived in relative ease and comfort on the island did, let it be and look the other way.

******

On November 1st, 1963 we joyfully welcomed our beautiful 8-½ lb. daughter Marie who, unlike her brother Alex, was born with no complications at the small island clinic. She was a mellow, happy baby and I began nursing her right away, taking a month off from work to help everyone, especially Alex who was still a baby in diapers, to make the adjustment of having a new family member. We patched phone calls through to Georgia and Ohio to let our families know our good news.

A week or so after Marie's birth, my friend Cindy who was a teacher, knocked on the front door.

"Come in, come in. What you doing here in the middle of the day? Is there a school holiday or something?" I asked, opening the trailer door.

"The most awful thing has happened," she said. "President Kennedy has been murdered."

"What? No. That can't be," I said.

"I just heard it. That's why they dismissed school."

On November 22nd, only twenty-one days after Marie's birth, we who lived on a tiny dot in the giant Pacific Ocean received the horrible news that President John Kennedy had been assassinated in Dallas. None of us island residents, numbering some 150 people, could make any sense of it and being so far removed from any major news services in "real" time, we ruminated among ourselves about who would want to do such a terrible thing and why. No one had any answers, but we were all saddened by what had happened, lamenting among ourselves that the world had indeed become a place where uncertainty and tragedy were playing themselves out, "like chess pieces on a remote, non-caring god's chessboard", I heard a Colonel say one evening while we were having dinner at the Yuk-We-Yuk club.

Soon after Maria's birth, we arranged for Alex, now fifteen months old, to stay with an American neighbor during the day while I went back to work. Our reasons for not allowing our Marshallese maid Jai to keep both children were anything but admirable and showed the extent of our own ingrained feelings of white superiority and prejudice.

"If we leave Alex with Jai, he might start speaking broken English or maybe even Marshallese Ebon," Saren said, as we sat outside eating dinner on a deck in front of our trailer that looked out over the turquoise waters of the lagoon.

"She's a wonderful caregiver," I said acknowledging his remark, "so I think it'll be okay if we let her take care of Marie since she's too young to pick up Jai's broken English."

I was conflicted. In spite of our racism and cultural biases, I hungered to know other cultures and their traditions. It was one of the reasons I had been so drawn to Saren, whose family were immigrants from Romania and had very different traditions and customs than my own as our engagement party in Ohio a few years earlier had shown. I was caught in a conundrum of being interested in the Polynesian culture but at the same time, worrying that my children would be negatively influenced by it.

That the South Sea Islanders might have a rich culture was in evidence all around us if we had been able to see it with a different perspective. I had an ah-ha moment of recognizing that the Marshallese had a more workable and nurturing solution to childcare than our own in the West. It happened one day when I was sick and had stayed home from work. I noticed that Jai and a number of other nannies had gathered under the palm trees by the beach lagoon next to our mobile home. Each had brought her charges of one or two small babies and young children. The women were singing, playing hand games, laughing, hanging out and eating their favorite food, canned tuna over white rice. As I continued to watch their activities out the window of the trailer, I noticed that if a child cried or was fussy, the woman nearest the child would tend to it. There seemed to be no individual ownership or responsibility attached to a particular child and their caregiver. The women responded to all the children and their needs as a group.

The special way South Sea Islanders formed their social structures for relating and living in communities, which bore little resemblance to those in the West, was the focus of a study done in the islands of Samoa by the famous anthropologist Margaret Meade. Meade had identified the Samoan culture as being a matri-focal society, one that instead of having beliefs in individual ownership and control, was based on everyone sharing in a commonality of vision and caretaking. I knew nothing of Dr. Meade's studies in Samoa but watching the Marshallese maids and nannies out the window of my mobile home, I thought it a fine arrangement to spread child tending to everyone in the group.

BIKINIS, BOMBS & BABIES

"I've got some exciting news," Chaplin Tinker said to me one Sunday after I'd been directing the Chapel choir for some months. "We've been invited to visit Ebeye by the Marshallese choir director who wants to collaborate with us for a joint choir concert."

Residents from Kwajalein were forbidden to visit the small nearby island of Ebeye, home to the Marshallese. The two islands were separated by only a mile-long stretch of coral reef, which you could walk during extremely low tides if you didn't mind the sharks that constantly patrolled the area. Once we'd arranged a time for our visit, the Chaplin, a few others and myself went aboard one of the flat-bottomed boats that brought the islanders to and from the island. I was so excited for this opportunity, having recorded the Ebeye choir on several occasions when they'd sung for Sunday morning church services on Kwajalein. The Marshallese sang mostly Christian hymns in two-part harmony, but occasionally would sing songs written in their language of Ebon. It was an energetic and emotional singing style known as "call and response" in which a lead singer would sing a few lines that were echoed or repeated back in unison by the choir, similar in musical style to many old folk tunes and African-American spirituals.

After a short ride, the flat-bottomed boat docked at Ebeye's harbor adjacent to the small village where we stepped out onto a dirt road that ran directly through the middle, with houses on either side. As we walked down the muddy dirt road, I soon realized that the houses were nothing more than flimsy structures made of cardboard, pieces of tin and wooden boards nailed together with holes left for windows and doors. Pigs, skinny dogs, chickens and naked brown children were running everywhere; garbage and refuse were strewn about on the road and in the yards. As I gazed at the poverty and squalid living conditions, I felt myself becoming nauseous.

Why would God allow such suffering? How could He allow innocent children and islanders to live in such abject poverty, even if they were living in sin because they hadn't accepted Jesus Christ as their Savior? Perhaps, I reasoned desperately, a miraculous way would be shown for their poverty and ill health to be eliminated. I sincerely believed that with God anything was possible. That the poverty and ill health of the Marshallese might be related to the United States' policies and actions in the South Pacific and have little to do with a punishing God never occurred to me. I was as naïve in my worldview, as spiritually impoverished and misguided as I reasoned that the Marshallese were.

I could feel Chaplin Tinker watching me out of the corner of his eye as I kept swallowing to ease my nausea. As I looked more closely, I realized that many of the children and adults were crippled and had deformities I'd never seen.

"Many of these children and adults got polio a few years ago," the Chaplin said, seeming to read my mind. "Officials believe that someone from Ebeye was exposed to a carrier on Kwajalein and took it back to the village where it quickly spread throughout the entire island atolls."

"What about the polio vaccine?" I asked, still trying to comprehend what I was seeing.

"They didn't get vaccinated until after the outbreak, but by then it was too late. Many islanders died or were left crippled and maimed for life."

"What about her and the little boy next to her?" I asked, nodding in the direction of two young children standing near one of the dilapidated houses. "What happened to them? Can polio cause such deformities?"

"Their deformities are from the radiation fallout many of the population suffered after the extensive nuclear testing the United States did here a few decades ago. A lot of babies born to mothers who suffered from radioactive fallout were born with no arms and no legs."

I struggled to understand what he was saying and how it related to what I was seeing. My heart ached knowing how the mothers must be suffering for their children whom they wanted to grow up healthy and have a good life... many of these same women were mothers who would leave their children every day to come to Kwajalein to take care of our healthy, white babies.

I smiled and waved to the deformed young children, who smiled and waved back with their knobs where arms should have been.

******

"What do you know about radiation fallout?" I asked Saren later that evening after I'd returned from Ebeye.

"Radiation fallout?"

"Yes. From nuclear bombs the military exploded here for years after World War II. The fallout from those explosions made a lot of the islanders sick and mothers are still giving birth to babies that are severely deformed. You should have seen some of those children with no arms that I saw today on Ebeye."

"I don't think those deformities were due to radiation fallout, though," he said with certainty born from a creed and devotion to the military as the only practical way for keeping peace. "The military's really careful in how they conduct nuclear tests. And if it hadn't been for those tests, well, it put us ahead of the rest of the world in building up a stronger military force than anyone else. Everything we're doing here now is a direct result of how successful we've been in the past. We need our large arsenal of missile weaponry to keep us safe, to keep the world safe."

******

It was the same argument that was used back in 1946 when the American military governor of the Marshall Islands, Commodore Wyatt traveled to Bikini Island where he assembled the islanders after Sunday church, asking them if they would be willing to leave their homes temporarily so that the United States could begin testing atomic bombs. "It's for the good of mankind and to end all world wars," he solemnly told the islanders.

"What is an atomic bomb," the islanders had asked in innocence and confusion? How will it end all wars?" After sorrowful deliberation, King Juda, leader of the Bikinian people, finally agreed. "We will go, believing that everything is in the hands of God."

The people of Bikini were soon removed by the US. Navy to nearby Rongerik Atoll and left there with food supplies sufficient for several weeks. They shortly discovered that the coconut trees and local food crops were scarce and yielded little fruit. As their food supplies quickly started to dwindle, they began to suffer from starvation and fish poisoning due to the lack of edible fish in the lagoon. Within two months after their arrival on Rongerik, the islanders were begging U. S. officials to move them back to Bikini, but their home island of Bikini was too contaminated for them to return after the nuclear testing.

One month later, in March of 1946, the nuclear legacy of Bikini Atoll began in earnest when the United States detonated the largest hydrogen bomb ever tested. Called the Bravo shot, it was a 15-megaton hydrogen bomb, *a thousand times more powerful than the atomic bomb dropped on Hiroshima.* The Bravo test exposed the Marshallese people to near-fatal amounts of radiation that resulted in widespread radiological contamination of the people and the environment. In addition, the military placed goats and pigs aboard Navy ships anchored in Bikini's lagoon to track the effects of radioactive fallout on animals and to see how military craft would withstand the detonations.

The Bravo test was called an unprecedented "success" and "beyond our wildest dreams" according to the American scientists who were involved in its detonation. One scientist described the aftermath of the detonation on Bikini this way: "The area was illuminated by a huge and expanding flash of blinding light. A raging fireball of intense heat that measured into the millions of degrees shot skyward at a rate of 300 mph. Within minutes the monstrous cloud filled with nuclear debris, shot up more than 20 miles and generated winds hundreds of miles per hour. These fiery gusts blasted the surrounding islands and stripped the branches and coconuts from the trees. Millions of tons of sand, coral, plant and sea life from Bikini's reef and the surrounding lagoon waters were sent high into the air by the blast."

The island residents of Rongelap Atoll, located downwind about 125 miles east of Bikini, said they were never warned to evacuate and were hit with direct radioactive fallout. They described the explosion very differently than the scientists. "Soon after the blast, we all watched as a white, snow-like ash began to fall from the sky. We didn't know what was happening and watched in amazement as two suns rose high in the sky. Soon the dust was so thick it covered the whole island and turned our drinking water into a yellow color. Mothers watched as their children played in the fallout because we didn't understand the danger. Soon people began to experience severe vomiting and diarrhea and our hair began to fall out, causing terror and panic. Two days after the test, our people of Rongelap were finally taken to nearby Kwajalein Island for medical treatment."

After the Bravo explosion, both U.S. and Marshallese workers cleaned radioactive debris from the ground-zero location, either bulldozing it directly into the ocean or storing it in temporary containment sites. It was the beginning of over sixty years of migration for the inhabitants of Bikini to various other islands throughout the Marshallese chain where they often lived in perilous and near starvation conditions while awaiting their return home to Bikini as promised by the United States. Experts have agreed their home island will be uninhabitable for the next 30,000 years due to the radioactive fallout and contamination still present.

******

In another part of the world in July of 1946, an extraordinary series of events unfolded which brought the island of Bikini into the international spotlight. A French fashion designer named Louis Reard had designed something he felt sure would stir the masses into a buying frenzy, but he didn't have a name for it. After searching diligently for just the right name to label his creation, in an unbelievable quirk of fate, the U. S. Military came to his rescue. Four days before he was to unveil his new creation to the *haute couture* world in Paris, a news broadcast announced that the U. S. Military had exploded a nuclear device near several small islands in the South Pacific called Bikini Atoll. On July 5th Reard showed his new creation to the world, calling it a bikini. When criticized for naming his creation after something so devastating, Reard claimed he had named his creation bikini after the islands and not the atomic blast.

But Bikini Atoll, the remote and little-known South Pacific Island, was far more than just a name attached to the daring, two-piece minuscule article of women's clothing created by Frenchman and designer Louis Reard. Bikini, the place, represented a darker side of the United States' foreign policy whereby military and government officials had taken over an entire region and carelessly, ignorantly destroyed its environment, its people and their way of life. Despite government propaganda to the contrary, the story of Bikini Atoll was the story of how the United States became a nuclear super power through its successful nuclear testing program conducted in the Marshall Islands at the expense of the islanders and the environment.

As a result of the nuclear testing program carried out by the United States, as I had witnessed for myself on Ebeye, Micronesia had continued to suffer one of the highest rates of radiation sickness in the world, leading to children being born with extreme deformities such as the infamous "jellyfish babies," where the child's body has no arms, legs and sometimes no head, and yet, to date, no epidemiological survey has ever been conducted. According to the stories and histories recorded by the Micronesian people, the United States' policy in the region had resulted in unspeakable genocide against the indigenous people of the Marshall Islands.

Now, some twenty years later, we found ourselves living in the same toxic environment and potentially suffering from its effects, just as the native islanders had suffered for decades. No one at the time seriously connected our baby Marie's breathing difficulties to the extensive radiation fallout from nuclear testing done in the area that might still be present in the coral dust. But when we returned stateside, as her baby teeth began to come in, they were the color of grey dishwater. When tested for allergies, she was so highly allergic to numerous food and environmental pollens that she had to suffer weekly injections for many years.

******

Shortly before we were due to leave the island, we were visiting our best friends Cindy and Bob who lived a few trailers down from us.

"What's that?" I asked, admiring an unusual object hanging on their living room wall.

"That's an authentic storyboard which the Marshallese sailors use for navigation. The Marshallese like all Polynesians were once master sailors. Some call it a stick map. It's made with string and tiger cowrie shells and various other shells like those you and Cindy collect on the reef. The best Polynesian sailors know how to read these storyboards like we'd read a map," Bob answered.

"You mean they use it to plot their navigational course when sailing?" Saren asked. He and Bob were both avid fishermen, loved flying even though they were in the Army, and had become good friends during our two-plus years on the island.

"Yeah. Each one of the smaller shells marks a certain small spit of an island or a coral reef build-up to be avoided. The large cowrie shells represent the larger island atolls and the strings connecting the different shells show the routes the boat can sail to get to specific locations. Some of the old Hawaiians I've met say that the first really good sailors stood naked at the boat's prow and navigated with their penis, depending on how the wind struck it, they'd know which direction to guide the boat," Bob said, and being the constant comedian, held his finger in front of his crotch and waved it back and forth to mimic sensing the wind's direction with his penis, causing us to roar with laughter.

In a few more years, both men would be heading out to serve their country in another far-off land we'd never heard of, signaling a time when we all would be asked to navigate the vast seas of change brought on by the Vietnam war with what would seem like little more than a stick map, a Marshallese storyboard of seashells and string.

VIETNAM WAR

"Don't go," I pleaded with Saren.

"What? Don't be ridiculous. I have to go. I'm an Army officer, remember?"

"I don't care. I want you to resign and we'll move to Canada and raise our family there."

"Are you crazy? I can't throw my career away just like that!" he said, snapping his fingers before turning to walk away from what he considered a ridiculous conversation.

"I don't care about your career. I care about you. Please don't go to Vietnam. You could die," I yelled after him, almost hysterical.

Saren froze. Turning back to me, his expression grim, he said stoically, "I chose the military as a career and I knew that one day I might have to go to war. That day has come."

And so it was that my husband, now a Major in the United States Army, went to war, just as thousands of other women's husbands, brothers and fathers did. It was incomprehensible that my husband might die but death became a living thing, like a succubus that attached itself to your shoulder or worst yet, got inside your head where you carried it around with you all day every day. The reality for the thousands who went to Vietnam to fight was that many would never return alive.

The Vietnam War was an unpopular war and there was little compassion for the soldiers or their families. Almost daily someone I knew was being informed of her brother, father or husband's death, messages which were delivered in cruel, unconscionable ways; it might be a knock on the door in the middle of the night to deliver a "your-husband-is-dead" telegram; or, a curt "your-husband-is-dead" telephone message, to a letter sent in the mail asking wives to pick up body remains from the airport on a particular date. We military wives all lived in a state of shock and perpetual anxiety.

Lives were being snuffed out with little regard or compassion for them or for surviving wives and families. Bitterness, rage, and resentment welled up inside us, turning many of my friends into widows at far too young an age. We held one another in silence, letting the tears fall down what had become stony, cold faces.

Our local group of military wives in Huntsville, Alabama where I'd chosen to live while Saren was in Vietnam, were young and on our own for the first time. Most of us had babies and small children. Without noticing, we had become mother, father, family counselor, nurse, budget planner, and sole decision maker; in short, independent single parents with one major difference: our husbands were in a remote jungle in a country we'd never heard of, fighting an unpopular war and getting killed by the thousands!

"We might as well be the enemy," my best friend Sharon said despairingly over lunch one day where a few of us had gotten together to talk.

"No one cares if our husbands live or die," I said, stirring my over-sweetened ice tea, a cultural tradition in the South.

"You know what happened to me yesterday at the grocery store?" asked Charlene, a mother of two young babies. "When the person behind me at the check-out line heard me say something about my husband being in Vietnam and how worried I was about him, she told me in a loud voice so everyone could hear, that I wasn't going to get any sympathy from her because "you knew what you were getting into when your husband signed up to be a soldier." Her chest heaved with a sigh of grief she knew only too well since her brother had recently been reported "killed in action." Breaking into sobs, she rushed off to the bathroom to get control of herself.

Later that week a few of us wives gathered again, this time at Helen's home. Helen was a personal friend and her three boys attended the pre-school on the Redstone Arsenal Army post where I was working as the school's director. I chose to work to stay busy and to be near Marie and Alex, now three and four and a half years old. Helen had just been notified that her husband had been killed and when we arrived, she was resting in the back bedroom after the Army doctor had given her a sedative to help her sleep. A group of us were there to watch her three boys and help them get through the next few days until family members arrived.

One of Helen's young boys had turned on the television just as the latest brutal scene of dead bodies in Vietnam popped up on the screen. Without a word, one of the women quickly scooped him up and took him outside to play with the other children while another silently walked over and turned off the television set.

"You never know what you're going to see on television anymore," she said, quietly pouring another cup of coffee from the coffee pot that we kept going. Many of the women had become smokers; many were drinking too much. I, who had insisted to high heaven that my husband never take another sip of alcohol, was having an occasional drink and smoking an occasional cigarette. My weight had dropped from 110 lbs. to 95 lbs. and I was anything but calm. In an effort not to transmit that anxiety to the children, I would read them stories every night from the Bible or children's books. Saren would sometimes write letters to them, which they loved and that helped to keep their dad in their minds. They went to pre-school every day and playing games, taking them to swim, and doing other activities with them also helped to mitigate the absolute terror I felt sometimes about the possibility of their father getting killed. How would I ever explain his death to them? They were only children; too young to have to bear such a reality.

"I mean, do they have to give us the body count every day on the nightly news? That's just the time the kids and I sit down for supper. It's awful!" Charlene said, crushing out her cigarette in the overflowing ashtray, spilling ashes onto the table. We were having a pot-luck dinner at her house and although we all noticed the ashes spilling over from the ashtray, no one said anything or made a move to clean it up. Sometimes we just didn't care if things were clean or not. What did it matter?

"Well, one good thing about the news, if there is one, is that we're learning the names of all those awful places in Vietnam," Sharon, a young twenty-two-year-old with a newborn spoke up.

We all nodded in agreement. If we recognized any of the places reported on the news that had suffered particularly brutal attacks and knew someone's husband was serving there, we'd pick up the phone and give a call. "Bring the kids and come over right now," we'd say to her. "Don't stay another minute by yourself!"

We comforted one another as women have always done in desperate times. We shopped at the Base Exchange, took the kids to the dentist and pre-school, and gave each other home perms. Some of us went back to school to stay busy; some worked jobs outside the home like I had chosen to do; others stayed busy with volunteer work or more involvement in their church, anything to keep our minds off what might be happening to our husbands. Some broke from the strain and suffered nervous breakdowns. Most of us waited in agony and quiet desperation. I was twenty-four years old, with two young children, and like all the other wives in our support group; my life had become a living hell.

All we wives pretended that everything was normal; pretended that we had happy, adjusted lives. After all, war was a natural thing, wasn't it? Were there any reasonable, viable alternatives to war? We had to have the upper hand on those who were seeking to kill us, didn't we? Didn't necessity dictate that our country had to have a strong defense against bullies and evildoers in other parts of the world that threated our national security? My military husband and the husbands of the other young women believed those things to be true and were putting their lives on the line to prove it. Was there any room for healthy doubt and questioning of the war if our husbands and brothers were fighting and getting killed? Certainly, most Americans at the time were questioning the presence of our military in the jungles of Vietnam. If we truly loved and supported our husbands and our country, however, could we do anything less than wait, be patient and pray that God would see us through the ordeal?

******

One evening in early January 1968 while watching television during the period of time that came to be known as the bloody Vietnam Tet Offensive, picture after horrible picture flashed across the screen showing Vietnamese women and children running into bomb-shattered streets, crying and tearing their hair as they stood over the bloodied dead bodies of husbands and fathers. In those brief moments of seeing women like myself literally tearing their hair out and screaming over their beloveds lying in the street, I felt a connection to them through time and space. They were the same as me.

Suddenly, I was overcome with a realization that these women were crying out for mercy and protection for the lives of their loved ones, the same as us American women were. Who would the Father God choose? Would He choose my family and me because we were white and Christian believers? According to my religious upbringing, that's exactly who He would choose because we believed and trusted in the one true God and His son Jesus Christ for our salvation.

With these questions about God and faith rumbling about in my brain, I decided to seek counsel, this time with the Army Base Chaplin whom I knew and trusted because, like Chaplin Tinker on Kwajalein, Chaplin Jones had also been a Baptist minister before entering the military service. This meant something to me because I knew his faith, like all Baptists, was scripture-based and that was critically important because it was the direct word of God.

We met in the Chaplin's office at the Army Chapel. The Chaplin, a very tall man who had to bend to get through the door, greeted me with his big-toothy smile, and pointed to a chair in front of his desk for me to be seated.

"Chaplin Jones, I hardly know where to begin..." was all I could say before I burst into tears.

"There, there. It's all okay," he assured me, pointing to a box of Kleenex on the corner of his desk. "You know Jesus always has an answer for us if we trust in him."

"You know my husband's in Vietnam, Pastor, and I'm really afraid he's going to get killed," I managed to say before breaking into sobs again.

He waited.

"I've been seeing all these pictures on television showing Vietnamese women and children running in the streets and throwing themselves on the bloody dead bodies of their husbands..." Once more I broke off, sobbing and grabbing more tissues.

"Go on, go on," he urged, folding his hands calmly and precisely on his desk.

"I don't understand how God is only going to protect me and my husband and our American soldiers just because we're Christians," I said, managing to regain some composure.

"Mrs. Canto, Mrs. Canto," he said several times barely hiding a slightly exasperated tone. "These are issues best left to us theologians. You shouldn't worry your pretty little head about such matters. Just trust in the knowledge that you are saved through your belief in Christ Jesus. Let Him take care of who goes to heaven and who doesn't. Now, I'm a busy man as you might well imagine."

He stood up, a signal our time was over. Grabbing my purse, I stood up too, taking in the not-so-subtle cue. Once again Chaplin Jones flashed his big-toothy smile at me, walked around the desk, and reaching out his hand, patted me on the top of my head.

"Now don't you worry about a thing, Mrs. Canto. Your husband's in God's hands and you know God is a merciful God. He's not going to let anything happen to your husband if it can be helped. Pray. Pray. Don't forget to pray!"

With these words, he took my elbow and steered me towards the office door.

"You just call me anytime you want to talk. Now remember; don't you go worrying about who or what God does or doesn't do. That's up to God. Just turn those questions over to God when they come up. Give them up to God!"

With tears stinging at the corners of my eyes, I finally found my sexy red MGBGT sports car Saren had bought me before leaving for Vietnam, a sort of *thank-you-for-being-such-a-good-sport-for-me-going-off-to-war-instead-of-Canada -like-you-wanted-me-to-do* present. I didn't know what had just happened in Chaplin Jone's office but something had played out terribly wrong. I had just poured my heart out to a minister of God only to have him reach over and pat me on the head? Only to have him advise me not to worry that pretty little head about such philosophical questions and to just let God take care of everything? Was I just a child in a woman's body to him and in the eyes of the church?

How could I worship a God who didn't love everyone equally and more importantly, unconditionally? How could I worship a God who put restrictions on what a person had to do to be saved and condemned everybody else to hell? Wasn't Jesus' message a simple one: Love one another?

Even though I wasn't in the mainstream of intellectuals who at the time were proclaiming that God was dead, that day sitting in the parking lot of the Army Chapel dedicated to God and His Holy word, I felt it in my gut.

******

Saren was due home from his tour of duty in Vietnam and I was marking off the final days on the calendar with a big red "x". It was April 3, 1968, and I was watching Dr. Martin Luther King give a televised speech, later referred to as "I've Been to the Mountain" in Memphis, Tennessee, where he'd gone in support of sanitation workers who were on strike.

Unexpectedly, tears of empathy poured down my cheeks as I listened and I felt myself being swept away by the purity and passion of Dr. King's words. He was right, I thought. I am a Southerner and a racist; I hadn't realized until now that I was a racist but I am. I am guilty of discrimination. Just as I'd been a racist in the Marshall Islands towards our maid and baby nanny Jai, afraid that her poor English would negatively impact baby Alex's speech. I was ashamed, sorry for the unintended harm I had inflicted on others through my ignorance and unquestioned superiority because I was white. Yet, my Christian faith and culture had always supported me in these beliefs and, in fact, had promulgated them.

Another shift like the one that had originally landed me in Chaplin Jones's office for counseling happened to me again during Dr. King's speech. An invisible threshold to a larger perspective was revealed to me and I had crossed over and through to the other side. Insights had been made. What exactly these epiphanies might mean in the future, I wasn't sure. But I knew I was a changed person. Little did I know that my exodus from a male God and male-dominated religion had begun in earnest and there would be no turning back.

At the end of Dr. King's speech, his words seemed to prophesize that he knew his time was short.

Well, I don't know what will happen now. We've got some difficult days ahead. But it really doesn't matter with me now, because I've been to the mountaintop. And I don't mind. Like anybody, I would like to live a long life; longevity has its place. But I'm not concerned about that now. I just want to do God's will. And He's allowed me to go up to the mountain. And I've looked over. And I've seen the Promised Land. I may not get there with you. But I want you to know tonight, that we, as a people, will get to the Promised Land. So, I'm happy, tonight. I'm not worried about anything. I'm not fearing any man. Mine eyes have seen the glory of the coming of the Lord.

The next day, April 4th, the news came that one James Earl Ray had assassinated Dr. Martin Luther King in Memphis, Tennessee, when he had walked out onto his motel balcony. I, along with millions of people around the world, was devastated. It was a cold-blooded murderous act. How could such a thing happen in America? How could there be so much hatred for a Christian man speaking out for racial equality?

I turned to relatives and friends for support and understanding. What I found astounded me. Many of my Southern neighbors and friends were passionate about Dr. King's death all right, but not in the way I had expected.

"I'll tell you what I think," a close friend said when I called her a few days after Dr. King's murder. "We were in church on Sunday and when our pastor prayed for God's mercy on those who killed Dr. King, why, everybody in the congregation stood right up and walked out the front door. We weren't sorry that man was dead! He deserved what he got! All those freedom riders coming down here from the North had better take note and learn from King's death and go home before something happens to them, too!"

Suddenly, I felt the world had gone quite mad! I was growing up quickly and being shown in no uncertain terms, the negative, shadow side of human beings, including myself. How was it possible that I had lived such a sheltered, protected life that I recognized almost nothing of this deep hatred, racism and violence that surrounded me? I and many other young whites in the South who were waking up were shocked and disappointed at our lack of awareness but also at the hatred we saw still being reflected around us. This extreme hatred for anything or anyone different than us whites was not a plague visited only on the South, of course; it was also rampant in the North, only there it was more discretely hidden and harder to see, but it was there, too.

******

Dressed in our best finery, the two children and I went to the airport to meet our father and husband, home from the war. We cried and hugged and were so happy. Saren was distant and somber and I was gaunt and skinny. We were both deeply changed people, inside and out. I soon realized I would never really know the trauma he had lived through nor would he know mine. Like thousands of other wives and soldiers who had fought in the Vietnam War, there was no counseling or gratitude for having risked their lives; nor was there any knowledge of the emotional and mental toll referred to now as PTSD. We did our best to pick up our lives on our own and move on.

During those first months after Saren was home, we lay in bed and held one another, often crying together.

"How can we ever catch up with each other?" I asked. "I feel so changed, like I'm a new person, like you're a new person. So many things have happened during these past eighteen months."

"It's going to take some time," Saren said, holding me closer.

"Did you ... I mean, did your unit kill anyone?"

He instantly pulled away. "I told you about the attack on our compound the week before I left. Some Vietcong got over the walls and were killed. It happened and now it's over. You don't ask about the rightness of war or if the enemy's a good guy or a bad guy when somebody's pointing a gun at you to kill you. Me? No, personally I didn't pull the trigger and kill anyone. But it's not something I want to talk about, okay?"

Saren got up from the bed, headed to the bathroom and closed the door. I thought I heard muffled tears, but I didn't really know for sure because I was sobbing into the pillow. Had we stumbled too close to the edge of a world in chaos and fallen in, destroyed in the end by all we thought would save us?

Soon we'd be heading out to another new post in the desert sands of New Mexico, White Sands Missile Range. Perhaps a new landscape along with time would help heal us both.

MRS. COMMANDING GENERAL HAS HER SAY

"There's going to be an anti-Vietnam protest rally this afternoon on campus. Let's go and check it out." It was my new friend Gail whom I'd met in Shakespeare class on the campus of New Mexico State University in Las Cruces where I'd returned to complete my undergraduate degree. "I'll meet you at 2pm in front of the student union," she called, flying off to her next class.

Putting on the rally were a group of people who called themselves hippies and peace activists. I'd stopped a few times between classes to listen to their speeches and loud music but still wasn't sure what to make of them or their raging anti-Vietnam rhetoric.

After my class, I walked to the large grassy area in front of the student union and spotted Gail, not a hard thing to do since she was a beautiful woman with long brunette hair, sparkling hazel eyes and curvaceous figure that turned heads everywhere she went. She was super smart, divorced, a single mom with three young girls and lived in student housing. We'd hit it off in English class when I'd made a humorous remark and she'd laughed out loud. After that incident, we'd become instant friends. We waved to one another and she signaled for me to join her near the front of the stage. One anti-Vietnam war protestor after another, all wearing black arm bands, filed across the stage, taking the microphone and blasting President Nixon and his Vietnam policies.

"Nixon's a liar. He told us he was going to withdraw American troops from South Vietnam but instead he's been secretly bombing Cambodia and Laos. There's proof he ordered the bombing and that he's not going to withdraw our troops," an articulate male, his long hair braided in "dread locks", argued into the microphone.

After a few more speeches, we decided we'd seen and heard enough and headed over to Gail's apartment near the campus.

"What did you think of the rally?" I asked as we sat in her small, modestly furnished living room sipping tea.

"Rallies against the war are happening all across America. I think there's ample evidence to support the protestors' claims that Nixon is lying about everything, especially Vietnam."

"If I'm truthful," I said hesitantly, "I thought the protestors were right about a lot of things. I mean, it doesn't make a lot of sense for us to keep fighting a war that's killing so many of our soldiers and never ends. I know all about that."

We were quiet for a few moments. Gail knew I was married to a career military officer who had just finished a tour in Vietnam.

"I feel guilty," I said, breaking the silence, "for agreeing with any of the anti-war protestor's ideas but I don't dare talk about it with Saren. He definitely would think I was a traitor after all he went through in Vietnam and he's not the kind of guy who welcomes opinions different from his own. He's still too close to all that happened to him in Vietnam."

******

After my visit with Gail, I drove the 65 miles from the New Mexico State University campus in Las Cruces to White Sands Missile Range, where we had been stationed after Saren's tour of duty in Vietnam. Driving with the radio off, with only silence and the emptiness of the remote desert landscape, there was nothing to distract me from obsessing over how the relationship with my husband was changing.

Letting out a heavy sigh, I watched as the glistening late afternoon light played off the majestic peaks of the beautiful Organ Mountains situated between Las Cruces and the military post. Although we had stepped into a new life in the remote desert region of southern New Mexico, we were still in recovery from the strain of Vietnam and in great transition, personally and as a couple. For the first time, I was feeling shaky in my marriage and wondered if Saren and I would make it through all the stress and changes we continued to experience. Before his time in Vietnam, we had shared everything but since his return we were keeping things from each other, or at least I was because I knew certain things would upset him. War changes you and I was well aware of the many friends whose marriages had ended in divorce after their husbands had returned from the fighting.

In part, the re-adjustment struggle had to do with a power dynamic. When Saren had first left for Vietnam, I put off doing things before writing to him to get his input but that became ridiculous because letters back and forth took weeks. In our husbands' absence, we wives had become sole decision makers, single parents managing home, school, a job if we had one and the million other little things required to keep a household running. Relinquishing that decision-making power and independence to our war-veteran husbands, some of whom were suffering from PTSD, wasn't an easy thing to do.

After eighteen months of running our household, it was awkward if not humiliating to ask Saren for money much as a child might ask their parent for an allowance. Finding ways to reach or appeal to Saren to consider something I thought important, like going back to university, was becoming more difficult and I began to resent that I had to figure out ways to approach him to get a favorable response or watch what I said to get him to see my point of view. It felt like manipulation and it probably was because I would plan out my approach, decide where it would happen, and rehearse what I'd say.

"Saren, I've been thinking that I want to go back to college and get my degree. You know that's been my dream even before we got married. I know it'll take a lot of adjustments but I think if we pull together, we can make it work."

"Yeah. Okay. I think we can work something out. Let's talk about it some more," he said, pushing back the empty plate from the delicious meal I'd prepared of the New Mexican style-cuisine I was learning to cook.

"I'm thinking about majoring in English and getting my teaching certificate and maybe teaching school in the future," I said.

It wasn't like Saren was always over me like a tyrant or despot. It was much more subtle than that. He was amenable to new things and ideas if it suited him, or if the thing at hand caught his fancy, or if it added anything like possibly more income for our family. It didn't mean that I didn't argue for my opinions. I did. But in a Southern Belle sort of way, which basically brings us back to manipulation.

It was clear to us both, however, that our discussions as to what to do in any given situation were power-based, me as the civilian, talking with an officer, Saren, whose opinion clearly outranked mine. He was, after all, a Lt. Colonel now.

※※※※※※

A few weeks after Gail and I had watched an anti-war rally, I stopped to listen to another rally happening on campus. I drew in a sharp breath. What's going on now? I wondered. The protestors had placed an effigy of a soldier inside a wooden casket and set it on fire to show their horror and non-support for America's continuing participation in the Vietnam War. It was a dramatic sight and brought to mind the images of the horrified Vietnamese women running through the streets, while fires from napalm bombs flamed around them. I continued to watch in silent agreement at the burning effigy mixed with feelings of guilt and a sense of betrayal. What about the men like my husband who had put their lives on the line by serving in Vietnam? Was there a middle ground somewhere in the War vs. Peace narrative?

I still thought hippies strange with their long hair, constant flashing of their two first fingers in the shape of a "v" to signify peace, and their tie-dyed, rainbow-colored clothes, but I liked some of their ideas. Some of the protestors were in classes with me and they asked interesting questions and gave insightful, informative answers in class discussions. In a certain way, they were brave people because NMSU was an agricultural school and extremely conservative; not known for taking on political or social issues. The protestors were risking expulsion from the university.

Hippies and peace activists weren't as interesting to me as a new movement called *feminism*, however, which was a topic in my sociology class taught by a brilliant woman professor whose lectures on women and women's rights both shocked and mesmerized me, so much so that I finally gave up trying to take notes and just listened.

"Feminism is a movement dedicated to ensuring women have equal rights under the law. It challenges the patriarchy and other all-male institutions that run our country. Social contracts such as marriage are a form of control created and championed by the patriarchal system to ensure that women are kept powerless," she spoke, striding confidently back and forth in front of the class in her smart two-piece suit and heels.

"They do this in many ways, one of the most popular being to inculcate women to the concept of romantic love. Women are kept trapped in submissive roles when they are conditioned to emulate fairy-tale lives; then they want to marry the Prince; want the Prince to take care of them, to make them happy. Everyone, men and women alike, pay a high price to keep women 'in their place', which for most women means staying at home, staying pregnant and being the happy little homemaker while the men go out and run the world!"

After class I raced to tell Gail about Professor Henley's latest lecture about women and marriage and something called "the patriarchy." She and I discussed these new radical ideas that were part of this thing called *feminism* during lunch at the student center, nibbling tuna sandwiches on stale bread and hardly noticing. "What is this feminism thing?" we'd ask each other, trying to assess if we'd been duped into the roles we were playing in our lives by a culture ruled and defined by an overarching form of control called the patriarchy. "Are we being manipulated? Do we have equal rights with men? What does Professor Henley mean when she says we need to exercise power over our own lives? And, what's wrong with romantic love?"

******

My friend Gail and I were both English majors and taking upper-level classes together. One day while having lunch again in the student union building, I shared with her that I felt I was living a double life. "When I'm not at school, I'm playing bridge with other Officer's Wives, or attending luncheons at the Officer's club. Sometimes my friend Jackie and I take the kids to the Officer's club to swim; or, I'm rehearsing the choir for Sunday's music at the chapel service. Then there's all the class work I have to do for school, the reading and writing. It feels like it's too much sometimes."

"I feel the same way," Gail agreed. "Even though I don't have the officer's wife duties you do, I'm a single parent and taking care of three young girls, working part-time, and going to school full time is exhausting. Sometimes I wonder why I'm doing all this or how long I can keep doing it all."

"You know, in high school, I loved achieving things because I wanted to but there was always this feeling I wasn't enough and that I had to strive to be the very best at whatever I did, whatever the cost. It was like I was this other girl who needed to do all these things in order to be loved and belong, and although I knew it wasn't me, I thought I had to become her," I said, sipping on my diet coke.

"That's sort of how it was for me in high school too. I was a cheerleader and class officer but even though I was popular and made good grades, I still felt that somehow that wasn't enough," Gail said.

"How come we think that as women we have to be perfect or excel at everything? Or, have to do everything a hundred times better than men? How come it's not enough to just be an ordinary woman?"

"I think it's because society tells us we have to be these perfect, amazing people to be worthy of love. Like you have to cook the perfect meals, have to have the perfect body, be the adoring wife and the never-get-angry mom. It's ridiculous!"

******

The reality of my living a double life hadn't gone unnoticed by an important other party, either.

One day my best friend on post Jackie and I had taken our kids to the pool and were having lunch poolside at the Officer's club, when the Commanding General's wife approached our table. Without so much as a "hello" or "how are you", she cocked her head back and delivered what seemed to be a well-rehearsed speech.

"I hear you're going to Las Cruces to the University," she said, crossing her arms in a deliberate gesture to show hands dripping with jewelry and long manicured nails. "I saw your picture in the newspaper for making the Dean's list. I just want to remind you, my dear that your first duty is to support your husband in having a successful military career. Just remember, that's your first priority! You'd be wise not to forget that." She turned precisely on her heels like a soldier in a marching regiment and walked off, leaving Jackie and me stunned and choking on our salads.

"How dare she talk to me like that," I protested with a lame bravado after I'd recovered enough to speak. "I mean who does she think she is?"

"She's the Commanding General's wife, which makes her Mrs. Commanding General, that's who."

I knew that Jackie, even though she was my best friend, didn't understand why I had wanted to go to university.

"Why do you even want a degree?" she'd asked when I first told her I was returning to university. "What are you going to do with it anyway? You'll be moving all the time making it hard to get a job. Do you want a job?" she asked, as though the thought of an officer's wife having a job was unfathomable. I explained that finishing college was always a dream of mine and that Saren supported me in making that dream a reality, even if I never worked at a job outside the home.

"I wonder if the General's wife will mention anything to her husband?" I asked Jackie as we rounded up the kids from the pool they never wanted to leave, and drove to our homes on "officer's row."

******

"Guess who got called into the General's office today?" Saren asked that evening after work, throwing his brief case down on the kitchen table with a thud.

"Oh, no! What happened?" I asked, hoping it didn't have anything to do with Mrs. Commanding General's advice to me at the pool earlier that day.

"He said he'd seen your picture in the post newspaper and congratulated me on having such a smart wife."

"Well, that's good, isn't it?" I said, relieved.

"Not exactly. He went on to say he did have a slight concern, however."

"What could he possibly be concerned about?" I asked, waiting for the talk on being a good wife as my first and most important priority. There was actually a book on how to be a good officer's wife and since we wives had already had a class on its contents, which was mostly about proper protocol in various situations, such as how to pour tea and how to tell the various officer's ranks, I knew getting an education wasn't in there.

"He advised me that it wasn't a good idea for you to be driving to school every day with an enlisted man's wife. Those kinds of relationships, you know, between officers and enlisted personnel, are *not* permitted. He suggested you should drive alone from now on."

"What? Are you kidding me?" I yelled. "He can't tell me who I can drive with in my own car... Can he?"

"He can and he did. You'll just have to tell Denise that you can't drive with her anymore. She'll understand. She's been in the military for years and knows the rules about officers not fraternizing with enlisted personnel."

"But it's not every day, and besides, it's almost 130 miles round-trip, and going over the Organ Mountain pass can be tricky at times and it's helpful to have someone with you. Besides, Denise is a good friend," I pleaded.

"We're in the military and those are the rules: no fraternizing with enlisted personnel."

"But we obey that rule, don't we? I mean, we don't invite enlisted people to our dinner parties. Driving in a car with someone isn't really socializing, is it? How does he even know who I drive with anyway?"

Saren made no comment but went to change his clothes before going out to the garage where he was completely re-building a classic Austin Healey sports car he'd just bought. In his mind, there was nothing else to talk about. The General had spoken, or rather Mrs. Commanding General had spoken. Kind of like the Wizard of Oz, I thought, only not as funny ... not really funny at all.

I fumed around most of the next day, digging furiously in my flower garden to let off steam. It's not fair I have to lose a friend over some stupid rule that makes no sense. Who makes up such stupid rules, anyway? I can't believe Saren would go along with such stupid unfair rules! Why does the military have all these ridiculous rules?

I did a load of laundry, started pulling things out of the refrigerator for dinner and checked periodically on the kids playing in their rooms. Finally, when I knew I couldn't delay the inevitable any longer, bracing myself, I reluctantly picked up the phone and dialed Denise's number. As I waited for her to answer, I rehearsed again what I'd say, all of which evaporated the moment I heard "hello" from the other end of the line.

"I can't believe what I'm about to say, Denise, but you and I can't drive together to school anymore," I blurted out, struggling to hold back tears.

"What?" Denise asked, not comprehending.

"The Commanding General found out that you and I were driving together to school. I'm pretty sure his bossy wife told him. Anyway, he called

Saren into his office and *suggested* ... and we both know that *Generals don't suggest* ... that he tell his wife that it wasn't appropriate for her to drive to school with an enlisted man's wife. Can you believe anything so outrageous? The General told Saren it didn't look good for an officer's wife and an enlisted man's wife to be fraternizing with one another, that it set a bad example. I'm so sorry Denise, but Saren says that because of what the General said, we can't drive to school together anymore."

My hand was shaking and I could hardly control the fury in my voice.

Denise said she understood. "It's okay. I've been the wife of an Army Sergeant for fifteen years now. I know how these things work, but I honestly didn't think driving in a car together would be a problem."

I hung up the phone in tears. I would miss Denise and all our conversations during the long drive to school, conversations where we had tried to make sense of how women's place in the world was changing and how it was affecting us, conversations that sometimes took a more philosophical bent on how it was that our individual lives were constantly shifting in weird and unexpected ways, and whether or not we trusted a God in heaven to direct them.

"Our lives are metaphors for the shifting white desert sands, don't you think?" Denise, who was a Christian and taught Sunday school at the Chapel, had once observed.

"I read Alfred Hitchcock said in an interview about the film or maybe it was a TV show he made near the white sand dunes, that he described this area as a seriously scary place and one he wasn't sorry to leave."

"I think he may have been right," Denise had said, gazing out the car window at the desolate desert landscape.

I missed Denise terribly on my drive alone to school and back, but I didn't drop out which I knew was what Mrs. Commanding General expected me to do. When I started senior year and began the semester of student teaching in English Literature to fulfill requirements for getting a high school teaching certification, I began to see less and less of Jackie and my other friends on post. Conversations with Saren about the new ideas I was being exposed to were almost non-existent. I began to feel isolated and alone.

DESERT AWAKENING

Archery Class 101: A boiling hot day in the Las Cruces desert where I am taking archery to fulfill a required PE class. Sweating like a first-time performer on opening night, I place the arrow in the huge bow, ignoring the black and blue marks on my wrists from weeks of the bowstring slapping against them, and take careful aim at the center of the circular target at the end of the shooting range ... but something's wrong, terribly wrong. I drop the bow and barely make it to the women's restroom before I pass out. Flat on the floor passed out.

Someone from the health clinic called Saren and a military ambulance was immediately sent to take me back to White Sands where I was admitted to the hospital for observation, and ended up staying a week, sleeping 8-to-10 hours a day, to recover from what the doctor diagnosed as *de-hydration, physical exhaustion and emotional strain.*

Rattling off a few details of my life and busy schedule to the doctor, he shook his head. "I'm strongly suggesting you see the post psychiatrist, Dr. Weinstein, who comes over from Ft. Bliss Army Base in El Paso to see clients here at White Sands. I think you would benefit from some time with him," he said, writing out a prescription for Valium. Just in case you change your mind," he added, giving me a reassuring smile. I'd already told him that even though I'd had a few anxiety attacks, I didn't want any medication because I didn't want to become a hypochondriac like my father who took pills for some aliment or another his entire life.

Alex and Marie, now six and seven, were waiting for me when I got home. "Are you okay, mommy?" they asked, wrapping their little arms around my neck.

"Mommy's fine now that I'm home with you," I said, blinking back tears.

"Do you want us to read to you so you can get some more sleep like you did in the hospital?" Alex asked, laying his head on my lap as all three of us snuggled on the sofa in the den. Their dad had brought them to visit me several times in the hospital, explaining that mommy was there because she's been working very hard and needed some extra sleep.

"What a great idea. Thank you. Go get your favorite book," I said, knowing it would be *Willy Wonka's Chocolate Factory* or *Charlotte's Web*.

As my two small children cuddled with me on the sofa, one on either side, reading to me from their favorite books in their sweet children's voices, I had the best feeling that no matter what I did with my life, giving birth to them would always be the greatest "achievement" of my life.

My joy at such a sweet homecoming was cut short when Saren reminded me that we had a trip to Las Vegas planned with best friends Jackie and Tom scheduled for the weekend, only two days away.

"I don't think I have the strength to go. I just got home from a week in the hospital," I pleaded weakly, having forgotten all about the trip.

"You can rest today and tomorrow and you'll be alright by the weekend. You don't have to do anything. I'll take care of the kids until then. All you have to do is relax. You'll be fine."

I had immediately begun to feel anxious. Saren had this awful habit of telling me how I felt, always assuring me I could do this thing or that thing, when often I just wanted to have some quiet, un-interrupted downtime. His constant urging me to do, do, do played directly into my already pumped-up Super Woman complex, which had landed me in the hospital in the first place.

Saren's idea of what was best won out and two days later, the four of us boarded a private Cessna airplane for Las Vegas with Saren, who had just gotten his private pilot's license, as the pilot. Once we checked into the fancy Las Vegas hotel for the weekend's festivities, I tried to laugh and have fun, because, I told myself, I'm with my husband and friends whom I love. Why am I so terribly anxious? I kept asking myself as I replayed over and over the scene in my mind when I passed out during archery class and the ambulance with its screaming siren coming to pick me up and the long, tortuous ride back to White Sands with me hyperventilating, worrying what everyone would think of me, what was going to happen next, and ultimately realizing I was absolutely overwhelmed by my life and was finding it ever more difficult to cope. Now, every time I heard a siren it would take me back to that whole series of events. It had become a trigger for my PTSD, a response to a traumatic event, something that hadn't been identified as a real thing yet. There were simply too many demands being made on me, many from myself but many from my husband and from the military environment we lived in and of course, from school.

Now, here I was, right out of the hospital, in the over-stimulating town of Las Vegas, trying to convince myself everything was okay, that I was okay, but rather than having fun, I was just enduring a weekend away, praying that the time would pass quickly so that I could go home to my children and familiar surroundings.

"What's wrong, honey?" Saren kept asking me.

"I'm afraid I'll faint again and have to go to the hospital or something," I answered, close to tears.

"Just lay down and rest by the pool this afternoon. That's relaxing. We've got the dinner and show tonight to see Tom Jones perform. You don't want to miss that. You'll be fine," he reassured me.

"But I don't feel fine. Why can't you understand that," I insisted, hoping that he might finally hear me, that he might see that I wasn't fine. He never did.

******

A week later, I sat waiting on a hard bench in front of Dr. Weinstein's office, the visiting psychiatrist from El Paso, anxiously wringing my hands and watching the minute hands on the hallway clock tick by, hoping to God I wouldn't see anyone I knew because I was so embarrassed and ashamed to be seeing a psychiatrist. Thirty minutes past our appointment time, a man opened the door and stuck his head out.

"Are you Mrs. Canto?" he asked.

I nodded.

"Come in. Have a seat. I'm Dr. Weinstein," he said in an unfamiliar accent I soon would learn belonged to a New Yorker. "How did you feel about having to wait thirty minutes past our appointment time?" he asked, jumping right in, without any small talk or get acquainted talk, something we Southerners always do.

What kind of question is that? I thought to myself.

"I didn't think anything really," I stammered. "Maybe that you couldn't break away from your client?... I mean, I didn't think anything," I said, my voice trailing off. I felt like a six-year-old.

"You didn't feel any anger?" he queried, staring hard at me.

"Anger?" I asked as though I'd never heard the word. In fact, it wasn't a word in my vocabulary or a subject I knew much about. Anger was forbidden, wrong. It was unbecoming to a girl or a lady of Southern Belle origins.

"You mean you didn't feel any sense of being disrespected or disregarded?"

"No, I guess I didn't. I just thought you had something important you were doing or, well, I don't know what you mean really," I stammered again. This was even more horrible than my obsessive and vivid imagination had imagined it would be. This man was a monster!

"Why are you here?" he asked, relenting on the question of anger that apparently, I hadn't been able to answer to his satisfaction.

"Because Doctor Middleton said I should see you."

"Anything else?"

I hated this man! Why had Dr. Middleton suggested I could benefit from seeing and talking to him?

"I've been having anxiety attacks and sometimes I get so nervous I can hardly function," I blurted out, reaching into my handbag for a tissue.

"Tell me about yourself. What's your life like? What do you do every day? Are you happy?"

"Dr. Weinstein, please. I cannot answer all those questions at once. You're going too fast," I responded, a hint of irritation creeping into my voice.

"Good!" he yelled.

"What? What's good?" I asked, my voice getting stronger at this man's incessant pushing me towards something I didn't understand. His pushing for something felt mean, making me feel I had to fight back.

"You had a real response just then. You didn't like what I said and you pushed back at me. That's what was good. So, please go on and tell me about yourself, your life."

I rattled off some basic details, "I'm a wife, mother, full-time college student, no longer a church person, have a few friends that…."

"Whoa! Back up. What's a church person?"

"I was raised in a very strict religious faith," I said, wringing the already damp tissue in my hands into tiny pieces, not sure I could explain something that was growing less clear to me every day. "It emphasized rigid adherence to church doctrine and Biblical scripture for morals and values. Since my husband's tour in Vietnam, I've been questioning the church's relevancy, especially how everything is interpreted and run by men."

"Go on, go on," he said excitedly, as if he'd finally struck pay dirt.

"I'm in university now, completing a B.A. degree and I've met a few professors on campus who have radically different ideas from any I've ever heard."

"Like what?"

"Well, like women have a right to choose what they want to do with their lives, like they don't have to be only housewives or mothers if they don't want to, and they don't have to ask permission all the time to do what they feel is right."

"Have you ever told anyone to go to hell?" he asked out of the blue.

"What? No! Never!" I replied, absolutely stunned at his question, flinging my words back at him as vehemently as someone might who'd just had a dead rat dropped in their lap.

"It might be a good idea for you to assert yourself once in a while and tell a few people to go to hell."

With that outlandish remark, he looked down at his watch, then his appointment calendar. "Let's make another appointment for next week," he said.

"Okay, I guess." As I stood to leave, he made another riveting remark.

"There's nothing wrong with you, Mrs. Canto; and, I'm not here to make you into a better Lt. Colonel's wife. Think about that until next time."

By the end of the shortened session, I was more confused than ever, but mysteriously I'd begun to think that just maybe Dr. Weinstein might not be as big a monster as I'd thought. Although I'd been completely shocked at his radical statements and questions, a part of me had felt heard, had felt seen for the first time in a long time and, like an emotionally starving person, I wanted more.

Needing time to think about the new ideas in the therapy session, I decided to go for a long walk on the road behind our house that backed up to the beautiful 9,000 ft. high Organ Mountains, named for their tall, slender peaks resembling the pipes of a pipe organ. Surrounded by the silent desert landscape, I reflected on how the magic of the desert had finally revealed itself to me after months of only being able to see shades of brown. It happened the first time I adjusted my sight enough to notice how light played off the spires of the Organ mountains in the early morning and twilight, creating a brilliant kaleidoscope of colors. Over time, I had also begun to appreciate the wide-open vistas that seemed to go on forever, much like the ocean, providing a perfect backdrop to toss out thoughts and let them wander off on their own into the distance; the desert contained a silence of such enormous magnitude that it had become like a medicine for healing my raw, sensitive emotions.

The desert was awakening something inside me, something new and unknown. It wasn't anything I could put a name to but once I'd married and left home, like Dorothy in the *Wizard of Oz*, I was aware I was no longer in Kansas or in my case, a small Southern town in Georgia. Like Dorothy, I too, had been caught up in a tornado of change that had transported me to new worlds filled with strange people with unusual beliefs and customs.

But who was I in this story? All my life I had been told what I was supposed to do, what I was supposed to want and supposed to become that I really didn't know who or what I was outside those definitions. For years, I had worked diligently to be all the things my culture had told me I needed to be, but something was still missing and it seemed to be the most important thing ... me!

With the strain of the conflict between my interior self and my outer reality, I had begun to have anxiety attacks. Maybe that's what I liked about what Dr. Feinstein had told me in our first session today; that it was okay for me to want to be something other than a good wife to my husband who might someday be a General. Maybe I didn't have to be a nice, smiley, Southern Belle Christian girl to be okay in my skin. Maybe I should tell someone to go to hell! At that thought, I laughed out loud, startling a small rabbit from its hiding place behind a clump of sage bushes, jarring me to recall the memory of the time my daddy told someone to go to hell. It was a story no one in the family told because, according to mother, "it's a shameful story about your daddy and his bad temper and I don't want you repeating it to anybody." But today, having just paid a visit to a person with radical ideas who'd suggested it might be good for me to tell someone to go to hell, remembering the story about daddy felt like an affirmation that I was on the right track with my life.

THE ROARING INSIDE

It wasn't a very long story. It had begun one Sunday morning when daddy and other men in his Sunday school class were standing outside the First Baptist Church, smoking their unfiltered Kent cigarettes before Sunday Church service. Baptists have a lot of "do's and don'ts" but no one knew until that particular Sunday that smoking in front of the church was one of the "don'ts." The preacher had preached a good sermon that morning, the offering plate had been passed and all was going along pretty well until the end of his message, just about the time the choir stood up, poised to sing "Must Jesus Bear the Cross Alone", when all of a sudden, the good Pastor Jones got a second wind and used it, not to condemn sin, but smoking!

"It just doesn't look good to anybody passing by our church to see a bunch of grown Christian men smoking outside the Lord's house! It doesn't set a good example for the young. It would be a whole sight better if you cigarette smokers, and you know who you are," he said, looking directly at the smoking offenders who all set together each Sunday in the second pew from the front, "it would be a whole sight better if you cigarette smokers," he said, repeating himself for emphasis, "to come inside the church and spend your time praying before the service starts instead of standing outside and smoking. Amen."

After church service, daddy had waited outside in the parking lot for Pastor Jones and that's when the incident happened. After the incident, he came on home, but took his time telling us what had happened. He waited until just the right moment to tell us, like any good performer who knows his audience, and daddy had a little experience with that because he played the piano with a "honky-tonk" group on Saturday nights until mother told him he'd have to give it up and get a real job or she'd leave him. Daddy waited until his audience, in this case the three of us, my brother Jack, my mom and me, were seated around our new square chrome-legged dining table with its chrome backed, plastic-covered dining chairs, where mother had laid out all the fixings for a proper Sunday dinner; fried chicken, mashed potatoes, green beans, cornbread, and for dessert, her acclaimed caramel cake, all served with tall glasses filled to the brim with over-sweetened ice tea.

With a bit of pride flavored with strong tones of righteousness, daddy told his rapt audience of three what had transpired at church that morning and afterwards when he'd met up with the good Pastor in the parking lot.

"After church service, I waited outside in the parking lot for the Pastor to give him a piece of my mind. I told that son-of-a-bitch I'd smoke my cigarettes anywhere I got good and damn ready to and he could go straight to hell if he didn't like it and then I told him it would be a cold day in hell before I ever stepped foot in his First Baptist church again!"

Mother, perhaps as a result of having had an immediate out-of-body experience on hearing daddy's story, jumped straight up out of her new dining room chair, almost knocking over her glass of ice tea and began screaming at the top of her lungs! Now it was her turn to forget the Bible's teaching on "thou shall not cuss."

"Johnnie Beene! You better get your sorry ass back out there and tell that Preacher how sorry you are for speaking to him like that! Johnnie Beene, if you don't go apologize right this minute, I swear I'll leave your ass and take the kids and go live with my sister Ellie!"

Ellie was mother's oldest sister who lived in Alabama, but thank goodness mother didn't have to make good on her threat to leave daddy because it wasn't long before he caught up with the Pastor and apologized like mother told him to. But daddy was true to his word and never did step foot inside the First Baptist church again. That is, until he died of lung cancer some eight years later from smoking his Kent cigarettes any damn time and place he wanted to; and the Pastor, being a man of God and holding no grudges, had preached the farewell sermon over daddy's waif-thin body that cancer had eaten up.

I guess my daddy had done a lot of thinking about hell in his life because when he died, among his belongings were his Bible and two of his favorite books, which Mother gave to me. One of the books was Mark Twain's

Short Stories and the other was Margaret Mitchell's *Gone With the Wind*. Inside the front cover of *Gone With the Wind*, daddy had written in what at the end of his life had become his shaky, scrawling hand, "Page 584. Scarlett's greatest hope accomplished. To tell the whole world to go to Hell." He had underlined the word "Hell."

But I wondered if daddy had really been happy after he'd told the Pastor to go to hell; if he'd felt remorseful, or guilty. Had it given him a bit of peace when he'd dumped out some of the anger he'd carried around with him for most of his life, anger that along with smoking and working with chemical fumes on the jet engines he repaired as an airplane mechanic for the air force, had caused him to be constantly sick? Was getting sick all the time the only way he knew how to deal with his anger? Was that what Dr. Weinstein was trying to tell me? That you had better get your anger out before it kills you? But how were you supposed to do that and still be a nice girl, especially when I could barely say the word "anger."

******

Spontaneous epiphanies became commonplace during my time of living in the remote desert, so much so that I began to refer to my time there as a desert awakening. New insights kept popping up like popcorn kernels in a hot skillet, often landing in strange and unexpected places. One religious epiphany of particular singularity came one Sunday while attending Chapel Sunday service, shortly after I'd started seeing Dr. Weinstein.

Since my time in the hospital due to mental and physical exhaustion, I had recently resigned as the choir director to focus more on my kids and studies; but other than sitting in the audience instead of up on the podium with the choir, this Sunday service seemed like most, the choir had sung of God and devotion; the offering plate had been passed; and the righteous congregation sat all proper-like and attentive while the Chaplin in his flowing robes, looked down on us from the raised pulpit from which he delivered his sermon, same as he did every Sunday.

Saren and I were sitting with a child on either side of us to eliminate arguments, when I nervously began to fuss with the crooked ruffle on the new dress I'd sewn for Marie. I can still pull it off, I told myself. No matter what the therapist says, I can still be the greatest ever mom and perfect wife to my husband; I know it's not too late. Weinstein doesn't know everything. I can obey my husband; I can be the perfect hostess who makes everything from scratch for our elaborate dinner parties that will make him look great and everybody will love me and they'll make him a General and we'll all live happily ever after. The End. That's the story, my story, no matter what the Sociology Professor or the hippies or Dr. Weinstein or anyone else says!

The organist began playing the majestic hymn "A Mighty Fortress Is Our God" written by reformist theologian Martin Luther. I didn't have to look at the hymnal because I'd sung it a thousand times, had directed choirs in singing it a thousand times. I opened my mouth to sing with the congregation in praise of a Mighty Father God, a mighty warrior God. "A Mighty fortress is our God; A bulwark never failing; and still our ancient foe doeth seek to work its woe; His craft and power are great and armed with cruel hate, on earth is not His equal." The words began to stick in my throat, gagging me like boiled okra. Why had I never noticed the militaristic language of the hymn before, which now seemed like blasphemy being uttered inside a sanctuary dedicated to the power of love and forgiveness?

The Chaplin rose to his feet and began to speak of the sins of *man*, and how Christ had come to save *man* and lift *him* up to glory. Where was *wo-man*? Was there salvation for wo-man inside God's plan for man-kind or was she forever doomed to be the outsider like Eve, or redeemable only in ways like the recalcitrant, humbled, repentant prostitute Mary Magdalene who myths say lived out the last years of her life as a hermit inside a remote cave in southern France, dressed only in rags with wild-looking hair that extended down her back to cover her naked body?

I squirmed in my seat, pinching myself, coughing and clearing my throat over and over, digging for Kleenex in my purse, anything to calm myself and keep me in my seat. I sensed that I was dangerously close to being fully popped, dangerously close to standing bolt upright and screaming at the top of my lungs. I was, after all, daughter of a woman who had made an art of screaming. Chaplin Mason, you don't have any idea what you're talking about, was what I wanted to yell. How dare you talk down to me, to us? Your message of one Father God who had only one offspring, a Son, is not the whole truth!

Where are the women who served Jesus and helped shape the Christian church? They are the people I want to hear about! Where are the women?

The longer I tried to ignore the overpowering emotions welling up inside me, the louder the roaring inside became, like an undetected tsunami swelling into massive waves before crashing down on a beach and thundering over the land. I've got to get the heck out of here before I start yelling. Who is this man standing high over us like a god, telling us we're sinners and living an un-redemptive life? This is not a religious message that uplifts women or men. Enough of this patriarchal bullshit that tells women who and what they can and can't be or do! Time to slide on out the front door of the church never to return, just like your daddy did at First Baptist.

I was like a person possessed, coming near enough to the description of women followers of the Greek god Dionysus, who myths said once overcome with heightened emotions, committed horrific acts of violence and cannibalism. I whispered to Saren, "I've got to go. I'll meet you outside after the service." He looked at me anxiously. The kids became concerned as I stood up to leave. "Where are you going mommy? Where's mommy going daddy?"

I stood outside the Chapel shaking like a leaf. Like my daddy, I, too was angry. I, too, had been angry for a long time and hadn't realized it. I was angry at my mother for not thinking more highly of herself and doing something with her life besides being an unhappy wife and mother; angry at my daddy for sitting on his talents and blaming the world for everything that didn't work out the way he wanted. I was angry at the United States for continuing a war in Vietnam that was taking too many lives. I was angry at a culture that encouraged girls and women to develop themselves only so far and no further; angry at my husband for being so unaware of a deeper meaning to life than his career and making the rank of General and most of all, I was angry at myself for not fitting in and being a better wife! Why did I have to rebel, make waves? What was wrong with me? Was I going crazy?

I was smack-daub in the middle of an inner battle between an emerging authentic self, yearning to be free to be herself and the "be nice and keep smiling" Southern Belle, one-dimensional-woman who wanted approval from others and would make enormous sacrifices and self-defeating decisions to get it.

Raising my outstretched arms high above me toward the wide open, blinding sun of the blue desert sky, I railed at God. I shall not return to Your House until it's a place for men and women!

In spite of therapy sessions with Dr. Weinstein who'd encouraged me to embrace my anger, instead, like the good little girl, the always pleasant Southern Belle I'd been raised to be, I calmed myself down, wiped my sweaty face and greeted Saren and the children with a smile when they exited the Chapel service. Once again, I stuffed my anger with all my other unresolved feelings into the sack I carried on my back, like a permanent Hunchback of Notre Dame.

All I knew was that I no longer wanted a relationship with a God who loved or preferred men; a God who could only be addressed through a man; a God who was always playing favorites to white, middle-class, western males.

What a lack of imagination! And I wanted no part of it!

SHAPESHIFTING

What to wear?" was the big question. While there might not be a lot of glitz or glamour at a banquet to honor students being admitted into the prestigious Phi Beta Kappa Honorary Society at a university that focused more on cutting-edge agriculture and cattle-raising than on cutting edge ideas in liberal arts and science, I had worked hard to achieve the 4.0 grade average necessary for admission. Besides, it would be fun to dress up. Pretty clothes were the one thing I had enjoyed about being in beauty contests and I still loved to wear the latest fashions. My closet was filled with shoes, handbags and multiple wigs. I chose for the occasion a medium-length blonde wig, a black velvet mini shirt tied at the waist with a multi-patterned, fringed scarf, a white long sleeve blouse with lace trim at the collar and sleeves and a black velvet jacket, black lace stockings and fancy black patent leather high heels.

The evening of the gala, Saren and I met up with my friend Gail who was also being admitted to the honorary society. She too was dressed to the nines, wearing a tight red-sheath dress, with her beautiful long hair spilling down her back and shoulders. Featured against the boring backdrop of the barren banquet room filled with round tables covered with plain white tablecloths, cafeteria style plates, ugly flatware and dingy glasses, were the students and professors who represented the crème de-la crème of the university. Gail and me ... were we both beautiful and smart? You bet we were and tonight we were strutting our stuff, looking like we'd stepped out of *Vogue* magazine, or at the very least, *Glamour*.

While Saren was chatting and being his charming self with Gail, I looked around the room to see if any of my three favorite instructors were there ... Dr. Joseph Knight, head of the psychology department, along with well-known poet and poetry instructor Keith Wilson and Dr. Hardin, Head of the English Department.

Unlike the poetry instructor Keith Wilson, Dr. Hardin was a very formal instructor. Her specialty was American literature and she often quoted entire passages from Walt Whitman, William Wordsworth and Emily Dickenson with a skill that any actor would have envied.

I continued to look around the room, secretly hoping to see Professor Joseph Knight, or Joe, as he liked to be called. Joe was tall and lanky, with a friendly smile and casual manner, smart, approachable, and easy to talk to. There was always a group of students waiting after psychology class to chat with him. I finally got up enough nerve to seek him out for conversation one day and soon, was visiting him regularly in his office, discussing at length diverse subjects from new ideas in psychology and sociology, to the continuing war in Vietnam, racism, and women's rights, all topics that I could find no audience with my husband to discuss.

"Would you like to go to lunch?" Joe asked one day after our office visit had run into the noon hour.

"Sure," I said. It seemed like the most natural thing to do. He was, after all, I told myself as I drove home from school that day, just a friend and my professor.

Of course, we were just friends, but there was no denying the attraction between us. I was starving to share my emerging journey into the new world of ideas that was sometimes as scary as it was exciting; starving for someone who wasn't judgmental or afraid; someone who was equally curious and interested in growing as a person. There was my friend Gail, who being a full-time student, worked part-time and single mom with three young girls to care for, had little time to visit and talk beyond an occasional lunch at the student union.

Joe, on the other hand, made himself available to talk and hang out, providing me the acceptance, understanding and intellectual challenge I was craving. One day after lunch together, he walked me to my car and leaned forward to kiss me and I didn't turn away.

"I want to make love to you," he whispered in my ear. My heart fluttered at his words, but I gave no reply. I felt totally conflicted as I got into my car and drove home.

"I'm so confused," I confided to Gail the next day at school. "I'm so attracted to Joe; he's everything Saren isn't, but I love my husband and family. I took a vow to be faithful to Saren and I could never cheat on him."

Gail listened, but as I would learn in the years following graduation during which time we remained friends, she had a very different take on what morals to use in guiding one's sexual life. During school, she'd always had several boyfriends, a fact that didn't seem to be a problem for her, but the sticky part to me was that none of them knew about each other, until they did and then everyone was involved in one great big drama.

"Are you suggesting I sleep with Joe?" I asked, horrified that she might be.

"It's your decision, of course, but sometimes sleeping with someone outside your marriage can breathe new life into it."

I didn't say anything because in that moment I realized I wasn't so sure anymore about a lot of things. Not only was I bordering on becoming a person with no faith in God, now I doubted how marriage to a person with such different values than my own could possibly play out in a good way.

Shortly after the kiss, Joe and I arranged to have lunch again and this time he had proposed a rendezvous afterwards. For two days prior to our scheduled romantic meet-up, I was in major conflict over what I was going to do. Swigging down a bottle of Pepto-Bismol to stave off a massive case of diarrhea should have clued me in that being a husband-cheater wasn't going to work so well for me. I managed to pull myself together enough to go meet Joe for lunch at the agreed restaurant, next door to the motel. As soon as I sat down, Joe saw how distressed I was.

"We don't have to do anything you know," he said reassuringly.

It was clear that it wasn't just my diarrhea that was the problem but my guilt; something I wasn't going to be able to shake off. Despite my attraction to Joe and my marital challenges with Saren, I didn't want to be sexually unfaithful. I excused myself and feeling enormous relief that nothing had happened between Joe and me, drove home.

******

A few days after my kiss with Joe in the campus parking lot and our failed motel rendezvous, Saren and I were returning home from a fun evening of dinner and dancing at the Officer's Club, where I'd gone over my drinking limit of two rum and cokes, leading me to confess that I was feeling attracted to someone at school.

He lost it in a flash.

"What the hell?" he yelled at me.

"We didn't do anything," I protested.

Once we got home, he grabbed my arm and forced me to the living room sofa. "Tell me everything. I want to know every last detail," he insisted.

"Don't be so mean," I said, jerking my arm away.

"Me? Me, don't be mean? It's you that's done the mean here. Not me. Who is he? How long have you been messing around with him?"

"He's my psychology professor and we're just friends. We haven't been messing around. We only kissed once. That's all we did."

"You kissed him?" Saren screamed, jumping up from the sofa. "You kissed him?" he yelled over and over, beside himself with anger.

He grabbed me and started kissing me hard on the mouth while tearing open my blouse and fondling my breasts. "Kissing like this," he kept yelling.

"Stop it, Saren! Stop it!"

"You're my wife, aren't you?" he yelled, taking me by my arms and dragging me to the bedroom where he threw me down on the bed, pulled off his trousers and soon was on top of me. I was crying hysterically.

It only lasted a few minutes, the non-consensual sex. I turned over afterwards not even washing myself and cried myself to sleep. We didn't speak for days. Sadly, I felt I deserved his hateful, violent behavior. I'm the bad one, I reasoned, the one who had crossed the line. I deserved to be punished. Like many women then and now, I took on the blame for whatever wasn't working in my relationship and also assumed it was my duty to fix it.

******

I saw Joe about a month later when I went to his office to make up a psychology test I'd missed after the fainting and hospital episode. I was so nervous that my knees were shaking when I walked into his office, but I needn't have been. He greeted me with gentleness and kind words.

"I never meant for our kiss that day in the parking lot or our proposed get together to cause you so much pain. I'm so sorry. I was out of line. Can you forgive me?" We looked into each other's eyes where I saw his love and respect being reflected back to me.

"Joe, there's nothing to forgive," I said quietly, my heart pounding wildly and tears forming in the corner of my eyes. Oh, how I wished in that moment that things could have been different. I didn't tell him about Saren's response when I'd told him about our kiss. It wasn't necessary. I took the test, made an "A" and Joe and I never saw one another again.

******

"Honey," I'd protest, "the kids are too young to be treated like soldiers. Don't be so strict."

"They've got to learn discipline. That's the way to get ahead. Discipline and doing what you're told."

We were having another disagreement about how to discipline our children. His way of disciplining them was to first threaten to spank them with his belt and, if he felt their behavior deserved it, he would follow through with his threat and spank them with his belt.

One of our biggest disagreements, which became a defining moment for me in seeing the differences in our values, happened one evening while we sat around the dining table discussing a rumor that was going around the Army post. The rumor alleged that the Commanding General's daughter had had an affair with an enlisted man and was pregnant. Not only was the guy an enlisted man, but an African American. The General immediately disowned his daughter and had insisted she leave home and live with a distant relative.

"I think it's awful that the General disowned his own daughter. I could never imagine disowning Marie if something like that ever happened to her."

"I think the General's decision about his daughter was the right one," Saren said in his stern, officer's voice.

"What? You can't seriously mean that? Disowning your own daughter?"

"She should never have slept with an enlisted man, especially a black man!"

"What does his being black or enlisted have to do with anything?" I asked, shocked.

"I don't want our daughter dating a black man just like the General didn't approve that for his daughter."

"Are you kidding me? Marie and Alex's best friend is our next-door neighbor Nelson, and he's a black person. Should they stop playing with him because someday he and Marie might end up dating?"

Socializing with our black neighbors had already been an issue between Saren and myself when he insisted that we not invite the Wilsons to any of our dinner parties and I had reluctantly agreed. Now this attitude about the black enlisted man and the general's daughter? Was he a racist?

"I guess it could all have been prevented if she'd been on birth control pills," I replied, searching for some middle ground. "I will definitely make sure Marie knows about birth control if she becomes sexually active with someone."

"No daughter of mine is going to use birth control! No way! She can wait until she gets married to have sex."

"You don't want her to know about birth control or use birth control?"

"No contraceptives for either of the children! That's how I feel about it and that's how it's going be. Period."

Saren was sounding like all the Baptist preachers and teachers I'd grown up with: *"a good Christian girl or boy should wait until they get married to have sexual relations."* Even though he'd been baptized in my own First Baptist Church in Georgia, and even though he was currently the Superintendent of Sunday School at the Post Chapel, I knew he didn't have deep beliefs in the Baptist doctrines. Where were all these conservative attitudes coming from? Was this more about what people would think and about him wanting to have control than it was about faith or morality?

******

"Here, I've brought you a book I think will help you right now," my new friend Leigh said, as we sat in my cheerful dining room with its red velvet curtains pulled back to allow the stunning view of the Organ Mountains behind our house on Officer's Row. I'd met Leigh at *Open Doors*, a non-profit school she'd help to start for mentally and physically disabled children of Mexican immigrants living in Las Cruces. I'd been working there part-time as a volunteer after graduating university.

We sat around the antique dining table Saren and I had bought and refinished together, sipping our tea and some "not homemade" cookies.

I glanced at the book she'd brought, my heart pounding hard when I read the title: *The Wisdom of Insecurity: A Message for an Age of Anxiety* by Alan Watts. Although my anxiety attacks had mostly subsided, I was still nervous a lot of the time.

Leigh read my worried look right away. "Don't be afraid," she encouraged me, in her always-gentle manner. "Read it a little bit at a time, that way you can digest it more easily and not feel threatened by any unfamiliar ideas you find there. We can talk about it anytime you want." Leigh was kind and caring, and had a brilliant, inquisitive mind. Right away she had become a mentor and friend to me, one whom I felt safe to confide in.

Leigh's husband was a recently retired Lt. Colonel from the Army and they had settled in Las Cruces. She assured me that as an officer's wife she, too, in her time had struggled with rules she didn't want to follow and with a husband, who like my own, was quite conservative.

"Forget being conservative," she laughed. "We're talking rigid. No other word for it. It's part of the military life," she said. "Here's something else I brought for you," she said, handing me a poem called *The Service Wife*. Here, read this out loud so we can have a few laughs."

"An ideal service wife," I began, clearing my throat, "has the patience of an angel, the flexibility of putty, the wisdom of a scholar and the stamina of a horse. If she dislikes money, it helps. One might say she is a bigamist, sharing her husband with a demanding entity called 'duty'. When duty calls, she becomes Number 2 wife. Until she accepts this fact, her life can be miserable. Sitting among her packing boxes with squabbling children nearby, she is sometimes willing to chuck it all until she hears the firm step and cheerful voice of that lug who gave her all this. Then she is happy to be his service wife!"

We howled with laughter at the absurdity of such limiting views of women who were military wives. But there were certain things in the military chain of command that military wives did have to obey.

"Can you believe the Commanding General told Saren that I'd have to stop driving to school with my friend Denise because she was an enlisted man's spouse?" I'd asked Leigh after telling her about the encounter with Mrs. Commanding General at the Officer's Club last summer and the follow-up results.

Leigh shook her head and, in an effort, to assure me I wasn't alone in my struggle against cultural and institutional rigidity, shared her own struggles with Army life, which had led her as it had me, to experience enormous anxiety, feelings of insecurity and aloneness. She assured me I was not going crazy!

"I've been going with a friend to California each summer for the last few years to hear a teacher from India named Krishnamurti who gives talks about ways to have a peaceful life while always questioning everything. We take our tents and camp out at night and during the day we gather to listen to his talks and then we ask questions."

I was amazed. A religious teacher who expected his students to ask questions? I'd never heard of such a thing.

"What kind of questions do you ask?" I wanted to know. "Did your husband Fred agree to let you go? Did it really help you with your life?"

We talked for several more hours before Leigh had to drive back to Las Cruces. I always felt so much better after an afternoon with her. My anxiety seemed to melt away and I was able to relax and breathe a bit easier when I was around her, much as I'd done with Joe. But Joe was out of my life now.

As Leigh and I hugged goodbye at the door of the comfortable, large home provided for officers by the Army, I felt so grateful to have met her. Not only did she share her wisdom and caring, but also many of the books that had helped her find her way when she had felt anxious, lost and alone. There was the Watt's book, which I could only read a few pages at a time because it elicited such anxiety in me, but I held onto it, hoping that one day I would be able to read it, cover to cover, without fear but with a confidence that my mentor and friend Leigh kept telling me, "If I can do it, so can you."

******

Nine months after I graduated university, we received orders that we had been assigned to the United States Embassy in Paris, France where Saren would assume duties as the U.S. NATO liaison officer to France. All our mottled, confusing emotions lifted amidst the ecstasy we felt receiving such a wonderful assignment and we happily began plans to move from our isolated desert home to yet another new world, this one inside a large, beautiful European city.

Before we left, our son Alex took matches and set fire to the desert scrub in the large open field behind our house. The fire department sent a fire truck to put it out and fortunately no one was hurt. Alex was severely punished by his father and soon afterwards began to have nightmares.

It is an illusion that our children don't know, absorb and are affected by their parent's problems. Saren and I both worked hard to be the best parents we knew how to be but sometimes that just didn't seem to be enough. It does take a village to raise a child and I only hoped we'd find the help we needed for our son Alex and for us as parents and as individuals in our new home in Europe.

PART TWO

BIENVENUE/WELCOME TO PARIS!

Upon our arrival in France, we stayed in an apartment in Rueil-Malmaison, a suburb of Paris where Saren's office was located, which also happened to be near the beautiful Chateau de la Petite Malmaison which Napoleon had built for Empress Josephine. We absolutely couldn't wait to visit the Chateau, so one afternoon we took the children for a tour in what would be the first of many excursions to learn the history of France and immerse ourselves in the French culture. The grounds were beautifully landscaped, and the Chateau was exquisitely decorated with the original furnishings, giving a feeling that Napoleon and Josephine might walk in at any moment.

"Is this the bed where Napoleon slept?" I asked the Chateau's tour guide. "Mai, oui, madame!" she answered. Saren and I looked at each other, perplexed. "I could sleep here mommy," Alex said, pointing to the bed. And he was right. The bed's size would fit a small child.

"So, the stories of Napoleon being short are absolutely true," I commented to Saren as we left, happy and smiling that we were learning in person the real history of our new home.

Saren's assistant director at his NATO Liaison office was Don Bernstein who, with his British wife Ruth, became immediate good friends, introducing us to France and the subtle ways of the French, particularly the Parisians. Both Don and Ruth had lived in France for many years and being slightly older, took us under their wing, helping us with everything from negotiating a complicated lease with a new landlord to advising us to immediately order the obligatory printed calling cards, names engraved in gold, and part of proper protocol to be left behind at official Embassy events and dinners.

While the men, Saren and Don did their thing at work—what they did at work was never discussed, because it was classifed as Top Secret—and once the two children were settled in their new school, Ruth and I took on Paris with the zeal of high school best girlfriends. Ruth had a dramatic flair about everything she did. Besides being attractive with her stylish short blond hair, fine jewelry, and fashionable clothes, she was fun, intelligent and had the British whit and sense of humor that kept me laughing. She worked part-time as the personal assistant to the U.S. Cultural Attaché to UNESCO and would often get us entry into places not available to the general public. Going with her to art galleries, museums, or flea markets and interacting with the Parisians was like being fast-tracked in learning the French language and culture. She became my enthusiastic tour guide taking me everywhere, often driving too fast in her Jaguar, which like all Brits, she pronounced with three syllables *Jag-you-are*; parking illegally without a thought, translating French life as we went along.

Surprises as well as beauty seemed to be waiting around every corner in Paris. One afternoon Ruth and I were shopping in an area off the Champs Elysee, when a loud commotion broke out. As we looked around to see where it was coming from, to our amazement, we spotted a large number of goats running helter-skelter down the middle of the street and they were being chased by a man dressed in black with a long pointy beard and curlicue mustache. As the spectacle ran past us, we burst out laughing. "This must be a performance for a gallery opening," Ruth said, "and I'll bet everything I know about art that that man chasing the goats is the famous surrealist artist, Salvador Dali!"

Laughing, we followed the screaming Dali and the goats as they disappeared into an alleyway behind an art gallery. We went inside the gallery and as Ruth had guessed, it was an exhibition of the artwork of Salvador Dali.

"Dali is a surrealist and uses a rich diversity of symbolism, often showing a sort of dream sequence with fantastical characters," the aloof, chic French art consultant informed us as we stared in silence at one of the most fantastical paintings I'd ever seen. Called *Swans Reflecting Elephants* it showed three swans sitting in a pond in an eerie, stark setting with leafless trees and two strangely-shaped clouds hanging in the sky and the reflections of the swans in the water were those of elephants. I was speechless and awe-struck at this new art form called surrealism.

It wasn't only art that teased and satisfied the senses in this new world we'd left the deserts of New Mexico to inhabit. Food, cheese and wine were inextricably linked and engrained in French culture and learning about them was an integral part of educating ourselves to the French way of life. As a wife-hostess to a diplomat, I signed up for French cooking lessons as a way to bring the enticing element of delicious food to our entertainment soirees. I gathered with a small group of other American wives who lived in the suburbs to take a series of cooking classes in French cuisine; basically, we talked story and drank a lot of wine but we did learn how to cook French green beans, make a juicy sauce to pour on the beans and prepare coq-au-vin. Cooking was never actually my thing, aspiring wife-hostess or not but I managed to pull it off for a short time before deciding it was best for everyone if we took guests out to eat, which we did.

Deciding to imitate the French, we soon learned to leave our kids at home and instead bring our new little Shih Tzu dog Oliver whenever we dined out, especially at the four-star restaurant owned by famous actor Maurice Chevalier located a few blocks from our new apartment in Ville d'Avray. We were so amused to see how the waiter's scowls turned to cordial greetings when we brought Oliver to dine instead of the kids.

Bonjour Madame and Mousier! Ah. Le petit chien! Tres joli, sa! The waiters would gush and immediately bring over a fresh bowl of water for Oliver to drink while we dined. Dogs no problem! Kids? Not so much. "This is not Italy," Ruth and Don reminded us. "Kids in France stay at home when the adults go out for dinner."

******

It was our first fall in France and we decided to go on a weekend trip to the wine country of the Loire Valley in the mid-section of France with new friends Elaine and Michael. Without noticing we passsed brightly painted Gypsy wagons standing motionless underneath a stand of tall willowy trees next to the river. The suddenness of their appearance on the landscape seemed no less magical than if we had happened upon a troupe of faeries. Saren drove a short distance past the colorful band before our senses registered what we'd just seen. "Stop," Elaine and I yelled in unison. "Those are Gypsies! We've got to go back!"

"I doubt those were Gypsies," Michael announced in his draconian *I'm-an-accountant-with Price Waterhouse* voice.

"Saren, we have to go back," I insisted.

Saren, who had a streak of adventure in his genes despite the rigidity of his chosen career in the military, turned the car around and pulled onto the narrow road into the Gypsy camp. The Gypsies, dressed in an array of colorful clothes as magnificent as the fall leaves, immediately walked up to our car, wearing wide smiles that showed off gleaming gold-capped teeth.

"We live in Paris," Saren said, speaking slowly in English. "We're here to see the beautiful French countryside and the vineyards." The Gypsies continued smiling and nodding, obviously not understanding much of what he was saying. Then, Saren in a moment of inspiration switched to his native Romanian tongue. The Gypsy faces instantly lit up, shocked and delighted that someone was speaking their Romani language. They began talking gregariously, spewing out their words in rapid staccato, as though they were with old friends who hadn't seen each other in years.

While Saren and the Gypsies continued their unexpected and congenial conversation, we got out of the car to walk around and enjoy the beauty of the Gypsies' camp, admiring the women's colorful skirts, embroidered peasant blouses and the abundance of gleaming gold jewelry that adorned their wrists, ears and necks.

A wizened old woman, her face etched with deep wrinkles, waved for us to follow her as she headed towards one of the nearby wagons parked under a large clump of trees for shade. Pointing enthusiastically to exquisitely painted scenes that covered the entire wagon, she told us in broken French that she'd painted the wagon herself. The wagon had been artistically decorated with flowers, trees, rivers and mountains drawn in a folk-style by her accomplished hand. She had used brightly colored paints of yellow, blue, and magenta to paint the swirls that encircled the entire wagon, like ribbons on an exquisitely wrapped package, I thought.

"How marvelous!" we exclaimed in genuine appreciation. We told her how honored we were she'd invited us to see her painted treasure, all delivered in our own broken French, a language we were studying but certainly could claim no mastery.

Saren was saying goodbye to the group of friendly Gypsies and motioned us back to the car, which by now was surrounded by a group of children giggling, laughing, and shyly pointing at us. The whole camp had turned out to wave goodbye as we got in the car to drive away.

"What else did they say?" we asked Saren, as he slowly maneuvered the car back onto the roadway by the Gypsy camp.

"They're from Romania and Bulgaria and they follow the grape harvest every year picking grapes in Italy and France. They told me how difficult their life is and how persecuted they are by most people. Some villages won't let them park their wagons anywhere nearby because they're afraid of them, afraid they'll steal their money or maybe even steal their children and raise them as Gypsies."

"What a hard life! Wonder if any of them ever leave and go off on their own?" I mused out loud.

"I bet they do," Elaine answered.

"I wouldn't trust them near my town either," Michael replied from the back seat where he sat, arms crossed tightly over his crumpled 6 ft. 3-inch body. I couldn't understand what Elaine saw in Michael. Elaine and I had originally met at the American School of Paris where we'd gone to attend a parent-teacher conference for our children. She was beautiful, smart and vivacious with a personality that tended towards the dramatic, and it was obvious Michael adored her and had put her on a pedestal. Maybe that's all that matters, I thought, being what your man wants and having him worship you, even if it is a false you. Of course, I didn't believe that for one minute, but I still had more questions than answers as to what made a good, solid relationship. The good news was that Saren and I had become closer since moving to France where everyone and everything was different and another language was spoken.

At dinner that evening, we recited some of the new wines we'd discovered during our tours of some of the many excellent vineyards in the area and ordered several bottles of those we'd liked. We were staying in a small, intimate *auberge*, a country inn, whose restaurant had received a 4-star rating in the Guide Michelin, the ultimate travel and reference guide for getting around Europe. We laughed, joked, ate and drank with gusto; felt the full weight of our privileged status as young Americans living abroad with the financial resources to enjoy the pleasures and beauty of the fabulous country of France. With full bellies and happy smiles on our faces, we said goodnight to Elaine and Michael and made our way to our small but comfortable room.

While falling asleep, I thought about what a great life we were living, traveling in France and Europe; about how confident Saren was that his position as U.S. NATO Liaison Officer to France was a significant step towards his dream of becoming a general in the U.S. Army. I thought of how proud I was of all his achievements and how lucky I was to be with him; he's smart, ambitious, and has a tender side towards the children and me, unless we "get out of line." That thought made me smile since he was already the General in our household, giving orders to his troops, the kids and me. Despite the warning from the therapist at White Sands that "I can't make you into a better Officer's wife," I still wanted to be a good Army officer's wife; wanted to help Saren achieve his career goal because I loved him and believed in him.

All the seeds of future transformation were there during that lovely weekend jaunt to the French countryside where we had met the Gypsies, mysterious and unique in their commitment to living life to the fullest and in ways chosen by them; they were living lives of freedom and authenticity we all wished we could live and thought we were living for a long time … until one day, the world shifted to what seemed like another dimension, and we couldn't go back to the old ways because they weren't there anymore, having disappeared forever like a lost Camelot or a band of Gypsy wagons that you'd seen parked by the Loire River and when you passed that way again, were gone, disappeared like a troupe of fairies in a stand of willowy trees next to a river.

"WHAT KIND OF SCHOOL?"

... from the musical *The American School of Mars*
by Marjorie Canto & Chris Bentley

"What kind of school do we want to send our kids to for their education?" was an important question and topic of conversation for Saren and me when we arrived in Paris. We both wanted them to have an experience of total immersion into French language and culture and were excited when we found an *ecole* or school not far from our new apartment in Ville d'Avray, a suburb of Paris and next door to its more famous neighbor Versailles. Our excitement was short-lived, however, when one of the teachers during their first week of attendance, slapped Alex on the face for not doing something she'd asked him to do speaking in French, which the kids were just learning. After we found out that striking or slapping a child was a permissible form of student discipline, we immediately took them out and enrolled them in the American School of Paris.

The American School of Paris was a private co-ed, K-12 school located in a nearby suburb. It was more like a college campus, sitting on ten well-manicured acres with numerous student facilities housed in multiple buildings. It was the first International School in Europe that offered English as the primary language, boasting a student body representing over 60 nations and where 95% of the students were children of diplomats or corporate families.

ASP hadn't been our first choice for our children's school but after the slapping incident at the French school, we felt we had to make the transfer. The children seemed more at ease in the American school and to our happiness, were studying French every day. After a few months at their new school, it was time for a parent-teacher conference, which is where new friend Elaine and I had first met.

"I think these parent-teacher conferences are a waste of time," Elaine had commented to me as we sat in chairs outside the classroom waiting our time to speak with the teacher about our children. Elaine was a striking redhead, very friendly and soon was telling me how she and her husband Michael had recently moved to Paris from Chicago with their daughter Laurie.

"I mean, why don't they call us to come in when there's something important to talk about?" she asked, complaining vigorously. As I was to learn, Elaine was never shy about speaking her mind.

I felt differently and was eager to talk with Alex's teacher because of recent notes saying that he was acting out in class and disrupting other students.

Later that evening, Saren and I sat talking after the kids had gone to bed. I told him about the conference and what Alex's teacher had told me. "She recommended we first check with Alex's pediatrician to eliminate any possibilities of a physical problem, and that we would go from there to find ways to help Alex succeed. She was very positive."

We both sat quietly for a few moments, sipping our wine, concerned about our son and wanting to do everything we could to help him.

"I've been thinking about becoming involved with the kid's school," I said tenuously. I could volunteer in the music department doing something, whatever they need, and that way I could see the kids at school, which might be re-assuring to Alex."

******

Chris Bentley, head of the lower school's music department was an affable, tall, lanky young man with a British accent and pleasing smile. He was warm and welcoming and I could see why the kids all loved him. "How absolutely splendid that you want to help out in the music department," he beamed when we first met and I told him of my musical background. "I'm willing to volunteer and help wherever you need me," I told him. After a few more conversations, we struck on the rather bold idea of creating a children's musical play, calling it *The American School of Mars*, an obvious reference to the children's real school, the American School of Paris. Working together over a period of weeks, we created lyrics and musical arrangements for nine songs. It was a win-win experience.

Not only was I having a wonderful time creating music with Chris, but also, I would inevitably run into Alex and Marie either at lunch in the cafeteria or the hallway and would give them a smiling hello and a hug.

"Maybe all those teacher education classes I took in university will be useful after all," I laughed, smiling at Saren over dinner one evening shortly after I'd begun to volunteer on a regular basis.

"I'm glad you decided to volunteer. It'll give you something to do and you'll get to see the kids as well," he said, pouring another glass of the fabulous Beaujolais we'd bought during our trip to the wine country.

"I've been working with some amazing children! You should see them. They're brimming with imaginative ideas about monsters and two kids who help to run the monsters off and start a new school on Mars. I've come up with a storyline for the three-act play and we're calling it "The American School of Mars."

"You're really into this thing, aren't you, honey?"

"You know, I am. I've always enjoyed working with children, you remember, when I was the director of the pre-school at Redstone Arsenal and you were in Vietnam?"

We both fell silent because we rarely spoke about Vietnam anymore but we had recently become friends with a Marine Officer and his wife and the topic had re-emerged.

Col. Donnelly was one of the interpreters at the Vietnam Peace talks, begun in 1968 and were currently still happening in Paris, with US National Security Adviser Henry Kissinger and Le Duc Tho leader of North Vietnam being the primary negotiators. We had met Col. Donnelly at the Embassy and were enjoying drinks with him and his lovely German wife when his stories of the peace talks had caused us to shake our heads in disbelief.

"You wouldn't believe how many hours, well actually months, we've spent debating what kind of table we should use and who should sit where," Donnelly told us.

"You mean at the Peace Talks they're debating what kind of table to sit at?" Saren asked Donnelly.

"Yes, they are. The North Vietnamese want a circular table so that all parties including NLF representatives would appear to be equal in importance.

The South Vietnamese argue that only a rectangular table is acceptable because it would show two distinct sides of the conflict. I think we're close to a compromise, though," he laughed, not seeming to be perturbed by the insanity of it.

"It's disrespectful to the thousands of Americans killed in that war that it's come down to the shape of a table before a peace agreement can be signed," Saren said with disappointment in his voice.

"What's the compromise?" I asked.

"Well, we're working on having the representatives of the northern and southern governments sit at a circular table with members representing all the other parties sitting on individual square tables around them. I hope it'll work because we've been stalled out now for months."

We stayed in touch with Donnelly and his wife who told us over drinks one evening that a Paris Peace Accord had finally been signed by the participants in the Vietnam war on January, 1973. We were all glad, relieved too, but somehow the event was anti-climactic, like applause being given hours after a performance has ended ... with only a few there to celebrate and appreciate the efforts or even to remember the sorrow of any of it.

******

Meantime, back at ASP and after weeks and weeks of rehearsing the nine new songs with the kids in music class...after creating the many costumes with the help of talented and devoted mothers...after getting the playbill for *The American School of Mars* designed and drawn by the kids ... finally the day of the performance arrived. The play was greeted with enthusiasm and thunderous, generous applause and was reviewed with a positive critique in the school newspaper. Of course, Alex and Marie got roles as two of the many monsters! Sadly, Saren was in Brussels and wasn't able to attend.

Although being at the children's school as a volunteer had ended, we knew we had to follow up on taking Alex' teacher's advice about seeing a pediatrician. Every so often we drove to an Air Force base in Wiesbaden, Germany to stock up on American-made items, to see American doctors and sometimes do some skiing with the children. This trip we had made an appointment for Alex to see a pediatrician.

"Your son is in perfect physical health," the pediatrician told us after examining Alex.

"Is there anything we can do to help with his acting-out and disruptive behavior in class," Saren asked.

"Put him on Ritalin," the pediatrician said matter-of-factly. "That's a drug used on a lot of kids who are having behavior problems."

"What? No! We can't drug our son," I protested to both the pediatrician and Saren, who was nodding in agreement with the doctor. "There's got to be a better way."

Saren relented to "no drugs" for our son but we both knew Alex needed some additional help that neither we nor his school were providing him. Did he need a different kind of school? Maybe a therapist?

Over the next weeks, I began to research alternative schools that educated children who were having behavioral challenges and had discovered a book called *Summerfield: A Radical Approach to Childhood*, which described a private school in England where students were given free rein to direct their own learning experiences. The school's philosophy was that by allowing freedom for the individual, which meant allowing each child to decide their own path in life by following their own interests, would lead them to develop into the person they felt they were meant to be; and that, in turn, would lead to an inner self-confidence and acceptance of themselves as individuals.

I showed the book to Alex and we talked about some of its ideas and the people there. "Do they really call the principal 'Neil, Neil Orange Peel'?"

"Yes, that's what the book says," I nodded.

"Then I want to go to that school. Please mom, can I?"

When I presented the idea of sending Alex to Summerfield, Saren wasn't in favor, saying explicitly, "No son of mine is going to go to some radical weird school where they don't discipline the students!"

"Can't we at least visit the school before you make up your mind?" I insisted.

"No. We'll look into military schools in the states. That's where he needs to be. He needs to learn discipline and be with teachers who'll hold him accountable."

Saren could be stubborn and hardheaded; it was understood that more important decisions were his to make and if he wanted to send our son away to a military school back in the states, I was going to have a hard time preventing it. But I wasn't going to give up so easily anymore if I disagreed with him. It was time for our family to incorporate some of my ideas, too. Regardless of what school we might or might not send Alex to, how to help him became a primary focus for our family.

CHARTRES CATHEDRAL & A BLACK MADONNA

Early one bright and clear spring morning Saren appeared at the doorway to our bedroom where I sat reading.

"Why don't we make that trip to Chartres and see the cathedral you've been wanting to see?"

"Sure, I guess ... I mean, why not?" I stammered, somewhat startled and surprised at the suddenness of his suggestion. We had steadily been moving apart in our values and what we wanted from life, arguing over trite things that were of little consequence to big issues such as whether to send our son away to military school. "A little outing might uplift the family," I replied. "I'll get the kids ready."

Saren's position as head of the U.S. Liaison Office of NATO France was much more demanding than we'd ever imagined, requiring long hours and constant travel to other European NATO allied countries and almost weekly trips to NATO's headquarters in Brussels. His frequent absences had put an enormous strain on all of us, but especially so for Alex. When Saren was at home, his scolding of the children for some misdeed or other created a tense home environment, with me always playing the role of peacemaker. It seemed that Saren and Alex were constantly engaged in a power struggle of wills, whether around the dinner table when Alex refused to eat his vegetables or his refusal to go on a family outing, declaring "I don't want to go!" to which is father would reply, "Oh, yes you will young man."

Although having Saren away so often on travel was challenging, the kids and I were far from miserable. We entertained ourselves during his absences by doing all sorts of fun kid things. We sang along to their current favorite songs like "I've Got a Pony I Like to Ride" or songs from the new children's album released by feminist actress Marlo Thomas, "It's Alright to Cry." We ate pizza and other junk food we've gotten at the commissary in Germany, or we'd go to the park to play ball with our little dog Oliver.

If it was rainy, which it often was in the winter, we'd play made-up games like "Alligator." This was a game where I would get on the floor and they would be on the bed. I was the alligator and would pretend to claw at them and they would scream with delight, trying to escape from the alligator. "Don't let the alligator get you," I'd say. We'd play that game until the alligator, me, couldn't go any longer.

But I was concerned. It seemed to me that the more sophisticated we were becoming, the more widely traveled, the more culturally-educated to great art and masterful cuisine, the more we were losing touch with what it meant to be a family in loving relationship with one another. Not only were there enormous demands on our time from Saren's job requiring extensive travel and entertaining high officials when they came to Paris, but also the pressures of adjusting to life in a foreign country, learning a new language, and the added challenge of a troubled child.

And it didn't help that I was increasingly questioning the role of the military in our lives, putting Saren and myself at odds with each other.

******

"Can Monique and Jacques come with us, please mommy, please?" seven-year-old Marie pleaded when I told the children we were going on a trip to see a very special church. Monique and Jacques lived downstairs and Saren and I had been pleased that they had found a few French children whose parents would allow them to play with Americans. It was tough to make friends with the French. After two years, I was still saying *Bon Jour* to our neighbor across the hallway when we happened to ride the elevator at the same time, and he was still greeting me with a heavy silence in reply.

Americans were still mostly *persona non gratia* when we arrived in 1970, an attitude the French people and current President Georges Pompidou had inherited from General Charles de Gaulle who was President from 1959-1969. Earlier in 1966, De Gaulle had opted out of the military side of NATO because he disliked what he regarded as American dominance.

"No darling," I replied. "This is a family trip for the four of us. We'll invite Monique and Jacques another time. Now go get dressed. It's going to be fun!"

I followed Marie into her colorful pink, orange and lavender bedroom where her family of stuffed animals, toys, and games were spread around the room. There was a small table and chairs where she did her homework; a carved trunk painted orange and pink that sat at the foot of her bed and book shelves stacked with so many books they seemed to be holding up the walls. She loved rocking her animals in the antique rocking chair purchased at the *Marché au puis*, the flea market, I'd painted a bright orange and pink. It was a bright, happy room that reflected her personality.

"Please wear something besides your cowgirl outfit sweetheart," I encouraged her, knowing it was of little use because she was currently in love with her cowgirl clothes and red boots; and, once she'd made up her mind to wear a certain article of clothing, no one could talk her out of it.

"And, don't forget your coat. It's still cold outside," I reminded her.

"Are you looking for your glasses? I asked Alex as I walked into his bedroom. After having suffered from severe headaches for months, he had recently begun to wear glasses and was always misplacing them. He'd also begun to have nightmares again and often pleaded to sleep with us at night.

His room was full of model airplanes and posters of some of his favorite cartoons and musical groups. He loved to read and his books filled two beautiful maple bookcases. There were matching bunk beds and a dresser with a mirror shaped like a boat's steering wheel...all things we'd shipped over from the states. There was a small desk and chair where he did his homework. It was a pleasant room and felt just right for the inquisitive, highly-intelligent boy that he was.

"Get dressed and wear something warm. We're going to make a little trip to a village to see this beautiful church mommy's been wanting to see. I think you and Marie will like it too."

*****

Arriving at the small village of Chartres, we parked in an area directly below the cathedral, a towering structure that dwarfed the surrounding landscape with its size and exceptional majesty. Having already trooped around Europe a good deal where almost every town boasted an amazing cathedral, each one seeming to be more grandiose than the former, we had grown numb, worn out from *here's-another-amazing-Gothic-Cathedral*. In spite of our cathedral-weary attitude, however, the extraordinary beauty of Chartres' façade captured us immediately as we walked up the mount where the famous Gothic edifice sat.

Before entering the church, we stopped at a souvenir shop near the entrance filled with rows of statues, rosary beads, ashtrays, and postcards lining the walls. Card after card showed the same image of a Black Madonna holding a child. How totally curious, I thought, picking up one of the cards, paying the cashier two francs, and sticking it in my handbag where I'd forget about it for years to come, unaware that the Once and Future Goddess, the Divine Feminine, had just reached out and placed a symbol of Herself directly inside my purse for my future self.

Inside the cathedral we signed up for a tour with a British guide named Malcolm Andrews, internationally recognized for his knowledge and expertise on Chartres and in particular, on the Black Madonna whose mysterious energy said to reside inside the cathedral he'd helped to perpetuate through careful research and talks he'd given to tens of thousands of tourists over the years.

"I came to Chartres to do research many years ago," Andrews began by saying to our small tour group, "and stayed on because of the energy of the Black Virgin of Chartres, one of many mysteries belonging to this sacred place. How could such a magnificent building have been built during the twelfth century? Who were its architects? Who had knowledge and skills necessary to design and construct such a great work? It was," Andrews declared with authority, "none other than the famous knights of the cross, the Knights Templar!"

"Follow me," Andrews said, as he guided our group to a stone carving of two knights on horseback wearing shirts that bore the symbol of a cross. As we stared up at one of many history lessons said to be carved in stone, he explained, "During the Crusades, the Knights Templar were monks who took up the sword to defend the thousands of pilgrims traveling the roads to the Holy Land of Jerusalem against the infidels who lay in wait to attack them and steal their belongings. Once Jerusalem was taken back from the infidels by the Christians, the Knights Templar were given housing for themselves and their horses on the very spot where Solomon's temple was reputed to have stood.

It was there, so myth has it ... and by the way, myths are not mere idle or made-up stories but are the repositories of ancient wisdom ... the Knights began to dig for the famed Arc of the Covenant, thought to contain not only the tablets of law God gave to Moses, but also something else that was unknown to the general public: the Arc of the Covenant also contained sacred tools of measurement used to build the amazing Chartres cathedral and all the other Gothic wonders in stone."

We all stared at the stone carvings, mouths agape, Christian-trained or not, we were dumbfounded by Andrew's information. History was being re-written on the spot.

"When can we eat mommy?" Marie asked, pulling at my dress to get my attention.

"We're hungry," Alex chimed in, "and this is boring."

"Just a little longer," I whispered. "We'll eat once Mr. Andrews has finished, ok?"

"Go walk the circle in the back," Saren suggested to the children, motioning towards the beautiful labyrinth at the back of the cathedral.

Everyone in the tour group was absorbed in the extraordinary information Andrews was giving us. "The actual builders of the cathedral weren't craftsmen at all," he continued, "but common folk from the surrounding villages. They followed a design given to them by the men who had found the hidden measurements inside the Arc of the Covenant which they brought back from the Holy land; it was the sacred measurement tools inside that helped them build the hundreds of cathedrals that sprang up virtually overnight throughout Europe."

"A sacred well was discovered on the mound where the cathedral now stands, which pilgrims came to visit for centuries. Before that, the well was a place where ancient Druids performed their ceremonies." Andrews was on fire now, as though delivering a great sermon, just as Pope Urban II had done in 1095 urging the Knights and common folk to take up the cross of Christ, join the Crusades, fight the infidels and take back the holy land of Jerusalem that rightly belonged to Christians. I thought we in the tour group were no less awestruck with Andrew's presentation than the people of the Middle Ages must have been centuries earlier by the Pope's injunctions to defend the Church and Christianity by taking up the sword. We strained to hear Andrew's every word, as though we were cramming for a test on material we'd never heard before and might never hear again.

We followed Andrews around the cathedral like a group of excited school children on a field trip to a dinosaur museum that featured a life-sized T-Rex. We were intensely focused on his presentation filled with strange ideas that made no sense. "There's an unexplainable energy which emanates from a dark-faced statue of the Virgin Mary found decades ago in an underground chamber of the cathedral; today that same statue is kept beneath the altar of the church and is a living presence."

No one said a word as we continued to follow Andrews who had now paused underneath the transept window from the 12th century called the Rose Window, a massive circular window, with a geometrical pattern of roses, like flower petals, made of thousands of pieces of stained glass.

We gawked at the magnificent Rose Window and the other stained-glass windows, so immense and profound in their beauty. The beauty of the windows set among the huge stones were like the bones of the cathedral. Andrew's weaving of amazing stories of the mysteries of Chartres, drew us into an unseen and un-scripted mystery of our own, one that seemed to emanate from the very stones themselves, seizing and holding us captive as we stood wrapped inside the cathedral's beauty and many mysteries.

The huge stones of the Gothic cathedral's ceiling appeared to be suspended mid-heaven by invisible wires. Like musical notes dancing across a musical staff of open sky, the height of the cathedral and the design of its ceiling literally pulled our attention and body upwards. I found myself standing tall and erect, aware that at the same time, my feet were planted solidly on the ground, under which a Black Virgin statue had been discovered. Was this the same Virgin whose energy presence permeated the great Notre Dame de Paris where I often went to listen to the ringing of the bells? I knew nothing of the Virgin Mary, or of energy, or a transcendent spirituality. Whatever the source of the feeling was at Chartres, I knew it hadn't been present in the all-male bastions of the Vatican in Rome, in St. Paul's Basilica, or in Saren's Romanian Orthodox Church in Ohio.

I thought about what Andrews had said earlier in the tour that had caused him to stay on at Chartres, an energy presence of the Black Madonna, and although I couldn't imagine anyone staying somewhere due to a feeling given them by a statue, I was intrigued by the palpable mysteriousness of the cathedral that had taken over all of us. I was still immersed in a lingering sadness and disillusionment from my withdrawal from the Christian religion, however, and wanted nothing to do with anything that stirred those spiritual fires so painfully extinguished, or so I thought.

Nevertheless, as Andrews masterfully guided us through the cathedral as a maestro might guide his chorus through a difficult Bach oratorio, I could feel myself alternating between maintaining a stiff, non-responsive body/mind, to relaxing into the strange, uplifting calm that was palpably present in the cathedral. Was this the effect of the mystical marriage of heaven and earth that Andrews said one could tangibly experience inside the cathedral? Such a concept was beyond my understanding at the time, but I was keenly aware that some force was acting on all of us.

Andrews gave a final explanation of the many mysteries associated with the Notre Dame de Chartres, saying they were connected to ancient rituals honoring a Great Goddess. "At different times the Great Goddess was called by different names, Isis, Demeter and Belisama. A stone dedicated to the Goddess Belisama was found lying on the mound where the cathedral sits today. Druids, as I mentioned earlier, used the site for their ceremonies, and inside the Druid grotto was a fertility stone altar dedicated to the Goddess Belisama. It was in this same Druid grotto that the statue of the Black Virgin was found. During the time of the Gauls and, even earlier when the Celts were here, pilgrims came to honor the Black Virgin and drink at her sacred well. Stories from that time tell of the many pilgrims who flocked to this very site, singing psalms to a dark virgin goddess whom they called, Our Lady of Under-the-Earth. During early Christian times, people continued to come on pilgrimages by the thousands, even as they do today. And with this, so ends our tour of Chartres. I trust you will take with you some of its mystery and sacredness as you go your way."

With these words Andrews took his leave and we gathered the children from the cathedral's labyrinth. We found a café nearby for lunch, and, still somewhat stunned by all we'd heard and experienced inside the cathedral, ate mostly in silence before driving back in the heavy Sunday-evening traffic along with the hundreds of other Parisians who had spent their weekend in the country.

"*Merci* for the lovely trip to Chartres," I said to Saren after we'd gotten the children to bed.

"Yes, it was a good day," he replied, putting his papers and other items into his luggage for a trip to Brussels the next day.

FEMINISM & NOW IN PARIS

Summer of 1972 marked our two-year anniversary of living in Paris.

"I think we should do something special to celebrate, don't you?" I asked Saren as he was preparing to leave again for Brussels. "Think of something," he said, pecking me on the cheek.

After getting the kids off to school, I poured myself another coffee and opened *The International Herald Tribune*, the only newspaper that reported the news in English. As I leafed through the newspaper, I noticed an unusual ad. What is this? I paused to read the ad that was announcing a meeting for anyone interested in forming an English-speaking feminist group in Paris and was being called by Lucy Komisar, a Vice President of national NOW, the National Organization for Women.

I hadn't heard the word feminism since a college sociology class but for some reason, my heart began racing as I read and re-read the ad. A meeting for women interested in forming an English-speaking feminist group... To be held at the American Cultural Center on the Left Bank.

I placed the newspaper on the small kitchen table, walked away, got dressed, came back and read it again. Probably no body would go except a bunch of dissatisfied, wealthy American women who don't have anything else to do, I thought. Or, maybe a group of students studying abroad who have to write a paper for their sociology class might see the ad and go. I remembered the sociology professor at NMSU who'd told us that feminism was a movement started by women who wanted to be treated equally and fairly as their male counterparts, and while I liked that idea, I wondered if there was an actual need for an organization to bring that about?

Still, I was interested in learning more and wanted to attend the meeting. I didn't think Saren would mind if I went. Sometimes he could be surprisingly flexible.

******

When Saren returned from Brussels, I'd made one of his favorite dinners, roasted chicken and glazed potatoes, green beans and a tossed salad fresh from the market and chilled a bottle of Beaujolais, his favorite wine. The children had already eaten and were in bed for the night.

"Is this our two-year celebration dinner?" Saren asked as I ushered him into the elegantly set dining table, complete with candles and fresh flowers from the market.

"Kind of. I thought it would be more intimate to stay home and enjoy some us-time together. I missed you and happy you're back," I answered honestly, pouring us both a glass of wine. As we relaxed over the delicious meal and good wine, we talked about his recent trip to Brussels. He never shared any details of what NATO representatives said or did in their meetings because everything was classified. He mostly only commented that things went well or they didn't.

"I found this ad in the newspaper for a meeting about starting a feminist group. It's going to be at the American Cultural Center on Rue Dragon. I'd like to go."

"Sure," he said, relaxed and leaning back in his chair. "I don't see why not. What's feminism anyway? Some woman thing?"

"I had a professor who talked about it in college but I don't really know much about it, so yes, I guess you could say it's a woman thing," I replied. "I'll tell you all about it after I go."

******

As usual, the Left Bank was crowded with students and tourists, but I found a spot to park not far from the meet-up at the American Cultural Center. I was surprised to see there was a line of women that stretched around the entire block waiting to get it. Once we got inside, it was so packed that Lucy Komisar had to often repeat herself.

"The National Organization for Women, NOW as it's called, was started in 1966 by author and feminist Betty Freidan," Komisar, a tall, attractive dark-headed woman, told us. "It was her book *The Feminine Mystique* that launched the Second Wave of the feminist movement. Freidan articulated the unease and dissatisfaction that many women are feeling, calling it 'the problem that has no name' which she identified as something that plagues millions of women dissatisfied with occupation: *housewife* although they're not sure why."

Right away, we women started nodding at her words, and could feel there was something deeper and more meaningful going on that affected all our lives.

We listened intently as Komisar shared how the Women's Rights Movement of the 1960s had grown out of a second wave of activism as a result of the convergence of numerous popular events. "In 1963, President Kennedy created the Commission on the Status of Women and named Eleanor Roosevelt as its chair. This was followed by the 1964 passage of the Civil Rights Act prohibiting employment discrimination on the basis of sex, race, religion, and national origin. A few years later the National Organization for Women was organized, followed by an array of other mass-membership organizations addressing the needs of specific groups of women, including Blacks, Latinos, Asian Americans, lesbians, business owners and professional women. And on college and university campuses, young women were organizing against the Vietnam War; and many women such as myself were also activists in the Civil Rights Movement."

I felt as though I was in a women's history class, learning how women's status was shifting and why it was important to all of us to absorb these new ideas.

There was a feeling in the room akin to a religious fervor of sorts, like we'd been brought together at this precise moment to be part of the newly regenerated work of women's equality, continuing what the women suffragists had begun during the early part of the twentieth century ... it felt like we were positioned on the crest of another big wave, one of historical significance, that would spread across the world bringing respect and equal status to women everywhere.

"What inspired you to call this meeting?" one woman asked Komisar.

"I'd recently published my first book, *The New Feminism,* and was in Paris doing research for a second book when I got the idea to call a meeting of English-speakers interested in feminism. Women throughout the world are realizing that having equal rights as men is important. And, here we are tonight. Thank you for coming," she said, smiling and bringing the meeting to a close. "Oh, there'll be a follow-up meeting next week for those of you who want to help organize an English-speaking feminist group. Hope to see you there!"

As we left, I was delighted to see the face of someone I knew. It was my friend Elaine from ASP whom I hadn't seen since our trip together to the Loire Valley.

"Hi Elaine," I greeted her enthusiastically.

"Hi Marjorie. How great you're here! Are you going to the meeting next week?"

"I sure am!" I replied.

"Then we should go together. I'll call you."

******

I was genuinely pleased to see Elaine at the meeting and welcomed the opportunity to renew our friendship. Within a few months' time, she and I would become part of a core group of eight women and one man who met regularly to organize and build a structure for the determined and committed English-speaking women from the countries of Sweden, Norway, Brazil, England, Italy, Mexico and Belgium as well as Americans living in Paris who wanted to engage in feminist dialogue and action.

During our initial meetings, the question arose immediately as to whether or not our fledging group wanted to affiliate with the National Organization for Women, or NOW in America. It was a question that continued to plague the group, because many of the women found the idea of joining a NOW group to be in direct conflict with their personal views of feminism, seeing NOW as being too conservative and having goals primarily directed towards the needs of white middle-class women.

In comparison to our European and Latin American Feminists, most of us Americans were new to social activism and feminism, and had little to no experience in organizing or working in protest groups pressing for social, political or economic change. This lack of experience didn't minimize the sheer brilliance of the incredible group of women from America who now called Paris home, if only for a few years. We were women from all walks of life and all ages. Although a few accomplished women in their own right were married to CEOs of large, international companies like Chrysler-Europe, Proctor & Gamble, and Price Waterhouse, the majority of the women were single, highly educated, adventurous and had immigrated to Paris on their own. They'd come to experience a more liberal culture where they could enjoy the freedom to express themselves both sexually and creatively, much as women had done earlier in the twentieth century during the *belle époque* of the 20s and 30s when women like Gertrude Stein, Alice B. Toklas, Natalie Barney, Sylvia Beach, and Janet Flanner had also fled America for the opportunities that Paris offered.

Most of the single women in the English-speaking feminist group, regardless of their country of origin, had to work and getting their green cards, finding employment and an affordable, safe place to live were daunting tasks they all faced. Those were things we could agree on and afforded us a few relatable issues, a place to start and we did become a NOW chapter, the first international chapter.

WHERE THE REAL PEOPLE LIVE

Our friends the Bernsteins lived in a lovely apartment near the Trocadero, an area in the 16th arrondisement situated on the oppositive side of the Seine directly across from the Eiffel Tower. One day while visiting Ruth, her youngest son Harry, recently graduated from the American University of Paris, offered to take me to a café where communist workers and sympathizers lived and came to talk politics. Harry had grown up in Paris and while a student at university, had become a leftist sympathizer, allying himself with the student and worker's revolts, all to his parent's shock and horror.

There had been mass student revolts and worker strikes in 1968 in Paris, similar to those in American cities and universities around the world. In Paris, there had been fighting in the streets, rioters setting automobiles and businesses on fire and intense police brutality, resulting in such far-ranging chaos that the entire country had been brought to a standstill. The sense of rebellion still hung heavy in the air and permeated the conversations of many Parisians.

"I'll take you where the real people live and hang out," Harry said with great enthusiasm. "Well, I'm not sure," I said, hesitating even though I was curious to see how and where the "real people" of Paris lived, at least, according to Harry. I knew the café was near the area where we had held a few of our feminist meetings because the rent was cheap. Maybe I'll learn something about the French feminists, I thought, since I knew that many of them lived in that part of the city.

"Harry will grow out of it. He'll realize that being poor isn't as romantic as he and those out-of-touch Marxist friends of his make it out to be. You should go with him and see for yourself," Ruth encouraged.

"Okay." I agreed.

******

Smoke from the overpowering, non-filtered French Galois cigarettes swirled around us as Harry and I entered the café in the working-class district.

"This is the real Paris," Harry again assured me passionately as we found a table in the back of the crowded café. "Not the one you'll find down at the American Embassy. They have no idea what's going on with the people on the streets who are the true backbone and heart of this city."

We were both in our twenties and I liked Harry very much and thought him quite intelligent. Tall, dark and with a prominent nose that made him look regal, he spoke with the same fiery determination about worker's causes that I was beginning to feel about women's equality and the feminist movement. Even though I was a diplomat's wife and he a diplomats' son, we were both young and passionate and seemingly immersed in the original energy of the rallying cry born of the French Revolution, *Liberte, Egalite, and Fraternite.*

Just as Harry had assured me, there was an electrifying energy and mix of people in the cafe, all talking loudly and making wild gestures. French people, I was learning, were anything but apathetic! Not only was the air heavy with cigarette smoke that left me coughing and eyes burning, but also the reeking smell from the older-style bathroom where you squatted over a hole in the floor to urinate, then pulled an overhead chain to flush. But nothing seemed a deterrent to the packed café's occupants, mostly sweaty, bearded men with a sprinkling of women, all hotly debating ideas and philosophy. It was politics and philosophy, the heady stuff that Frenchmen and women had nurtured and challenged themselves with for centuries.

"They understand the value of continuous dialogue and individual participation at the grassroots level, which is what eventually shapes government and economics at the highest level," Harry explained, now puffing on his Galois cigarette like one of the "real" people in the cafe.

The café's energy was flavored with the same intensity I'd experienced recently with friend Lisa when we attended a meeting of the French radical feminist group called *Choisir* started by activist lawyer Gisele Halimi and novelist/philosopher Simone de Beauvoir. Neither Gisele or Simone was present at the meeting, which was a disappointment because our primary intent had been to meet them, especially de Beauvoir. The women who were present were so rude and loud with their talk of resistance and revolution that neither of us had any intention of ever going back.

"Have you heard of the French feminist group *Choisir* or activist *Simone De Beauvoir?*" I asked Harry.

He nodded. "Yes, I know something about them."

"Yeah, I should have thought you would," I said. We ordered espressos and soon were talking loudly, our voices joining in the roar that engulfed the cafe.

"Are you a part of the French feminist groups?" he asked, surprised.

"No, no. I've only been to one of their meetings. Actually, a small group of English-speaking women have recently come together and we've formed our own feminist group. Our meetings are loud and go on for hours but aren't nearly as explosive as the French feminists, where the women continuously scream and insult one another. The French are so emotional and excitable."

"Yes, I can imagine. That's what I like about them!"

"Really? I'm not so sure."

"I would have thought you'd like that kind of excitability," he said, grinning.

"My goodness, are you flirting with me, Harry Bernstein?" I asked, smiling back.

"Maybe a little," he replied sheepishly.

I smiled and took another sip of my espresso. "The truth is, French feminists don't really welcome Americans in their groups and they're too radical for me, but you'd probably like them since they're committed to Marxism and other extreme political views."

"Marxism isn't extreme," he said defensively.

"What? Well, to most people it is; maybe not to you and certainly not to the feminists who call themselves social feminists. They want to create what they call an 'integrated Marxist and feminist analysis', which I have no idea what that is except it challenges capitalism and male supremacy."

"I could support that," Harry said with sincerity.

The café had filled to overflowing and we could barely hear one another.

"Why don't we go for a walk and continue our conversation outside," he suggested.

"All right," I agreed, knowing the kids wouldn't be home from school for several more hours and that I had to pee and wanted to find another toilet somewhere, one that didn't require squatting over a hole in a dirty floor and pulling a dirty chain to flush.

Spontaneously, we decided to take the metro across town to the Bois de Boulogne, one of the most popular parks bordering the city; with over 2,000 acres, it boasted wide roads, numerous walking paths and seven lakes, an open-air theatre and two racecourses. It was a sunny day, still a little cool, but perfect for being outdoors. Laughing and momentarily forgetting radical politics, workers and women's rights, we were just two people enjoying ourselves in the beautiful City of Light.

We grabbed an espresso at one of the outdoor café-restaurants in the park, and took up our conversation where we'd left off.

"I have something to admit to you," Harry said, lighting up another Galois and sitting back in his chair.

"Sounds mysterious."

"When you and your husband first came to our apartment and my parents introduced you as the wife of my father's new boss, I couldn't believe it. I thought you were the daughter and it took me a while to sort it out. I thought you were very pretty, too."

"*Merci beaucoup,*" I said, averting my eyes from his frank and admiring look. "I liked you too. You reminded me of photos I've seen of Lord Byron. Do you write poetry?"

"Me? No. I'm too in my head to be a good poet but I like poetry."

The mutual attraction between us was palpable as Harry reached out his hand and lightly touched mine for a few brief moments. We sat in silence, staring out over the park's beautiful green landscape and the elegant people riding their horses off in the distance; reveling for a brief time in a mutually recognized attraction that perhaps had once been but could not be in this time and place.

Of course, I'm attracted to Harry, I thought. He and I are both young, full of ego and youthful rebellion, wanting to topple the old systems and ways of doing things, thinking we know better ways to improve humanity and the world.

Mostly, I'd never rebelled, I thought as I glanced at Harry, probably the closest person I'd ever have to a college boyfriend, even if only for an afternoon. Mostly I'd only listened to what adults had told me was good for me while I was growing up. There were a few things I'd learned, however, during my one year of fake independence ... fake because everything was so tightly controlled at Mercer, the private Baptist University I'd attended for one year before getting married. I'd learned that Baptists could send missionaries to Africa but when Africans wanted to come to their university in Georgia, which a few converted Nigerians tried to do, they were turned away. I learned that only the "right" students, the popular students, the ones who partied and were deemed handsome or sexy or religious, but not too religious, were invited to join the sororities and fraternities that populated the Christian campus. I had refused to pledge even though I got invited by Chi Omega Sorority, which led to an article being written about me and published in the college newspaper for being an independent person who thought for herself, which was far, far from the truth because I'd wanted to join a sorority but mother said I couldn't and I listened to her even though I was paying my own way.

I learned how to masturbate because church doctrine forbade nice girls and boys from having sex before marriage and I listened even though I was hormonally-ready to do every sexual thing I could imagine which wasn't a lot; I learned how mean young men could be when one accused me of being a witch saying I'd made him fall in love with me, while another rich arrogant lad from Atlanta going to the law school on Mercer's campus said every derogatory thing he could think of about my past and the things I'd accomplished when he saw the charm bracelet I wore jangling with icons of those achievements, and I listened and took off the bracelet. I learned how people could manipulate you for their own ends even if they said they loved you, which Saren did at Christmas break when we went to Ohio and he proposed to me and refused to wait until I had finished college to get married, telling me it was "now or never" and I listened and took his engagement ring.

My history of rebellion hadn't gone missing because it never existed. Although giving birth to two babies by the time I was twenty-one had given me an intense experience of being a grown woman, because as every woman who's given birth knows, it is a life-altering experience because it means taking a serious plunge down the rabbit hole of potential life and death, but it wasn't really an act of rebellion. Which is not to say that giving birth isn't a big deal, because it is, as I'd found out when I nearly died giving birth to Alex at the Army hospital in Aberdeen, Maryland after pleading with Saren to let me have my baby with a doctor in the nearby town so I could get to know him and feel confident and not be so scared, which I was, but he refused saying, "free medical benefits are part of the perks of being in the military. What does it matter if you see a different doctor every time you go in for a checkup? Women have babies every day. You'll be fine." Always telling me what I felt, that man did, but I'd listened and almost literally died because the baby was breech and a forceps delivery with two young doctors I'd never seen before who basically didn't know what they were doing. I lost so much blood I had to have numerous blood transfusions and baby Alex suffered a lack of oxygen and was kept in an incubator for days.

When is it the right thing to stop listening and start acting? When is a rebellious act really an act of courage and compassion? Was this spirit of rebellion what I liked about the hippies at the university who'd protested against the Vietnam war; was it what attracted me to Harry and the women I was meeting in our fledging English-speaking feminist group?

******

"I've got to get home to the kids but I had a nice time today, Harry."

"I wonder where we'll both be in twenty years," he mused, giving my hand another squeeze.

"*Mai oui,*" I exclaimed, happy to be with someone who thought about such things.

"I have an idea," he beamed, pausing and drawing in his breath like the French do.

"Please, tell me."

"Let's agree to meet in Paris, just the two of us, no matter if we're married or not, in twenty years. We'll meet under the Eiffel Tower. Twenty years! Let's promise."

"I thought you weren't a poet!"

"I'm not!"

"You certainly sound like one of the romantic poets. OK. Harry Bernstein. I promise. Under the Eiffel Tower in twenty years! Let's shake on it!"

We shook hands, laughing and sighing at the same time. Paris was known for lovers and sitting with Harry in the marvelous sparkle of a pristine Parisian afternoon in the park, where at every glance there were lovers embracing and kissing, we were caught up in our own brief and wistful Kismet.

We left one another, laughing about the promise we'd made to meet again in twenty years at the foot of the Tour Eiffel. Would we really meet up again in twenty years or even ever? I wondered as I waved goodbye before heading out to catch the metro to the *Invalides* where I had illegally parked my Austin Mini Princess on a sidewalk, knowing that because the car plates bore the two letters "CD", meaning corps diplomatic and under no circumstances was to be given a ticket or stopped by the police or gendarme. It was a privilege I and other members of the elite folk belonging to the diplomatic corps often took advantage of when we couldn't find a parking space.

Shortly after our café outing, Harry moved back to America to continue his education and I never saw him again. Ruth told me he was doing stupendously in graduate school where he was studying for a career in politics. I was grateful for the short time we'd spent together, two idealist souls sharing a few sweet innocent moments. It was poetry at its finest I decided, like "poetry written with the heart wide open" like poetry instructor Keith Wilson at NMSU had told me was the only poetry worth writing. I knew I wanted that kind of mutual respect and understanding in my marriage but worried that the closeness Saren and I had once shared was melting away, like ice cream bought from vendors in the Luxemburg gardens where I'd take the children on a hot summer's day to sail their small bateau and watch the marionette shows.

WHAT WOULD JOAN OF ARC DO?

The challenge over leadership and organizational structure was a major issue for feminists' groups everywhere because women didn't want to duplicate social hierarchies or top-down leadership, the primary patriarchal model. We English-speaking feminists in Paris wanted something less formal and more inclusive so we had thrown out *Robert's Rules of Order*, but the difficulty of making decisions while also ensuring that everyone had an opportunity to be heard was challenging, time-consuming and often exhausting.

We finally decided on a structure where leadership roles would rotate among as many members as possible and last for a term of six months. Every six months a new person would be selected to serve, ensuring the rotation of all leadership positions. This rotation of roles was done intentionally so that no one person could take over the group, however experienced they might be, and it would also provide every woman an opportunity to be a leader and learn whatever skills were necessary to perform that role. Taking on a leadership role in a group that was evolving and viewpoints were often politically fractious, was complicated and required enormous energy and time commitments. When the vote was taken and roles were assigned, I was honored but dubious when asked to take on the role of President and to lead the fledging NOW group for six months.

What would Saren say?

******

I was both proud and nervous when I told Saren about this opportunity to be the first president of the Paris NOW group that was being formed.

"I'm excited for you but I'm not so sure you should do this," he said, frowning. "I mean, it'll take a lot of time and energy and you already complain we don't spend enough time together as a couple or a family because I travel so much. How is this going to work out? What exactly is feminism anyway? What is it you women want? Don't you have everything already?"

"We want the same thing men want, equality!" I retorted, feeling the blood rush to my head. I knew instantly I was going to need some time to think about what to say to him when I wasn't so angry.

"I'm going for a walk," I said, grabbing my jacket and heading for the door. "I need to think about a few things, ok? The kids have already had their dinner."

Street vendors were roasting chestnuts and their fragrant aroma wafted through the cold December air as I briskly made my way to the Notre Dame Cathedral about a thirty-minute walk from our apartment. We had recently moved from the suburbs of Paris to the Left Bank to have an experience of living in the city and to enroll the children in a small private school called Pershing Hall. Alex had continued to have behavior problems at the American School of Paris and was now in therapy with an American psychiatrist after he'd taken some toy soldiers from a toy store. The psychiatrist had convinced Saren that sending Alex away to military school stateside wouldn't be a good idea since Alex, in his opinion, was feeling alienated, angry and vulnerable. Saren had initially protested but relented and agreed to keep Alex at home with us and hopefully, in the new, smaller school he would do better.

Since moving into the city, I often went to the Notre Dame Cathedral for quiet reflection; much as I'd done growing up in Georgia when I'd sought refuge inside the Baptist church to escape my parent's incessant arguing. I found a seat in the back of the grand cathedral and closed my eyes, ignoring the chatter of tourists walking past. My mind was racing with Saren's questions. He's right about being the leader of the feminist group taking enormous time and energy, even if it's only for six months, I thought, blinking back tears.

It would be easier to sit on the sidelines, complain and criticize others who had jumped in and were working to make a difference, but I couldn't be complacent in the matter of equal rights for women. There was too much at stake, not just for myself but also for my daughter and all the other daughters and women who would follow in the future.

During these quiet times at Notre Dame, I often thought of Joan of Arc, the famous Maid of Orleans who had fought and defended the throne of France in the early 15th century against the invading British. During her long trial for heresy, she had testified that her voices always came to her during the ringing of the church bells in the small village of her childhood, Doremey. "The sounds of the bells opened me to my visions," she'd said, "and they help me to hear the voices that come to me, telling me what I must do and where I must go." Joan was eventually burned at the stack as a heretic because she wouldn't deny hearing her voices or cease dressing as a man. While no voices spoke to me as they had to Joan, I did experience clarity of mind and a renewed sense of strength in the cathedral.

As I sat quietly, my eye suddenly caught sight of a banner at the front that I'd never noticed before. The banner, embroidered in gold featured the majestic figure of Joan of Arc, dressed in the forbidden clothes of a man, riding her faithful steed and carrying a sword and her own banner decorated with *fleur de lis*, the sign of French royalty.

What would the Maid of Orleans do? I asked myself as I studied the banner. I was pretty sure she would have encouraged me to take on the challenge and stand up for what I believed since that's exactly what she did.

Affirmed in my decision to take up the leadership position in the NOW chapter for the next six months, I left the cathedral and hurried home to talk with Saren again, whom I wanted to win over and gain his acceptance. Although he finally agreed, I knew he was conflicted about it and I understood because I knew it was taking on a lot. I found it interesting, however, that he would often brag to our friends that I was a feminist and "wasn't that great?" but when the truth of what embracing feminism meant in our daily lives, it was proving to be a challenge for him.

******

The biggest challenge for me as we approached the middle of our two years of living in Paris continued to be the changing dynamics between Saren and myself. The growing tension I felt about having to gain his acceptance and approval for doing something I wanted to do that might be different from what he thought was right, was proving to be exhausting and challenging. It was the same seeking or justifying of yourself and your ideas that women everywhere had to perform out in the world if they wanted a seat at the table. We women were struggling to be seen and heard at home, in the work place and the world. We were also struggling to un-yoke ourselves from the devastating attitudes and misogyny of centuries of belittling women and considering them as inferior to men.

Dissolving the old forms, the old ways and replacing them with more respect and equality for women was creating turmoil for everyone in what came to be called the Second Wave of feminism; it was a similar kind of turmoil that had arisen when integration came to the South when I was growing up; the same kind of turmoil that had arisen when the institution of slavery itself was challenged; the same turmoil that arose after Abraham Lincoln ran and won the Presidency on an anti-slavery platform in 1860, which was soon followed by the secession from the Union by eleven Southern states, leading to the ultimate turmoil and destruction of the Civil War.

Yes, feminism as a vehicle for social change and freedom had come to the streets, the town square, and to institutions everywhere; it was inevitable that it would gain the momentum that it did, but it was hard to step across the old threshold into the new ways of being and seeing the world. As regards the feminist movement, some of us were up for the challenge and some were not, as seems to be the case in any struggle. It didn't mean we were better or that we'd win but we were committed to making progress, however slowly towards our ultimate goal of equality and freedom. We were naïve, however, in thinking that once we'd seen things change that they'd never go back to how they used to be!

I did accept the leadership of the NOW Paris group and eventually our meetings settled down as the more radical women left to join other groups while the more moderate feminists stayed on. Because many of our group's problems in Paris were directly related to being foreigners, we eventually pursued goals that were meaningful to us as feminists and foreigners living in France. We published a booklet *How to Get a Job in Paris*; published a monthly newsletter with updates on women's films, books and articles on women's health; listed apartments for rent and other feminist issues, plus, we started a number of Consciousness-Raising and Self-Help groups.

I thought Joan of Arc would have approved and I planned to tell her next time I saw her in the Notre Dame!

MY BODY BELONGS TO ME

Heads turned and a deadly silence fell across the theater. A man had entered a sacred space intended only for women. It was an affront to their sensibilities. I should have known better ... *no men allowed*, and for some, *no children allowed*.

Saren and the children had come inside to drop me off for a women's event before heading out for an evening of fun on their own. "Come back in a couple of hours, but don't come inside. Meet me out front," I whispered to Saren as he quickly gathered up the children and left.

Heart pounding at my *faux pa'u*, I found a seat at the back of the small theater and sat down. As I began looking around for anyone I knew, I saw that the two French women who had given me killer stares were seated only a few rows in front of me and were making out, kissing passionately and caressing one another. It was my turn to be shocked. While I supported women's right to love other women, I simply had never seen women kiss one another in public. I felt uncomfortable. Should I move or stay put? I wondered. Public displays of kissing, caressing and showing affection happened everywhere in Paris but I still wasn't used to seeing them since I'd grown up in a culture where public displays of affection were considered vulgar behavior; however, since I'd begun to consciously work on rejecting the etiquette of proper behavior presented in the Southern Belle's playbook, I decided that *so what if two women were kissing in public!* Big deal! I would be staying put, right where I was.

The evening's event about menstrual extraction as an alternative to having an illegal abortion was a joint effort of our POW group and the French feminist group MLF to bring Carol Downer, leader of the Self-Help Abortion Movement in California, to Paris to demonstrate how menstrual extraction could be performed.

"I've been arrested in California for practicing medicine without a license," she began, matter-of-factly. "It was a sham because all I was really doing was teaching women how to perform menstrual extraction using simple, affordable materials you can easily find. A lot of pro-choice organizations don't like what I do either, but I know how many women have been helped with unwanted pregnancies using this simple method, so I say to hell with them." With this remark, we all loved Carol instantly! She was one of us.

One by one, Carol picked up every item on the table, explaining how it was to be used and how the menstrual extraction method could also prevent unwanted pregnancies.

"Listen, you've got to learn about your bodies," she shouted from the stage. "You shouldn't trust your health solely to doctors who are mostly men and don't give a shit!"

She picked up an item that looked vaguely familiar but I wasn't sure.

"This," Carol said, holding the item high above her head for everyone to see, "is a speculum. This item will become your best friend for making sure you have healthy vaginas. Speculums are those cold, steel objects the OB-GYN doctor pushes up your vagina to determine the health of your woman parts. Now do you recognize it?" Everyone shouted, "yes, yes!" as if any woman could ever forget a freezing cold object inserted up her vagina during a pelvic examination.

"I'll give you the address where you can order plastic speculums so you can do your own vaginal self-examinations. You've got to get to know your own body, what it looks like when it's healthy and what it looks like when it's off. We've got to learn to love our bodies and stop being afraid of them."

The menstrual extraction procedure wasn't anything I felt any desire to use if I were to become pregnant again, something I wasn't planning on doing. To me, legalized abortions were the best and safest option for women. My support and that of our feminist group remained primarily focused on ways to ensure that abortions became legal and available to all women. Fortunately, interest subsided in self-performed abortions when they were legalized in the United States in 1973 with Roe v. Wade[1], and in France where they were legalized in

---

1   As I was preparing this book for publication, sadly the U.S. Supreme Court overturned the almost 50-year old Roe v. Wade decision that gave women the right to have an abortion ; a legal right that we women of the Second Wave feminists had worked tirelessly to secure.

1974. But vaginal self-examinations using plastic speculums seemed beneficial when used to assess your vaginal health.

******

After Carol Downer's talk, my CR group decided we wanted to do vaginal self-examinations using plastic speculums. Excitedly, we each ordered a speculum so that we could begin to teach ourselves about our female anatomy and the beauty of our vulvas and vaginas by doing pelvic self-examinations.

Consciousness-raising groups, or CR groups as they were called, were transformational experiences for most women and my CR group of nine women was no exception. CR groups had become vital in shaping and identifying a feminist consciousness which was often the result when women came together, opened up to one another and shared at a deep personal level about themselves, and in particular, learning what it meant to be a woman in a patriarchal society that oppressed us. CR groups gave us the opportunity to talk about our feelings and experiences in a setting of acceptance with other caring women. Most groups were small, for women only and usually met in member's homes.

Our CR group often met in my apartment in the 7th arrondissement since it was central to everyone and had a large living room where we could sit comfortably. Each CR group decided on its own guidelines and it was through the process of CR groups that we learned to speak from the personal "I" point of view, meaning we learned to say, "*I feel* this way or *I think* this," which allowed us to "own" whatever statement we were making rather than making generalized remarks. We were learning to be our own authority for making decisions in our lives. Perhaps even more importantly, we were learning to trust women again, and for many women, it was the first time!

Consciousness-raising was not encounter group, which was a popular method of self-discovery and self-assertion during the 60s and 70s that used confrontation techniques for getting to know the *real* you; a CR group on the other hand, was a positive place where we felt supported and listened to as we sought to build our self-esteem as individuals. We encouraged each other to be our authentic self by recognizing and letting go of old values that didn't support us anymore.

******

A big grin spread across my face when I picked up the box of plastic speculums delivered to my APO address at the Embassy. The American Embassy in Paris! I felt like I was participating in a secret mission to assist women in freeing ourselves and our bodies, and it was being carried out right under the noses of the ruling patriarchy inside a bastion of male authority whose entrance was guarded by tough-looking, no-nonsense marines.

"What are those things, anyway?" Saren asked in bewilderment later that evening when I took out a plastic speculum and held it up for him to see.

"This is a speculum. *Spec-u-lum*," I said, slowly pronouncing each syllable. "It's what doctors use to examine women's vaginas; only theirs is metal and freezing cold." Just saying the word vagina and speculum made me feel powerful.

"What are you going to do with all of those spec-u-lums anyway?" he asked, letting the word roll carefully over his tongue.

"Our CR group is going to do pelvic examinations," I said proudly as though a woman had been voted President of the United States!

"You're going to look at each other's privates?" he asked, incredulous. "Are you becoming a lesbian or something?" he asked, stumbling over the word *lesbian*. "It all sounds a little perverted to me."

"No, no, it isn't. We just want to educate ourselves about our bodies. Learn what's down there; see what's down there," I protested, already feeling misunderstood.

"I hope you're not telling all those women in your group about our sex life. That's none of anybody else's business," Saren insisted.

It was a comment every single woman in the CR group had heard from her partner. "Don't fuck and tell!" Of course, we did tell and along with reading books on women's sexuality and health, referring often to books like *Our Bodies, Our Selves* published by a Boston's women's health collective and by sharing our personal sexual experiences, we were learning the anatomy of our bodies, what area to massage or caress to bring ourselves or our partners to orgasm; we learned that a clitoral orgasm was not an inferior orgasm to a deep orgasm inside one's vagina; we learned what to do for yeast infections or bladder infections after having sex with a new partner.

In preparation for our pelvic self-examinations, we'd devoted an entire CR meeting reviewing New York photographer and women's pleasurable-sex advocate Betty Dodson's book with drawings of female vaginas, and afterwards sharing how we felt after looking at an entire book of photos of vaginas. "They're like flowers," we all agreed. "They're beautiful! And every single one is so incredibly different. Who knew women's genitalia were so amazing! It's like looking at a flower garden where every flower is unique." We were in absolute awe and felt so proud to be women. We'd all heard about penis envy, but now we were sure that it was really vagina envy that the good doctor Freud should have been talking about.

At first, we were all nervous about doing the pelvic self-examinations and after passing out the speculums, no one moved. "Maybe we don't want to do this after all," Janice said with notes of apprehension in her voice.

"Of course, we want to do this. We've got to be brave. We can do it," I said, motioning for the group to follow me to the master bedroom.

Like shy schoolgirls in a locker room for the first time, we undressed and sat on the king-sized bed, awkwardly holding our speculums in front of us.

"OK. Who wants to go first?" Cassandra blurted out.

"I'll go first," Lisa said, stretching her 5' 9" body out on the bed. We all watched as she rubbed Vaseline on her speculum before inserting it into her vagina.

"Are you ready to see," I asked, pointing a small flashlight on her pelvis while Cassandra held a mirror up to Lisa's vagina. Holding a mirror up to the pelvis allowed Lisa to see inside her vagina once she'd inserted the speculum.

"Wow!" We all exclaimed in unison while Lisa kept saying, "Oh my god; oh my god!" It was a mind-blowing experience for all of us! Discovering and seeing with our own eyes the *oz*, the small opening to the womb that was considered so important in experiencing a deep vaginal orgasm. It was like witnessing some miracle part of our bodies that few of us even knew existed until recently; it felt like *woman's pelvic anatomy 101* or, finally owning our own copy of the *Kama Sutra* and realizing the subject was us, a multiple-orgasmic woman.

After everyone had a turn at viewing her own vagina, we lay quietly on the bed together basking in our own intimate experience of sisterhood is powerful. We had reclaimed our bodies in a way we'd never imagined! We had seen "down there" and it was beautiful! No longer were our female bodies ugly or off limits to anyone except our male doctors, lovers and partners. We had owned our bodies in a profound, intimate experience with other women, our trusted sisters and friends. From this time forward, we would decide with a heightened confidence how to care for our bodies, how to pleasure them, how to use them and how to honor them. Woman Power was alive and well and on proud display! None of us were aware at the time that we had tapped into the energy of an ancient ritual known as Yoni worship that had been practiced in India and China for thousands of years.

******

Along with the newly reclaimed idea that our bodies belonged to us and no one else had the right to tell us what we could or couldn't do with them was the phrase *biology is not destiny*. This phrase became a liberating idea for many women because it not only meant taking back control of our bodies but choosing whether to have children or not. Janice, an articulate woman from New York, member of our feminist group and editor of our newsletter, decided she wanted a child even though she was a lesbian and wasn't in a relationship with anyone. Embryo implants weren't an option then, that didn't happen until 1983, so she arranged to sleep with a husband of a good friend who supported her in her desire to have a child of her own. "I'll raise my child by myself if it turns out that I don't meet another woman to be with," she told us. We were in awe of her strength and conviction to be a mother and her courage to make it happen.

What made these and other ideas about women and our bodies so compelling was that they weren't intellectual concepts but actual things we were dealing with and experiencing in our lives and in our bodies; bodies that society was trying to control in a variety of ways intended to take away our right to decide what was best for ourselves.

For many French feminists who identified as radical feminists, however, the phrase *biology is not destiny* took on a very different meaning. They believed all male and female roles were learned, male political constructs that ensured the power and superiority of men; in their view, men were not superior *because* of their biological difference but because of the *rationalization* that they were supreme *due* to that biological difference. Proponents of radical feminism saw men as the oppressors of women and often viewed women's role in reproduction as continuing to enable men to take power over them. They felt that women's struggle to overthrow patriarchy and oppression was best obtained by working, living and existing in women-only groups. French author and radical feminist Monique Wittig in her book *Les Guerilleres* first published in 1969, had written: "If you're in relationship with a man, it's a betrayal of feminism." *Les Guerilleres* achieved international acclaim and became a primer for the emerging feminist consciousness, although it gave a narrow definition of woman: the most famous being "lesbians are not women but a separate class of people unbound by traditional notions of gender."

We feminists of whatever persuasion were highly volatile and passionate about women's role in society and the world. We didn't always agree, far from it, but we were committed to fighting for women's equality and viewed having control over our bodies as an inalienable right.

DE BEAUVOIR, SEXUAL POLITICS & FREEDOM TO CHOOSE

"The women here tonight have all had abortions ... illegal abortions," the dark-haired woman said. "It's time we changed the law to allow legal abortions. The women you'll hear tonight will tell their stories of fear, trauma and for some, near death, in getting an illegal abortion." It was Simone de Beauvoir speaking, the most influential and visual feminist during this period. She had guided the French feminist movement into the twentieth century with her international best-selling book, *Le Deuxieme Sexe*, or *The Second Sex*. First published in 1953, it had become a classic in detailing how women had historically been regarded as secondary citizens, something de Beauvoir said remained true in present-day Western culture.

De Beauvoir had called for a rally to support legalizing abortions in France after she, along with hundreds of other French women, had signed a document called the *Manifesto of the 343*, acknowledging they all had had an illegal abortion.

Elaine and I had heard about the rally in our feminist POW group and decided we would attend. We huddled closer together for warmth against the freezing cold night air as we watched one French woman after another take the stage and speaking into the microphone, told the large crowd of mostly women about her terrifying experience of having had an illegal abortion, a procedure that had left many of them permanently sterile or having narrowly escaped death at the hands of incompetent people using dirty instruments in back alleyways where illegal abortions were performed.

I struggled to make sense of many of the details the French women shared of their experiences, often couched in Marxist or psychoanalytical terms. In the 1970s, while many social feminists in France were intent on creating what they called an integrated *Marxist and feminist analysis of society*, other feminists focused on developing a psychoanalytical theory for better understanding the continuing dominance of patriarchal ideology. I was more interested in how we could make immediate changes in the day-to-day lives of us ordinary women, reflected in one of several letters to the editor of *The International Herald Tribune* I'd written on the need for making their classified job ads gender neutral and another letter condemning them for not including girls in stories about sports, both which they'd published. Simple things we could do.

"Sometimes I feel I have more in common with the women of Micronesia than I do with French women," I said to Elaine, pulling gloves onto my freezing hands. "I don't really understand why developing a psychoanalytical theory to understand male dominance helps ordinary women. I don't really understand how Marxism and feminism work together either."

"You don't have to be a Marxist to be a feminist," she replied in her usual authoritarian voice.

"What about the *personal is political*?

"The personal *is* political because it influences society and changes the way people think and act, especially when it comes to women's rights over their bodies, but you don't have to be a card-carrying Marxist."

I hadn't dressed warmly enough and was still shivering from the cold and now from Elaine's icy remark and superior attitude. Although I had once been sexually attracted to Elaine, her authoritarian personality of knowing everything had caused me to feel differently very rapidly. Big egos know no gender, I thought to myself, and Elaine can be a real bitch. But I said nothing, having seen her wrath when anyone crossed her. I had begun to feel compassion for her husband Michael whom she had told to move out of their home so her lover Sophia from Sweden could move in with her.

Driving home from the rally to legalize abortions, I thought about how passionate the French feminists were in achieving their goals of equality regardless of their own particular societal perspective. It didn't hurt that they had de Beauvoir at the helm either but what was this *feminist consciousness* that women worldwide were trying so desperately to develop, bring forth, shape and hone to create a new and better society for women? Would it be expansive and open enough to hold our widely divergent views socially and politically as well as our emerging collective consciousness leading to a ripening wisdom? Would political ideologies squelch a feminist consciousness from blossoming into a paradigm of inclusiveness where everyone, including men, could find a place? Where did sexual politics and individual freedom fit into it all? How were we supposed to develop a *feminist consciousness*?

******

Feminism wasn't an idea shared by only one or two women, I reminded myself. It was a movement, a swirling energy of bright, beautiful colors being painted by the women of the world around the wagon of feminism, much like the one the old gypsy woman had shown Elaine and me. Women were thinking and writing their way into history and society with their creativity, energy and their diverse voices demanding to be heard. There were feminist films, books on feminism, feminist groups, rallies and demonstrations...all of these were helping to raise our consciousness regarding how women had been treated as secondary citizens both historically and currently and how we would have to organize and work hard to gain equal status with men in society.

Film and filmmaking were highly regarded as both liberating and necessary in developing a *feminist consciousness*. In the spring of 1974, our feminist group POW joined with French feminists to bring the first of many women's film festivals to Paris. The event was held at the Paris Museum of Modern Art and featured films that focused on exposing women's sex-role stereotyping and the masculine myths that accompanied them.

Paris feminists made or appeared in a number of the films on the festival program. *Three Lives*, a film by American feminist Kate Millet, author of *Sexual Politics* (1970), documented the lives and experiences of three women, showing their struggle to break away from traditional roles and live according to their own definition of themselves. Although I didn't see that particular film, my good friend Lisa did. She told me that one of the three women featured in the film had recently moved to Paris and wanted to join our POW group. I was looking forward to meeting her and hearing about her experience of being in Millet's film.

About half a dozen women, including Jane who had appeared in Millet's film, had shown up in response to a call for help that Janice, the editor of the

POW newsletter had put out. Everyone had gathered around a long table where Janice had laid out papers and pens and cups for coffee. As we began to read, discuss and sort out what the various sections of the newsletter would be, without forewarning or reason, Jane began to make inflammatory remarks.

"Monique Wittig's got it right, you know," Jane asserted. "If you're in relationship with a man, it's a betrayal of feminism!"

For a few moments, no one said anything because we were so shocked at her statement and how out of place it was since the majority of the women in the English-speaking feminist group were married or in relationship with men. With her words, tempers flared.

"How can you say such a thing?" one woman fired back at her.

"That's nonsense," someone else shouted.

"Did you read Anne Koedt's article *The Myth of the Vaginal Orgasm* in the rag *Lesbianism and Feminism* where she says that a woman's life is not the political property of the women's movement?" Janice, our articulate editor, asked, hurling her words like darts at Jane. "Koedt specifically says that slogans like the *personal is the political* becomes a perversion when women use them to pass judgment or attack other women for sleeping with men or for wanting to have children. I am a lesbian, and I'm insulted by your remarks that if women sleep with men they're betraying feminism, or if we want to have children. I am a lesbian who wants to be a mother."

"I don't think you understand the real issue here," Jane shot back. "I think Wittig made it clear in her highly acclaimed novel *Les Guerilleres*—did any of you happen to read it?" she asked sarcastically. "Well, if you did, maybe you'd remember she made it very clear that women have to be warriors who aren't afraid to fight with men in order to triumph over male domination. Lesbians aren't women; they're a separate class of people ... they're beyond traditional notions of gender. Wittig rejects 'woman' as a social construct and believes it is inherently oppressive."

"I guess you'd better go join Wittig and her group of lesbian guerillas then. You definitely don't belong here with us," Janice struck back, standing up and slamming her chair under the table.

In response, Jane angrily threw her papers across the room and stormed out, never to be seen again at any of our meetings. She did join Wittig's radical French group, the *Feministes Revolutionnaires*, whose later attempt to place a wreath for "the unknown female soldier" at the Arc de Triomphe caused a public outcry throughout Paris. We feminists in POW admitted that placing a wreath at the Arc de Triomphe, where a fire was kept burning perpetually for the unknown soldiers, presumably males who fought and died in wars, had been a really bold, courageous thing to do and we were proud of our French sisters. But we didn't miss Jane.

"I'M STILL THE SAME"

"We need to find a marriage counselor," I insisted to Saren one day after we'd had another heated argument. We'd been in Paris for over two years and during that time our arguing had become increasingly unbearable and we were rarely able to resolve anything without berating one another.

"I haven't changed since the day we got married. I'm still the same. I'm not unhappy with our marriage. You are. You go to counseling if you feel you need help. I'll pay for it."

Did "I'll pay for it" mean he gave his consent as the holder of the checkbook and the high god of our finances? Should I be shocked that he was taking pride in not having changed since the day we met? I had grown to suspect that Saren was happy being in the military because he liked giving orders and being obeyed, which meant he was in control.

"How can you possibly think that in a relationship of two people, it's only one person that has problems? Even if that's true, the one who's 'still the same' should care enough about the other one to come along for support, don't you think?"

"Marjorie, you know where I stand about therapy or counseling or anything like that. It's not for me, okay?"

Saren had made up his mind. I felt disheartened but if I had to go alone to marriage counseling, then I would. At the time I did't realize how ridiculous the idea of going alone to marriage counseling sounded. I knew it wasn't going to be easy to find someone to work with in Paris because only a handful of analysts spoke English, something I had found out when searching for someone to work with Alex. No one in Paris even spoke of therapy or marriage counseling since most practiced some variant of analysis in the tradition of Frenchman Jacques

Lacan, a psychoanalyst who had influenced French intellectuals in the 60s and 70s by advocating a return to Freud's ideas. The widely held view in the French community was that analysis, possibly lasting for years, was the only reliable and worthwhile method to make positive and lasting changes to one's psyche. Obviously, not a time frame that we Americans liked, but this was Paris.

******

Friends gave me names of three analysts who spoke English and I made appointments to see each of them for an initial interview. The first analyst I interviewed was a woman originally from Great Britain who had settled in Paris decades earlier and worked almost exclusively with French clients. A tall, skinny woman wearing a long black dress, with her black hair pulled back in a tight bun, and lips painted a bright red emphasizing her pale-as-snow white skin, answered when I rang the doorbell.

"Please wait here, Madame," she said, motioning me to a Louis XV chair in the shadowy, long hallway. "I'll be with you a *bientot*."

I must have stepped into a Gothic novel, I thought as I settled myself and surveyed my surroundings. "The long hallway was lined with ornate tables holding enormous candelabra whose tapers were lit and burning brightly. Black velvet curtains with gold braided trim and tassels were drawn tightly closed over the windows preventing any light from entering.

This was kind of creepy, like a scene inspired by tales from Edgar Allen Poe. Who kept their curtains closed and burned candles in the middle of the day? Clearly, the lady of the house had some kind of aversion to light.

When the dark lady finally called me into her office, I sat on the edge of a long green velvet sofa, barely moving for the entire twenty-minute interview, more fearful of her than I was of the analytical process itself. She began to tap the desk with her long, brightly painted red fingernails that matched her lipstick, and spoke English with a French accent.

"*Maintenant…mai oui*, Engleesh, yes. I forgot already to speak Engleesh. What is your purpose you want in analysis? What can I help you Madame?" she asked, still tapping the desk with her red fingernails that I now noticed had been filed into a sharp "v" shape.

"I'm married to a man who works for the U.S. Embassy. We have two children, young children, and we, my husband and I, have been having marital problems for some time now and I was hoping to get some help, some clarity about how to communicate better." I straightened my shoulders hoping that would help to establish I wasn't just some wimpy, spoiled American but a person of substance who was serious about getting her counsel.

"*Alors*, Madame, I'm not so sure I would help you much. I see patients who have more psychological issues. I don't marriage counsel," she said, nervously patting her perfectly coiffed hair with her sharp, v-shaped fingernails.

We both hemmed and hawed a few more minutes before I finally stood up, and thanked her for her time, all the while thinking, you scare the heck out of me lady. As I hurried out of her apartment onto my next interview, I busied myself with thoughts of what character she most resembled...the headless horseman who chased Ichabod Crane in *The Legend of Sleepy Hollow*; or, *Cruella Deville* in 101 Dalmatians? I couldn't decide. All I knew was that I had no intention of going back to her real or imagined vampire den.

The second interview took me to an apartment belonging to an elderly British gentleman who had also lived most of his life in France. He welcomed me into a modest-sized room where he sat down behind a large, elaborately carved desk and I sat opposite him in a stiff, over-stuffed chair with brass tacks decorating the arms and back. Archaeological artifacts and other *object d'art* from Egyptian and Grecian cultures were displayed on his desk and around the room.

"Why do you want to see an analyst, Mrs. Canto, and what do you hope to gain from this experience," he asked in a formal manner, accentuated by his thick British accent.

I gave my rehearsed reply. "I want to get to know the authentic me; I want to be a less-anxious person; I want help to understand what's happening in my marriage." All the time while calling out my concerns like items on a grocery list, I was squashing my real desire to tell him outright that I wanted to save my marriage from going to hell in a hand-basket! But no. That would leave the wrong impression.

He listened intently for the first few minutes and then something ghastly happened ... something you could never imagine would happen in a professional's office, especially a therapist's office.

He began picking his nose and wiping the boogers on a paper lying in front of him on the desk, presumably intended for that purpose!

I was horrified and didn't know what to say. Was I supposed to ignore it? Was it a test of some kind to get a certain response? I tried to read his face. Nothing there; face like the stone sphinx sitting on his desk. With no clue as to what might be expected, I rushed through the questions I'd rehearsed to ask all the analysts, keeping my head down to avoid looking at the piece of paper with his boogers on it! I raced out of there as soon as I could, wishing I'd had the courage to say something, anything.

On the way to my car, I busied myself with things I could have said. "Excuse me, Mr. Analyst sir, bet I can pick more buggers than you can in one minute;" or, "Do you mind not picking your nose while I'm scratching my arse?" or, "Picking your nose makes me want to fart, so please do stop!" The list was endless and the entire scenario so ridiculous that I was absolutely giddy and laughing out loud by the time I arrived home, thinking of all the things I could have said and even though I hadn't said, it was still funny. Despite my giddiness, I was beyond discouraged because clearly, I was in better shape than the two professionals I'd just seen.

Resigned and with little hope, the next day I rang the doorbell of the third and final analyst on the list, my mind filled with negative thoughts. I'll never find anyone who isn't crazy. Everybody in Paris is slightly crazy and hysterical, right? Who are these weird people and how could they ever help anyone come into a mentally and emotionally balanced life?

To my surprise, a pleasantly handsome, middle age American man opened the door and greeted me. He looked exactly like a person you'd want to be your father or favorite uncle, with his slightly graying hair, glasses and a pleasant face with a warm smile that said "Hello. It's so nice to meet you." His manner was gentle and kind, and when he asked me the usual questions of why I was there and what I wanted from being in analysis, they seemed genuine. I was so excited. I'd finally found someone I could work with who might be able to help me navigate the choppy waters of my life and marriage.

"I have no room to take on any new clients for the next year," he informed me when our time was up, "however, I can put you on my waiting list."

"One year," I stumbled on the words. "I was hoping to start right away."

"I'm so sorry," he said sincerely, as I fumbled to put on my fashionable, floor-length coat trimmed in fake fur.

The next day I called Helen Feinstein, a Jungian analyst trained at the Jungian Institute in Switzerland and a member of our English-speaking feminist group. Helen was my last choice, not because she wasn't good, but because I didn't want there to be any justification for Saren to accuse me of having chosen someone to work with who was "a feminist and against men," which was beginning to be the way he described feminists and feminism.

******

During my first session with Helen, she asked why I wanted to be in therapy. "I want to save my marriage," I said simply and honestly.

"Do you feel it's your responsibility to make your marriage work?"

"Well, yes, I do. I mean, who else can make it work?"

It took some time before I realized I had to be in therapy for myself, not to save my marriage, which might be "saved" in the process, but the goal was to understand myself better and work to make changes in myself. Saving my marriage would be something both partners would have to undertake together and so far, Saren wasn't interested.

It was a huge step for me to be in private therapy where I would once again be asked to confront my ambivalence about my own self-worth. The idea of recognizing myself as a separate individual with my own needs and desires and working to gain the confidence and strength to express those needs to my partner became a key factor in learning to accept myself, warts and all. The therapy sessions were difficult because I was filled with guilt about focusing so much energy on myself, something I'd been taught was selfish because I should be putting the needs of others first.

"I want you to start recording your dreams when you wake in the morning. Get a journal just for that purpose. We'll do some analysis work based on your dreams. We'll use symbols that appear inside your dreams as a guide to understanding your deep psyche," Helen instructed me during our first session.

Afterwards, as I began to recall my nightly dreams, I was horrified and didn't want to write them down, much less talk about them. They were taking place in caves where I would struggle to make my way among dismembered, bloodied arms, legs, heads and other body parts.

"I hate those bloody, horrible parts of myself," I said vehemently to Helen once I'd begun to keep a dream journal.

"What parts of yourself do you think you've rejected?" Helen asked.

I gave long pause to her question. "Everything," I wanted to say but knew that would be avoiding the question. With Helen's help, however, I began to see how the bloodied body parts in the dreams were symbols of those parts of myself I'd discarded, thrown away or kept hidden in my deep psyche where no one could see them or be affected by them. It would take a long time of examining my psyche before I'd begin to understand that I was, in fact, retrieving and reclaiming lost parts of my soul that I'd discarded, thinking them too horrible and ugly to be loved.

Rejection of parts of myself that I thought made me unlovable was to some extent a direct result of my growing up years where I'd heard sermon after sermon by Baptist preachers who preached constantly about sin and how everyone was a sinner, a lowly worm unworthy of God's love, and those messages had sunk deep into my psyche, causing me to believe myself to be unworthy and a monster of sorts. Confessing myself to be a sinner, asking Jesus for forgiveness and accepting him as my personal savior had been the churches' solution to keep such an unworthy one as myself from going to hell, but I didn't hold to that belief anymore. Now, I realized it was up to me to learn to love all the parts of myself; the good, the bad and the ugly.

Also with Helen's help, I was learning how to *burst the bubble of perfection*; of thinking I had to be perfect in order to be deserving of love; it was a perfection bubble that another Jungian analyst Marion Woodman had made the subject of her book *Addiction to Perfection*. Women suffer from their addictions to being perfect, Woodman had said, and they want to achieve perfection in all they do and it kills off their inner self-acceptance and joy. They feel at risk of losing love and acceptance from everyone and everything they care about. When I read Woodman's book, I knew she was describing me.

Therapy was giving me a way to find and accept those parts of myself that fell short of perfection and using dream analysis was giving me a new framework to look at my life. It was difficult work and painful to have so little support or understanding from my husband.

MARRIAGE, MONOGAMY & BELONGING

"There's got to be another way to partner with someone you love other than marriage, don't you think?" I asked my friend Lisa one day as we sat having espressos at our favorite café.

Lisa had been considering marriage with her long-time French boyfriend but they had broken up recently. She was working on releasing her anger about the break-up with a new technique that involved taking a bat or tennis racket and hitting a futon while screaming out your rage. She had borrowed my tennis racket and unfortunately it had broken during one of her sessions. "Listen," she said, "I'll buy you another one."

"That's okay. I never play tennis anyway," I'd told her.

"I thought Jacques and I had figured out how to live well together without getting married but for some reason it all blew up when the idea of marriage came up and we started talking about it. How weird is that?"

I, too, was feeling restless and weird these days, fatigued from the ongoing conflict I felt regarding monogamy and the idea that marriage meant belonging to someone else who could exercise control over you and the choices you made. Of course, a couple had to talk about this power dynamic but what if your partner didn't want to talk about it or didn't even know there was such a thing? Although I had become aware that it was possible to feel sexually-attracted to another woman, I was more interested in having my sexual independence than getting into relationship with anybody else.

"Do you ever think about being with another woman as your partner?" I asked Lisa.

"I don't know. Maybe. I think I like men too much although they can be pains in the derrière!"

"Yeah, I feel the same way. You know I was attracted to one of my university professors when we lived in New Mexico. We kissed once and then broke it off because I was so full of guilt about even the notion of having sexual relations with him; and unfortunately, confessing to Saren that I had kissed him didn't work out so well."

"Why do men think we belong to them once we get into a relationship with them?" Lisa asked.

"I think it has to do with the patriarchy. 'Belonging to another person' is at the heart of the marriage ceremony. When you get married, think about it. They call it 'the bonds of matrimony.' For the woman, it means another person, your husband, has control over you, control over your decisions regarding what you can or can't do with your body and even your feelings. You can argue that these things are all symbolic, but are they really? In my marriage ceremony, my father walked me to the altar where he literally handed me over to another man who, with that one gesture, was given authority over me ... authority over me because now it was his responsibility to take care of me and not my fathers. The churches' marriage ceremony is patriarchy made visible, down to the woman changing her last name from her fathers to her new husbands!"

"Yeah. I'm kind of happy I haven't gotten married yet, if I ever do. I agree with you though, about the patriarchal part. Marriage is a legal contract that says you are willingly bound to another person, that you're monogamous, and if you step outside those rules sexually, you're considered an adulterer, an act punishable by death in some cultures, that is, if you're a woman."

"So, if it's a legal agreement, then who gets to decide who you can sleep with?"

"Men are excluded from these rules, and in some cultures, it's expected that men will have mistresses," Lisa spoke, leaning back in her chair and readjusting her 5'9" body-beautiful, a visible result of her daily yoga practice. But, if you're in a relationship with another mature, responsible, sensitive adult, you would talk with them about it, wouldn't you? But I think most marriages favor the man who can have his cake and eat it too. Know what I mean?"

I loved these conversations with Lisa, even though her predilections towards a preciseness of details sometimes drove me a little crazy. We'd met at the first planning meeting to organize a NOW chapter in Paris for English-speaking feminists. She was also in my CR group and we'd become good friends. She was like another member of my family, coming over often for dinner and, taking a liking to my kids, would take them out to the park or other fun kid outings.

"Have you heard about open relationships?" I asked her.

"Yeah, I know a couple who have an open relationship. It seems to be working for them. I don't know any details but I guess if you're emotionally mature and aren't the jealous type, it's probably a good way to keep your relationship fresh sexually. Are you thinking about trying it with Saren? He doesn't seem the type that would be open to that," she said, emphasizing the word open and we both had a good laugh.

"Hey, let's order some lunch 'cause I've got to go in about an hour to teach my English class."

"Yeah, me too. The kids will be home soon."

I liked the idea of an open relationship and decided I would bring up the idea of sexual independence and having an open relationship with Saren, thinking that as adults we could talk rationally about it whether we acted on it or not. It was a bombshell of an idea from the get-go! Think Godzilla meets the tooth fairy. And, no I wasn't on drugs or any other life-altering substances, though on reflection, I'm not sure it would have made any difference because I was on my "free and independent" journey, which was by definition messy, scary, and bat-shit crazy at times.

******

One such episode happened one evening when Saren and I had gone out to dinner and afterwards were strolling down the elegant *rue de Rivoli* gazing at the beautiful items of jewelry in one of the lavishly-decorated windows of the expensive *magasins*, or stores.

"I have something important to tell you," I blurted out, not having intended to bring up such a delicate and important subject in such a public setting, but never being much of a drinker, I was emboldened and slightly inebriated by having drunk three glasses of wine at dinner.

"What is it?" Saren asked, wrapping his arm around my shoulders.

"I've been thinking about this for a long time," I began. "It has to do with our marriage; well, actually, with our relationship. You've heard of couples having an open relationship in their marriage? Well, I want us to have an open relationship and ... I can't ... I can no longer promise to be sexually faithful to you," I said in a halting voice.

"What?" Saren said, dropping his arm from my shoulders and stopping dead still on the sidewalk.

I repeated my sexual declaration. "I can't promise to be sexually faithful to you anymore. I've taken off my wedding ring because it symbolizes that I belong to you and that you belong to me and I don't believe that anymore. I believe we're both free people who have a right to make our own choices, and that includes our sexual choices."

"What are you saying?" he gasped. "Are you saying you want to sleep with other men? Or maybe it's women you want to sleep with? I don't understand where all this is coming from." He was clearly agitated and I instantly regretted my poor timing in revealing my new, bold view on sexuality and open relationships on a busy Parisian street.

"No! There's no one I want to sleep with but you! But I want to have an agreement that we have sexual freedom to be with anyone else if that should ever arise, which I doubt it will," I said, trying to do a bit of back-tracking.

"I don't understand," he said again, shaking his head. We had both stopped and were standing in front of another gorgeously decorated window full of gold jewelry and diamonds. "And you took off your wedding ring? What did you do with it?"

"It's at home in my jewelry box. It's safe. It feels like a symbol of something I can't embrace right now."

Saren was visibly shaken and I, too, had begun to shake in my boots, chic purple suede ones I'd bought to match my ankle-length purple tweed skirt, stylish clothes that I would soon stop wearing, seeing them, too, as a way to be attractive in a way that labeled me with an identity I no longer wanted: sexually desirable to men.

"Let's get the hell out of here and go home," he said, grabbing my arm and walking towards our car.

****

"What was I thinking? I must have been out of my mind!" I said, as I shared my whole sexual declaration scene with friend Lisa the next day when we had met up again at our favorite café for espressos. "I should have known the idea of an open relationship wouldn't be received well. And certainly not the idea of being free sexually. But you know, our attitudes on sexuality couldn't have been any more different even before this happened."

"Yeah. Like what?" Lisa asked.

"Like our first big blow-up around sexuality happened in New Mexico before we moved to Paris. We disagreed about a decision made by the Commanding General regarding his daughter."

"I'll never understand the military thing, but go ahead," Lisa replied.

"Yeah, well, it is another world, that's for sure. Rumors had been circulating on the Army post that the General's daughter had had an affair with an enlisted black man and was pregnant. And would you believe it, the General disowned her and sent her away to live with a relative? When I told Saren I thought that was awful, he came right out and said he agreed with the General's decision. Then, when I said I'd make sure our children knew about sex and birth control, his comment was that no child of his would ever be given birth control."

Lisa shook her head. "Saren's a good guy but boy he's more conservative than anyone I know!"

"Right? I asked him the other day what happened to the art book of nudes that was on the coffee table and he told me he'd put it away because the children weren't old enough to be exposed to anything like that!

"Did you guys even talk about it?"

"No! That's what made me angry. He just put it away without even asking me what I thought. My idea was that looking at beautiful images of the human body in a book from an art museum would be a wonderful way to explain human anatomy and sexuality in a positive and respectful way. You know that he told the kids that they couldn't take baths together anymore, right?

When I asked him why, he said it was because they might be too inquisitive about differences in their bodies and might start touching each other."

"Oh my god! And you didn't object to that?"

"Of course, I did but you know how Saren can get when he's made up his mind about something. In the past, I would have let it go, let him have the final say, but I'm standing up for what I believe these days. I'm beginning to assert myself and make messy instead of making nice. Arguing instead of acquiescing. I honestly don't know how to reach Saren anymore or how to communicate my ideas or feelings to him. He wants everything to be the way it always was; and he doesn't want to make any changes," I complained, blinking back tears.

"You should both be going to couples' therapy and if you can't work it out, then you may have to think about the "d" word," Lisa said.

"Does becoming a liberated woman mean I have to give up my husband and my life? I don't want a divorce. There's got to be some middle ground here. Maybe I was wrong to talk about an open relationship or sexual fidelity with Saren. I mean, he's a great person and we have two great kids together. I wish he'd get out of the military but there could be worse things, I guess."

"Wish guys would organize their own CR groups and work out some of their hang-ups about their identities and sexuality," Lisa said as we ordered another espresso and continued to watch the people passing by, a constant pastime for Parisians that we'd happily adopted.

******

Summer of the beginning of our third year had come to Paris. Although it could be sweltering hot in the summer, today was cool and I'd arranged for Lisa to take the kids for a swim on one of the bateau-mouche pools on the Seine. "Such a nice day, I think I'll take the metro to my therapy session with Helen," I told Lisa. "You guys have a great time at the pool and we'll do something fun together when you get back."

As I casually strolled to the metro, I walked past the Catholic Monastery for Nuns located three blocks from our apartment in the 7th arrondissement. Today, I paused to look at the brass plaque on the front gate that gave the Monastery's history. Since its inception, the plaque read, it had been a sanctuary for blind nuns. I had often seen nuns dressed in their habits coming and going in small groups to the nearby metro, using canes to negotiate their way down the stairs onto the platform to catch the metro. I found myself wondering what it might be like to be blind.

When I reached the entrance to the metro, I imagined how I might descend the steps if I were physically blind. I thought of the H. G. Well's book *The Country of the Blind* that depicted a country where blindness was the basis of its morality; where the greatest crime was to see because to see was to be able to know what others didn't know and that was considered impious.

But didn't most people live in some version of the country of the blind where they were forbidden to "see" what was actually there because then they'd know things, important things that might set them apart from everyone else and they would no longer belong?

I felt determined to regain my own internal sight of all the hurtful attitudes I'd been blindly holding onto for the sake of a false sense of security and identity, or of belonging. Energized by this clarity, I bounded up the metro stairs to the street, eager for my session with Helen to tell her the latest events unfolding in my life.

Helen lived in an older apartment near Montparnasse with a nice view across the city. No elevator in the older apartments, but I was energized today so climbing the six flights of stairs felt good. I took my seat in the familiar overstuffed chair opposite her, and excitedly launched into my story, hardly pausing to breathe. "I told Saren I can't promise to be sexually faithful to him any longer and that I want us to think about having an open marriage. I've taken off my wedding ring because I want to belong to myself." I held up my left hand, without the large diamond-encrusted band I'd worn for fifteen years.

"How does that feel to take off your wedding ring?" she asked in her usual friendly but detached manner that showed no emotion.

"I'm happy but I'm also scared," I answered.

"Why?"

"Because I don't know where this might lead."

There was the usual long pause after I said something during which time Helen would say nothing, waiting for me to reflect on what I'd just said. At first the long silent pauses made me uncomfortable and anxious until I was able to use the long pauses to reflect on what I'd said and possibly discover a deeper meaning on my own.

"I've always belonged to someone or something other than myself," I said tenuously. "When I was a child, I belonged to my mother and father, and, of course, to the Church and to school. Then at my marriage ceremony, I was legally and contractually given over by my father to another man, my husband, whom I promised to obey and who vowed he'd take care of me, which meant he was the director, the one who authenticated my life. I was probably too young to get married because I never had a chance to get to know who I was on my own or what I thought about things. In truth of fact, I've never belonged to myself. I didn't even know it was possible."

Long uncomfortable pause, then... "I have no idea who I am beyond society's defined roles of a mother and wife and I have no idea what I might be if I didn't have those roles to define me. I mean, I'm trying to understand what kind of identity I could have from a feminist perspective ... like if I belonged to myself first and foremost."

"Has there ever been a time when you made a decision solely by yourself and lived the results?" she asked.

"Only once, really. When I decided to marry Saren, no one in my family or his supported it but I did it anyway. Of course, we did it anyway," I said.

"Actually, he gave me an ultimatum," I continued, recalling that day in the Baptist church in Ohio when Saren had told me that if I didn't marry him immediately, he'd break off our engagement. "So, I agreed to marry him. Ever since, I've pretty much let Saren make all the important decisions. I mean, he's older and has seen so much of the world and I was, well, I was a teen-ager when we married. I was nineteen and he was thirty-three. I mean, I had opinions but what did I know of the world?"

And has that changed now?"

"Well, yes. I think so. I've been learning to trust that even if I am 'just' a woman, I've been learning that my thoughts and ideas even if they are different from my husbands, or society or the church or anybody else, they're just as important and deserve to be heard. I know it's important to believe in myself."

"What do you expect to happen as a result of your sexual freedom declaration and desire to have an open marriage?"

"I honestly don't know. I've never been sexual with anyone but Saren and although he's a sensitive lover, I sometimes wonder what it might be like to be with someone else and then I judge myself for even having a thought like that. It's not like there's anyone I want to be with sexually. I just wish I could be with my husband and be my own person whoever that might be, and talk about my feelings even if they do seem scary. But Saren has no interest in the journey I'm on and has zero desire to look at anything in a new or different way. He has rules for everything and he takes pride in saying 'I'm still the same.'"

Helen sat erect in her chair, her face showing no emotion, no approval or disapproval.

"And I feel guilty for even saying those things; like I'm a bad person."

******

When Saren returned home from work later that evening, the tension from our heated argument about sexual freedom a few nights earlier was still palpable between us. My head felt like it was exploding. Should I say anything? What should I say? What is there to say? Hadn't I said everything to him a thousand times before? How could I explain my feelings about wanting to belong to myself, which included my body and my sexuality? How could I defend something I was only barely beginning to understand myself?

"I think we should talk after the kids go to bed, okay?" I threw the idea out as he put his briefcase down on the beautifully carved antique table in the entry hallway and went into the living room to relax as I made dinner.

"Sure. Whatever," he said nonchalantly.

After dinner, he helped me clear away the dishes and after getting the children to bed, we sat down at the kitchen table to talk. I'd painted the entire kitchen bright colors, with the table a bright orange to match the gold and orange kitchen cabinets with their purple accents. The kids loved the brightly painted kitchen but Saren was less than enthusiastic. "It looks like a kid's room or something at Disneyland."

"Where should we start?" I asked, nervously pushing at the bamboo placemats on the table.

"You're the one who wanted to talk, so talk." Saren said gruffly, crossing his arms and sitting back in his chair. I had recently been learning about body language and how you could tell how a person was feeling by looking at the way they held their body. Crossing your arms was a sign of not being open, of protecting yourself, and sometimes of hostility.

"Why don't you ever read any of those magazines on psychology in the bathroom?" I asked, which seemed an odd question considering the presumed subject of our talk would be about sexual monogamy vs. an open relationship.

"What? Those are your magazines. I don't have any interest in all that psychology stuff. Just because you like it doesn't mean I have to like it," he said defiantly.

"I know that but I thought you might be interested just a little bit in something you know means so much to me. I read your aviation magazines," I said defensively.

"Look, you're going to that therapy thing of yours. You talk there to that feminist who, if you ask me is putting all these strange ideas in your head and you think everybody ought to go along with them. Well, I don't. I don't even understand what you're talking about half the time, except that now you tell me you want to have sex with everybody you meet."

"What? That's totally outrageous and it's not true. That's not what I'm saying at all. I'm saying I want to grow as a person, get to know who I am and what I want, not what some church or institution has taught me to want or to be. You haven't changed or done anything to grow as a person since we first met fifteen years ago. At least that's what you said. Don't you want to know about your inner self, why you do what you do?"

"No, I do not! And, you're right. I haven't changed since the day you met me and that's the person you fell in love with."

"Please, Saren," I pleaded. "Our son is having behavior problems. We're fighting all the time about almost everything. I think we need to go to marriage counseling together. We love one another but we need to stop arguing and fighting about everything. We've got to get some help, find better ways to communicate with one another, to tell each other what we're feeling, how to get our needs met." Tears were streaming down my cheeks.

"Don't cry, honey," Saren said, instantly changing his tone. "I love you. You know that. I just don't think we need any marriage counseling. Alex is seeing a therapist. You're seeing a therapist. We're okay. Don't cry," he said, coming around the table and putting his arms around me.

"We didn't even talk yet about having an open marriage or even what that means," I murmured into his chest.

"I know we didn't. We'll talk about that later," he said reassuringly. Soon we were in our bed caressing one another and making love. Afterwards as we lay in the bliss and afterglow of lovemaking, he whispered in my ear, "How can any couple who make love like this be in trouble? We don't need marriage counseling. Make love, not war, like you used to say, remember? Sometimes I'm just afraid I'm losing you."

"You're not losing me. But if you keep resisting every new idea I have or want to talk about, you are pushing me away."

I lay quietly in Saren's arms thinking about what he'd said. He's probably right, I thought as we dozed off to sleep. No couple could be this passionate with each other and need to change anything. Right?

DANCING WITH ARISTOTLE ONASSIS

It was Ruth's idea to go to the exclusive *New Jimmie's* nightclub. "It'll do you both good to get out and have some fun," she assured me, knowing Saren and I were having marital difficulties. Besides, I've heard that Aristotle Onassis goes to *New Jimmie's* when he's in Paris; maybe he'll be there with Jackie. He's been spotted lately at many of Paris' hot spots with her."

Who knows if that's true? I thought, disgusted with Ruth's constant obsession with the rich and famous. Who even cares if Onassis shows up or not at *New Jimmie's* with Jackie by his side? After weeks of listening to Ruth's pleading, I finally gave in and agreed that Saren and I would go with her and Don to the nightclub. *New Jimmie's* was a members-only club, but Ruth, through her connections as personal assistant to the U.S. Ambassador to UNESCO, was able to gain us entry.

New Jimmie's was a popular nightclub boasting the same exclusivity as the fashion show Ruth had dragged me to see earlier in the year where famous Paris designers showed their *haute couture* spring collections. At the fashion show, she'd arranged for us to be seated directly in front of the runway, close enough to hear the swooshing sounds the gowns of satin and silk made as the anorexic models paraded up and down the runway. I found it sad that women were killing themselves to be models, reminding myself however of the many contestants in the *Miss Georgia Beauty Pageant* I had participated in whom I felt confident would gladly have starved themselves to be a model on the Paris runway.

According to Ruth, fashion houses and fashionable nightclubs were the domains of the rich and famous, people whom you wanted to know and stand close to, maybe even touch. Ruth loved this world, longed to live there. "I feel at home with them," she'd say. According to her, these were the people who created the world in their own image; people to emulate, to get close to in any way you could; in short, these were the people she most admired.

Ruth was full of tales of glorious times when she or one of her family members attended or shared a moment at some event where one of the rich and famous had been sighted; these chance encounters formed the bedrock of her identity and persistent storytelling. Intelligent and sensitive, she peppered her speech with outrageous name-dropping and detailed descriptions of the grandiosity of these chance encounters that brought her near to the aura of these semi-divine beings; she lived for these moments.

As much as I wanted to dismiss Ruth's adoration of the rich and famous as shallow and naive, her enthusiasm and delight were infectious. Her British sense of humor and generous heart more than offset her obsessive fascination and enchantment for the elite of the world. If Ruth liked something, I couldn't help but feel that there was something there to like, too.

******

Could anything be worse than trying to find something stylish to wear in a closet that now contained no designer or dressy anything? I'd given away all my clothes that bore any resemblance to anything a woman of taste or style might wear to an elegant affair, replacing them all with plain, uniform-like sweaters, pants and jeans in monotone colors of navy, gray and black with the exception of an orange and navy striped coat that even I had to admit was hideous; then there was my favorite suede hippie-style floppy hat that I wore over my recently cropped hair dyed an orangish color. A black leather purse with fringe finished the look.

But I liked my new non-wardrobe; liked that I was dressing only to please myself and not to gain approval from others, meaning men mostly, or to conform to some image of what fashion designers or fashion magazines declared was in good taste, sexy or attractive for women. Dressing to suit my own taste in this androgynous looking way definitely was an unusual look to the Embassy crowd or those who attended the American Church of Paris. But they weren't my tribe anymore. My feminist group was my crowd and few of them wore anything closely resembling the latest fashions.

Nothing left of the beauty queen or the Southern Belle now, I thought, but that's just fine. Grabbing a black jacket to go with my black turtleneck sweater, I threw on a pair of jeans and black boots. Ruth won't like this outfit, I thought, but that's too bad! Ruth was constantly shocked when I tried to explain my interest in feminism and its goals of women's equality, and would only shake her head and mumble, "I just don't understand. You've got a husband who adores you, two brilliant kids, you travel, are taken care of, have a beautiful home. What else is there?"

"My friend Ruth needs to come to a CR group," I'd once told my good friend Lisa.

"Why don't you invite her to come to a meeting?" Lisa asked.

"I've invited her dozens of times. She just doesn't want to come. Period. She thinks we're crazy!"

I finally decided that Ruth really didn't understand feminism, just as I didn't understand her enchantment with the rich and famous, but I was committed to keeping our friendship, and I loved her.

******

"What should I wear?" Saren called from the other room. I paused before answering his question; letting it linger in the air for a moment, savoring the memory when we were first married and how much pleasure I'd derived from helping him choose his clothes, just as I'd enjoyed dressing the children when they were young, often sewing their clothes. It had given me a sense of pride and sewing was something I enjoyed. Once I'd consumed fashion and home decorating magazines much as I now consumed magazines and books on psychology, women's issues, and self-help.

"Wear that patterned jacket, the tailor-made one from the fancy men's store on the Champs-Elysee and the green shirt and paisley tie."

I checked myself in the bathroom mirror, put on some mascara and fluffed out my baby-fine hair so it didn't cling to my head like fuzz on a Georgia peach. Well, this is it, I thought, turning to join Saren. Looking beautiful and physically desirable to men and society was part of my old identity. Now, I had entered the world of women's liberation and it had electrified me; catapulted me into realms of thinking and discovery that excited me far beyond anything that being fashionable or beautifully-attired had offered, at least for the present.

******

We took a taxi to *New Jimmie's* where we met Ruth and Don. Ruth showed the doorman an official membership card and he waved us into an elegant, marbled foyer. Entry to the club located on the subterranean level was via descent in an ornate, beautiful art-deco elevator. Bright lights and blaring music greeted us as we exited the elevator and stepped into another world, one where the air was infused with expensive perfume worn by stiletto-heeled women with flawless skin and men whose carefully put-together look signaled wealth.

Saren was an excellent dancer and once we had enjoyed regular evenings out dining and dancing until the wee hours of the morning. That all seemed like an eternity ago. As Saren led me out onto the small dance floor of *New Jimmie's* a feeling of such complete sadness and nostalgia engulfed me that I bit my lip to fight back tears. At first, I didn't notice that everyone on the dance floor had paused and were standing still, as though frozen in time. Soon, I too was staring at the same glittering sight. A short man with grey hair and wearing enormous glasses had walked onto the dance floor with a woman draped on each arm. On one arm was a stunning Caucasian woman dressed entirely in black and on the other arm, a beautiful African woman dressed in white. Shimmering particles of glamour from the stunning spectacle seemed to fall like fairy dust on everyone, swooping us up and away on a magic carpet ride to a realm inhabited by the super-rich and famous. Was it real? Were they real?

As I turned towards the distinguished man, our gaze met and for a few moments that seemed like hours, we looked directly into each other's eyes.

Maybe it was an obvious invitation for him to notice me, maybe even ask me to dance with him. As though on cue, he dropped his two beauties and walked directly towards me, extended his hand and soon I was smiling as he waltzed me around the dance floor. Then, returning me to Saren's side, he bent over my hand and kissing it, murmured "*merci, Madame*." With that, the spell was broken, people began to dance again and Saren and I returned to our table.

Ruth was beside herself, barely able to contain her ecstasy that her friend had just danced with Aristotle Onassis! I sat quietly for some time, sipping my wine while Ruth gushed. I honestly didn't know how I felt. I hadn't wanted to be impressed by any of the glamour and glitzy spectacles of the wealthy on display in *New Jimmie's* that formed the core of Ruth's *raison d'être*, but in truth, I had experienced genuine excitement and sensuality on the dance floor with

Mr. Onassis. With Ruth's ramblings fading away into background noise, I glanced furtively to the table where Aristotle was sitting. He was looking back at me and smiled, as though there were only the two of us in the noisy nightclub; then he raised his glass of wine in a salute. I nodded and smiled in return. In that moment, I knew something had shifted, much as I'd felt after making my sexual freedom declaration and of wanting to belong to myself. Exactly what lay ahead, I didn't know. But things would be different now, very different. I was sure of that.

LILITH & EVE:
A NEW STORY OF SISTERHOOD

Not long after the titillating night at *New Jimmie's* nightclub and my brief dance with Aristotle Onassis, my mother and aunt, solid steel-magnolia women from the Deep South, came to Paris to pay a visit. I lost no time in letting them have a heavy dose of my newly-found feminist swagger, insulting them with innuendoes and not so subtle remarks pointing out their outdated and narrow viewpoints belonging to Christianity and its failure to embrace women's new emancipated role in society and the church.

To bring the finer points of feminism to bear on the occasion of their visit, I invited them to attend our monthly feminist meeting; actually, it was more like I dared them. "The program will be a psychodrama, called *Defending Feminism: What do you say when somebody says..?* and the participants will fill in the blanks," I explained. Then a few members will explore their feelings in various situations through role-playing." I felt fairly confident that my mother and aunt had no idea what a psychodrama or role-playing was but I wanted to take every opportunity to show them the error of their small-minded beliefs.

To my surprise, they agreed to go. This was going to be great, I thought gleefully as we loaded into our new Volvo station wagon to drive into the city.

For our feminist meeting, we'd rented a large room in Paris' rundown, working-class district which fed the illusion for some that we were part of the worker's revolution, which clearly most of us were not, and that we were supporters of the idea of a new economy focusing on *downward mobility*, which clearly again, most of were not. This diversity of women's political and social views in our group, however, was only one of many problems I'd written about in an article called "Difficulties in Starting a NOW Chapter in a Foreign Country," which was published in the handbook distributed to attendees at the *First International Feminist Planning Conference* at Harvard that I, along with my friend Lisa and hundreds of other women from around the world had just attended.

Once we arrived, I helped mother and my aunt get settled in chairs at the back of the room, while others on the program helped to get everything ready for the meeting. One of our members, a practicing psychotherapist, was going to lead the psychodrama for the group after I'd given my report about the feminist conference at Harvard. As the meeting was starting, I noticed a few new women who had entered with one of our Latin American members. They sat off to the side, in the back near my mother and aunt.

Our meetings had settled down a lot but were still somewhat on the chaotic side, although this one had gone smoothly at first, and I even got to give my entire report on the Harvard conference and some of the resolutions; but the calm was definitely one that precedes a storm. As the therapist member stood to announce the psychodrama, one of the new women sitting in the back suddenly stood up and in a loud, booming voice announced that she'd just arrived from Amsterdam where she'd been working the streets as a prostitute. "You women know nothing about my life and the issues of real women like me who have to use our bodies to earn a living!" she exclaimed. An audible gasp went up around the room.

"I've been living on the streets of Amsterdam for years now. I suck cocks, large or small, the cost is the same. I fuck in alleys and filthy rooms; use dildos or whips; front or rear penetration; cost still the same. There's plenty of women like me and we're constantly getting vaginal diseases and anal lacerations for all the fucking we do for a living. Once you're in this world, there's little chance you'll make it out alive."

Several lesbians spontaneously jumped up and joined in the diatribe to convince the obviously distressed woman that her problem was due to her having fallen victim to heterosexual propaganda that had fostered her addiction to masturbating herself with the male penis!

"What you need," Arlette said, "is a woman lover who will treat you with respect and give you all the good loving you deserve."

"Caroline and I will demonstrate," she said, motioning for her partner to stand up, and they began kissing and caressing one another.

"See," Arlette said to the woman from Amsterdam, "we don't violate one another, and female being with another female is completely satisfying. You don't need a male penis. You've just been brainwashed!"

Caroline continued the conversation intended to enlighten the new woman, while everyone else in the meeting space remained more or less comatose. "A woman with a woman can bring each other to orgasm over and over again and orgasms between women are far superior to the illusion of a good orgasm with a simple, over-rated male penis fucking itself to orgasm inside the female vagina."

The evening's agenda had taken on a life of its own and soon the entire group was participating in a spontaneous, real-time psychodrama. There was hardly a woman present who eventually didn't have something to say to the, by now, overwhelmed woman from Amsterdam. Personally, I was so thrown off guard that I couldn't speak, especially since my mother and aunt from Georgia and Alabama respectively were sitting in the back of the room. What had been an initial effort on my part to embarrass and humiliate them had totally backfired and I had "egg on my face." I'd never imagined that a prostitute from Amsterdam would appear out of nowhere and incite such frank talk about sex at an "ordinary" feminist meeting.

******

Only the sound of the windshield wipers swishing away the Paris rain falling on the car window penetrated the silence during the drive home. The moment we hit the door of our apartment, however, mother and aunt couldn't stop talking, giving Saren a detailed description of everything that had transpired at the meeting, including what was said and by whom.

Unfortunately, they had regarded the evening's events as simply an outrageous show, producing no more than a titillating story, one which they could delight in telling and retelling to select friends once they returned home to Alabama and Georgia, minus some of the frank details, too delicate for most Southern matrons, even the "steel-magnolias."

That evening demonstrated to me, however, that it wasn't only my mother and aunt but all of us women who'd missed seeing the deeper wound being offered up for healing by the despairing prostitute from Amsterdam and her story of a life in the streets. It certainly went deeper than how to have an orgasm or which gender gave the best orgasms. I felt it called for a deeper understanding of what she'd shared and the need to become more aware of the diversity of women's realities, which often depended on their economic, social or racial status; and finally, to ask ourselves how we might work to help improve women's lives, whatever their status.

******

One of the feminist newspapers many of us read in Paris was the New York feminist newspaper *Majority Report*. In the early 70s a short story appeared that gave a "sisterhood is powerful" version of the Fall Myth of Adam and Eve. Author Claire Randall called her article *Applesource: The Coming of Lilith* in which she completely revised and re-visioned the Fall Myth. In Randall's humorous account, she details a friendship that develops between Lilith and Eve, which changed the entire storyline to one of women empowering women. In the beginning of Randall's story, Eve doesn't know anything about Lilith until one day Lilith returns from her home in the faraway desert and sets herself up outside the Garden of Eden. That's when the two women begin to talk, share many wonderful ideas, laugh and cry together, and eventually become friends, all to the puzzlement of both Adam and God. Randall ends her revised story with, "And God and Adam were expectant and afraid the day Eve and Lilith returned to the garden, bursting with possibilities, ready to rebuild it together."

Women empowering women was a new idea to many in the feminist movement. As the responses to the prostitute from Amsterdam had shown, most everyone was still embracing an "us-against-them" adversarial attitude, whether that was women against other women or women against men. To me, holding such attitudes meant there was no possibility of healing or equality. I knew that the phrase "sisterhood is powerful" had to mean more than "us-against-them" if any equality, reconciliation and transformation was to be possible. But how to help bring that about was as controversial as the challenge itself. A continued separation and condemnation of one half of humanity over the other, regardless of gender became unacceptable to me and literally made my heart hurt.

YOKO ONO: WARRIOR WOMEN

Warrior Women: A Song by Yoko Ono

...from her 40th Birthday Concert

Harvard's First International Feminist Planning Conference—1972

"I say:

Enough.

It is time to cry: enough

And form a block with our bodies"

...from *New Portuguese Letters*, by the "Three Marias"

"A rock star? Who?"

"Yoko Ono! She was there for the entire feminist conference. One day after lunch I decided I wanted to meet her so I went up to the table where she was sitting and introduced myself. She invited me to sit down and we ended up having a two-hour conversation and missed the entire afternoon session."

It was a beautiful fall day and Danda, a feminist friend from Brazil, and I were having lunch at a popular outdoor café on rue de Bac in the student district of the Left Bank. After ordering lunch, we'd settled into an easy conversation about our recent journeys aboard. I had been in Boston attending the First International Feminist Planning Conference at Harvard University, followed by a grief-filled trip to visit my family in Georgia where my father had had lung surgery and was slowing dying of lung cancer.

Danda had just returned from a trip to Portugal where she'd seen the Three Marias, three women writers all named Maria, who had been jailed for writing a feminist book *The New Portuguese Letters*, that had immediately been banned by the Portuguese government as "pornographic and an outrage to public morality."

"Really? What did you and Yoko talk about?" Danda asked.

"After I introduced myself, we just started talking about our lives as women. She said she was interested in talking with me because she wanted to meet someone who was married with children and living a normal life, if there is such a thing! Of course, I was interested in her life as a famous artist and how she was able to keep her own identity while being married to an internationally famous person like John Lennon. Oh! John was there and filmed our entire conversation. He wasn't allowed to attend any of the meetings, though. No men were allowed. Yoko told me that only a month or two ago, she and John had been served deportation papers by the U.S. Immigration Department because President Nixon and his supporters wanted them out of American since they were considered dangerous persons with their anti-Vietnam stance."

"Yes, I had read something about that in the papers. Did she share anything else about what's it like to be a feminist and to be famous?" Danda asked.

"Yoko and I came to the conclusion that no matter who we are, famous or not, our lives as women are ruled by the patriarchy and that we have to fight for our equality because no one else is going to do it for us."

Danda nodded in agreement. "Did Yoko perform?"

"She did! She gave a fabulous concert on the last night to celebrate her fortieth birthday! She sang an outrageous song called *Warrior Women* that talked about the struggle women everywhere are going through, one that can sometimes lead to bloodshed. Many of her songs have a dark undertone, like *Coffin Car*, but by the end of the concert we were all holding hands, dancing and circling around the church auditorium and singing freedom songs to the top of our lungs. Lennon was at the concert, too, but he hung out in the background the whole time, sometimes playing guitar or discretely taking videos of Yoko singing."

"I want to hear all about the conference at Harvard, especially if any decision was made about the affiliation of our Paris feminist group with the National Organization of Women in America. Does anyone in Paris still want to be part of NOW? Were there any surprises?" she asked, laughing mischievously, as we sipped the house wine, a mellow-tasting Beaujolais.

"The decision is still out regarding our English-speaking group's affiliation with NOW in America," I laughed. "But I suspect we won't be affiliated much longer because too many women don't like NOW and what it stands for, although I didn't mention any of that in the article I wrote for the Conference's handbook. Were there any surprises at the conference? ...only if you consider arguing and heated debates lasting all night, trying to define what the real issues for women are. The most heated debate was whether or not the feminist movement is centered primarily on middle-class women and their needs and how the movement should become more inclusive. Not much different than our Paris feminist group meetings."

We both laughed again at the reminder of the constant chaos at our feminist meetings. "The debate about the feminist movement being inclusive reminds me of Cecilia. You know Cecilia, don't you?" Danda asked. She's the woman in our group from Mexico; she really believes that too many feminists in the movement work on the theoretical and intellectual level only. She calls it feminism for the elite. I think she's right. That brand of feminism is doomed because it isn't supported by any grassroots reality." My mind flashed to the conversation I'd had with Harry at the workers' café, remembering his words, "It's all about the working class, the ordinary people on the streets, the real people," he'd called them.

"Many women in our feminist group are from developing countries," Danda continued, "and are very aware of how political movements fail when people from the bottom level aren't involved. In the case of feminism, women from all socio-economic groups need to be involved and their needs have to be addressed if the movement is going to make any lasting and meaningful change."

I felt a twinge of guilt about my white middle-class status and the fact that I didn't have to work; also, I was straight and married to a man, all factors that had become defining and problematic characteristics for me and other women of similar circumstances in our Paris English-speaking feminist group, especially to the lesbian and working-class women.

The waiter brought more wine and we paused to savor our time together and enjoy the lovely afternoon. I wondered if Yoko Ono ever felt guilty about her status as a rich and famous woman? I doubted it. And anyway, no one could be any wealthier or happier than I was right now, I decided.

Danda and I had become so caught up in our conversation that we'd almost finished the carafe of wine before even tasting our lunch. We ordered more wine and dug into our delicious salads of fresh greens, garnished with herbs and the perfect simple oil and vinegar salad dressing. The warmth of the day felt good on my skin, which along with some help from the wine was immensely relaxing.

"Of course, our own Gilda and Faith were at the conference telling everyone about the Three Marias and promoting the idea of an international campaign on their behalf," I reported, knowing that Danda would be pleased. She was heading up the Latin American feminist group working to bring together the disparate feminist groups in Paris in creating an event to raise funds for the legal defense of the three Portuguese women authors.

"Oh, Betty Freidan gave the opening address, calling for full equality for women in equal partnership with men. Of course, most of the feminist groups in Paris don't even want partnership with men," I said.

We both laughed, knowing the drama and backbiting that continually erupted among the various feminist groups in Paris over politics and ideology.

"Have you ever been married Danda? I asked, changing the subject to something I'd been curious about for some time. Another Brazilian feminist had told me that Danda had grown up as the daughter of a wealthy and influential political father in Rio de Janeiro and I wanted to know more about this fascinating woman.

"Yes. I was married very young and my husband and I lived the ideal romantic married life for a few years. We were both active in the political left but after a military coup in Brazil, I wondered if it was only my disappointment in the coup that filled me with such deep sadness or if it was the state of my marriage. It was during this confusing time that my husband and I moved to Europe where we had scholarships to study at the Sorbonne. But once in Paris, nothing seemed to change and so I left Paris and went to study at

Columbia University. My husband told my children that I would never make it; that I would be back in less than two months. But I did make it. When I came back to Paris, we divorced after fifteen years of marriage and I married a second time to a man in political exile from Brazil and became involved in politics again. But I found that the same discrimination against women still existed. Three years later I divorced my second husband, became a feminist and a lesbian and ever since that time have allied myself with other like-minded women. And here I am!" she smiled, lifting her glass of wine in a salute gesture.

I raised my glass in return. Smiling at Danda, I saw a beautiful, intelligent woman in her early forties whose face radiated a sense of well-being and self-confidence. Feeling at ease with her, I shared my concern about the future of my own marriage.

"I'm so confused about what to do right now. I've been in personal therapy with a woman from our feminist group and I'm learning so much about myself. I'm not sure if I have the strength or desire to struggle on with my husband whose values are so different from mine and who doesn't want to make the effort to change. I am emotionally exhausted," I said, giving a brittle laugh.

Later, over the restaurant's famous crème caramel desert, I decided to share with Danda my growing interest in exploring my sexuality with others, including women.

"I'm just so tired of men, their big egos and eternal pre-occupation with their big, or not-so-big appendages!"

Roaring with laughter, we raised our wine glasses in another toast.

"A lot of women don't know anything about lesbianism and because they fear what they don't know, they condemn it. It's sad really. I turned to being with women because it was easier, less stressful in many ways, though it has its problems too," Danda assured me.

"Recently, a number of the more radical lesbian women in our group have been giving us married women a hard time, chiding us that we're sleeping with the enemy, that sort of thing. It hurts."

"Don't listen to them. They're unhappy with themselves and try to make everyone else around them unhappy too. It can get very complicated with a woman, same as with a man."

As I drove home from lunch with Danda, all I could think about was what a great life I had and how, despite our many differences, I loved Saren and our family; that in spite of whatever desires I might have to experience myself sexually with women or other men, that at my core I wanted to throw myself completely into making my marriage work. Despite my renewed optimism, my world was about to come crashing down, and the shift began the moment I arrived home.

PART THREE

RAGING RIVER OF CHANGE

Oliver, our dog, was waiting by the apartment door and started barking the moment I walked inside from my lunch with Danda. "Why haven't you been walked?" I asked, looking around for the children whose chore it was to walk him as soon as they got home from school.

"Alex? Marie? Where are you?" I called out but when no one answered, decided I'd better walk Oliver before he had an accident. Mumbling under my breath about children who don't do their chores, I strapped the chain around Oliver's neck and took him outside to the grassy area that extended down the middle of the entire length of avenue Breteuil, before coming to a dead end at Napoleon's famous tomb, *Les Invalides*. As I crossed the street with Oliver, the concierge from our building ran after me, waving a note in her hand. "*Il n'pas grave, Madame; il n'pas grave!* It's not bad, Madame. It's not bad."

"*Merci beaucoup, Madame. Attendez. Attendez.*" I said, thanking her and urging her to pause a moment while I read the note.

Your son has been in an accident when a car struck him and the police have taken him to the hospital for children, Enfants Malade in the fifth arrondissement. That was it. Nothing about his condition or what had happened to Marie. Shaking, I quickly grabbed Oliver and took him back into the apartment and headed for the hospital that fortunately I knew was not too far away. A million anguished questions raced through my mind as I struggled to remain calm. How serious was the accident? Was my son okay? Where was my daughter? Was she all right?

At the hospital, no one seemed to know anything about a young American boy brought in by a police officer. Finally, a nurse arrived who led me down a long corridor to a small room where Alex was lying motionless on an x-ray table. He started to cry when he saw me. Running to his side, I leaned down and kissed him, noticing that his head was bloody and blood was oozing from his nostrils.

"How are you, sweetheart?" I asked in a determined calm voice, wiping the blood from his nose on my sleeve.

"My head hurts a lot, mommy," he whispered.

"Mommy's here now. Everything's okay," I reassured him, stroking his brow.

A nurse stuck her head in the door and told me that the doctor would return shortly to look at Alex's x-rays and diagnose his condition. As the reality of the situation slowly began to take hold, I felt myself starting to shake uncontrollably.

This was my child laying on the hospital table with blood all over him. Not a statistic, not an item for the evening news, but my child who was so small and so young, and possibly badly injured.

"What happened sweetheart?"

"I don't remember."

"That's okay. You just relax." I suddenly thought to ask the nurse if anyone had seen Alex's sister but in my shocked state, I couldn't remember the French word for "sister." Miraculously, Saren whom I'd called before coming to the hospital, walked into the room at just that moment and was able to ask the nurse more questions. "Your daughter is safe and at your friends the Bernstein's apartment," she answered in perfect English. Most Parisians spoke good English but refused to speak it most of the time, which in certain situations like this one, was exasperating.

"Alex, you can squeeze mommy's hand if the pain gets too bad."

"I can take it, mommy," he said bravely, fighting back his tears.

"It's okay to cry Alex." My heart ached to see that in spite of all my insistence that it was okay for boys to cry, he had already taken on the cultural belief that it wasn't okay for boys to show their emotions.

Finally, the doctor arrived, carrying x-rays in his hands. "Your son has suffered a severe head concussion after being struck by a car," he said in French. He'll have to stay in the hospital for several days for observation. Since there's no room here at the *Enfants Malade*, you'll have to find another hospital for him."

In France, hospital stays were free, but it was the individual's responsibility to find a hospital with an available room. While Saren went to sign papers and locate another hospital, I stayed with Alex.

"Mommy, can I have my glasses? Maybe they'll help my head stop hurting so bad."

I searched around the room and found his glasses that were fortunately not broken, and helped him put them on. "Turn on your side, sweetheart, and let mommy scratch your back," I said, knowing this always helped him to relax.

After three more excruciatingly long hours, Saren returned. "I finally located another hospital that has a room for Alex but it's several hours away from here across town."

An ambulance was arranged to take us to the other hospital. When the ambulance assistant put Alex in a wheelchair, Alex joked, "I wish I'd broken my legs so I could ride around in a wheel chair all the time!"

I was happy to see that he was conscious enough to make jokes, even if they weren't very funny right now.

After checking Alex into a private room at the new hospital, he began to cry when we told him he would have to stay alone overnight because hospital rules wouldn't let us stay with him.

"I know it's very hard to be here alone, but you're very brave and the angels will be here with you, I promise. We'll be here very first thing in the morning."

As soon as we left Alex in the hospital room, I began to openly weep. I insisted on talking to the hospital director again to inquire if there was any possible way we could stay overnight with our son. The answer was a resounding, *"non, Madame. Il n'pas possible!"* he responded vehemently. Later, I was furious at myself for accepting "no" for an answer. Where was my warrior woman, the one Yoko Ono had bellowed out praise for during her concert at the *International Feminist Conference*; where was the warrior woman French feminist Monique Wittig had celebrated so convincingly in her book *Les Guerillas* that had inspired thousands of women? For that matter, why hadn't Saren's warrior-trained self stood up to the hospital director and demanded that we be able to stay with our son?

******

During the long taxi ride from the hospital to the Bernstein's apartment where our daughter Marie was waiting, Saren and I sat in the back seat in absolute silence. I muffled my tears with a tissue clamped over my mouth and watched as my ecstatic intentions for reconciliation with him from earlier in the day dissolved and flew out the taxi window like mere wisps of dreams that disappear with the morning dawn. Saren and I had become so estranged from one another that we never once consoled each other or reached out a loving hand during the two-hour ride. Did he blame me for Alex's accident? Did he blame himself? I felt we had let our son down in so many ways; that in fact, we had let ourselves down in so many ways.

As tragedy so often does, what's important becomes crystal clear. My son's accident cleared my mind of any lingering confusion and doubt about Saren's and my relationship. It brought me to the painful realization that the man sitting next to me had become a stranger, that we had become strangers to one another. If during such a tragedy we couldn't turn to one another for comfort and solace, then what was left of our marriage?

After arriving at the Bernstein's apartment, I was relieved to learn Marie was not only okay but had been a real hero during the ordeal of her brother's accident. It was her clear-headed thinking, in fact, that had prevented more serious complications for Alex.

"Alex just ran out in the street in front of the car and it hit him and threw him up on the hood and then he fell down," she explained in a tiny voice quivering with the horrible memory. She was only eight years old, fifteen months younger than her brother.

"I ran over to him to see if he was okay. At first, he didn't say anything but then he just kept asking what happened. The lady in the car told somebody to call the police and they came and put Alex in the police van and I rode with him to the police station. I gave them all the information they wanted about where we lived and who our parents were. Then they took Alex to the hospital and I just stayed there at the police station until the Bernsteins came and picked me up."

"You are the bravest little girl I know," I said, holding her close and marveling at her composure and common sense at such a young age and in such a terrifying situation.

That night after arriving back to our apartment, I slept with my little girl to comfort her but there was no sleep for me, as my mind was filled with worry about Alex. What was happening to my son? Who was watching after him? Did they care that he was shy and wouldn't ask for things? I felt helpless as I imagined how lonely he was, laying in a strange bed in an ancient old hospital in a dilapidated part of the city so far away from his family and people who cared. I began to cry softly into my pillow when I suddenly remembered the re-occurring dream I had had again only last night.

In the dream, I am standing at the edge of an enormous precipice and I know it is time for me to leap off into the unknown but I'm frozen stiff with terror. Somehow, I summon the courage to leap. Once I leap, I am free falling and although there is fear and nausea in the pit of my stomach, it is bearable. When I land, I'm in a new landscape and filled with joy and confidence that I have finally taken the leap and can fly.

Like so many women in the seventies and eighties, I was caught in a wild, raging river of independence and change, while still clinging to capsized boats made of old ideas and ways of being. We had choices, of course, but they weren't choices of turning back or staying the same. Becoming brave and a warrior woman meant holding yourself together and also supporting other women in their process, like we military wives had done for each other when our husbands were off fighting in Vietnam, or, like women were learning to do in feminist circles and self-help groups. Maybe I wasn't the warrior woman I wanted to be, at least not just yet; but I was becoming braver and my thrice-repeated dream seemed to support my taking a leap and becoming a woman with wings, able to fly with confidence into the unknown.

We were all tired and still stressed from the car accident involving Alex and were eager to see how he was holding up, having spent the night alone in the hospital. We drove across town again to the hospital where he had been admitted, following the doctor's orders that he should stay a few days for observation after his accident and head concussion. We brought him a change of clothes, some of his favorite things and his *Tin Tin* books. To my relief, Alex was in good spirits, having become a favorite with a few of the French nurses. When we entered the room, they were all laughing together.

We were able to see his primary doctor who assured us that Alex was fine and hadn't suffered any permanent damage from the head concussion. "I still want to keep him here one more night to make sure he's completely healed."

To our surprise and relief, Alex seemed okay with spending another night in the hospital, surround by newly-made friends who were enjoying the novelty and charm of a sweet American boy in their charge.

After Alex's accident and the insurmountable distance between Saren and myself that it had revealed, I felt affirmed in my decision to proceed with filing for a divorce and made a call to the U.S. Embassy's legal department.

"It's best to wait until you're re-assigned to the states," the legal officer advised. "Current U.S. laws only allow a woman to be granted a divorce in the state of her husband's legal residency; and if you try for a divorce in Paris, you're looking at international law and you don't want to get into that can of worms."

"You've got to be kidding me! Divorce papers have to filed in the state where a woman's husband is a resident?"

"Yes, I'm sorry madame, but that's the law."

Disappointed in a legal system that perpetuated the inequality of women, I knew I'd have to wait until we returned to America to file for divorce. After all my experiences in the feminist movement and seeing how women everywhere were at risk and needed legal counsel, I'd been thinking that becoming a lawyer would be a great career for me to help women and children while providing for my children and myself; and this insane, biased law I'd just learned about was simply another affirmation to do something to change it. My next call was to the American Cultural Center to ask how to sign up to take the four-hour LSAT series of tests necessary to apply to law school.

AN UNKNOWN TERRITORY
OF THE HEART

During the strained time of preparing to leave Paris after three years for a new assignment stateside and facing an imminent divorce, I came home one day to find Saren sitting at our dining room table with one of his flying students named Paul. Saren had started an American Flying Club a few years earlier and was a private pilot instructor to several student pilots, training them to qualify for their private pilot's license. Once I found out that his new student Paul was CEO of a Paris company, single and an ex-pat American, I immediately thought to introduce him to my friend Lisa, who was constantly complaining there weren't any eligible American bachelors in Paris. I warned her I found him to be a bit arrogant. "But it could also be my sour attitude about relationships and men at the moment," I told her. "Shall I give him your phone number?"

"Sure. You never know."

A few weeks later, Lisa and Paul had arranged to go for a ride on his motorcycle and were going to meet at my apartment because it was central to both of them. She called at the last minute, saying she couldn't make it. When Paul showed up moments later, I told him Lisa had called and wouldn't be able to go.

"Well, since I'm here, would you like to go for a ride?" he spontaneously asked.

"Me? Gosh. I'm not sure," I said, hesitating, surprised that he was asking me to go. "I've never ridden on a motorcycle before. I don't know. Is it safe?"

"I've got an extra helmet and I've never had an accident, so I think it's safe."

"Okay but I have to be back before the kids get home from school."

After putting on Paul's extra helmet, jumping onto the back of his motorcycle and putting my arms around his waist, off we went whizzing through the streets of Paris, heading for the Bois de Boulogne to get out of the city traffic and into the serenity and beauty of the park. I was surprised at how exhilarating it was to be riding on a motorcycle; how it felt so different than riding in a car. You could experience the smells, feel the wind on your face and body, experience people being right next to you, all of which gave a feeling of being connected to everything around you. I loved it!

Once inside the Bois, a sudden massive downpour caused Paul to quickly park his motorcycle and we ran for shelter under a grove of trees. Paul took off his jacket and put it around my shoulders as we huddled together for warmth against the hard pellets of falling rain. I had lost a lot of weight in the last few months and was visibly shaking from the rain and sudden cold. "Here, you're shaking," Paul said, as he stood closer, wrapping his arms around me. I was horrified when I realized I was feeling sexually attracted to him! As though I don't have enough problems, I thought. I don't need another man in my life in addition to everything else!

Once back at my apartment, we were both soaking wet. I offered Paul a towel to dry off while I went to change clothes. When I returned, he was taking off his soaking wet shirt. Trying not to notice how sexy he looked, I quickly averted my eyes. It was a moment of extreme awkwardness during which a palpable sexual attraction vibe shot between us again. He quickly left and I hoped we wouldn't ever meet again.

******

Saren and I had decided he would take the children to Greece for two weeks while I stayed home in Paris and continued sorting and packing for our move back to America, which was still some months away. "It'll give us time to think about whether or not we really want to divorce," he said, obviously in denial of our many conversations making it clear I wanted to divorce and move on with my life because nothing had changed between us. Part of me wanted to go to Greece and "break some plates" in one of their cafes where customers did that sort of thing. It would be cathartic; a way to mark the ending of what had been a rather wonderful marriage overall but one that had played itself out and wasn't working for either of us anymore. But I really did need some time away from Saren to clear my head even if it wasn't the six months separation I'd requested.

Shortly after he and the kids left for Greece, Paul called out of the blue, asking me if I'd like to take another ride on his motorcycle and have lunch in the Bois. My friend Lisa from the CR group had seen Paul a few times but told me she wasn't interested in him and anyway, I didn't think I'd be betraying a friend if I went for a ride with Paul because it wasn't like a date or anything ... just a ride on a motorcycle. After a long hesitation, I agreed. "Yes, I would like that. It could be fun."

What are you thinking? I asked myself the moment I hung up the phone. You've got more packing to do before Saren and the kids get back from Greece. You'll be moving in a few more months. You don't have time for fun.

******

My heart was beating monstrously fast when I answered Paul's knock at the door. I barely looked at him, locking the apartment behind me as we left to go on our non-date. I jumped on the back of his bike, wrapped my arms around his waist and soon we were speeding through the streets of Paris again, riding this time without a helmet, allowing my hair to blow helter-skelter, giving me an exaggerated sense of freedom much like I'd felt the first time I'd ridden on his motorcycle.

We stopped at one of the many fine restaurants in the beautiful Bois, and after a few sips of wine, I shared with Paul about my impending divorce and immediately started to cry. I was so embarrassed, since I hardly knew him and didn't really know why I was there with him in the first place. He reassured me it was okay and offered his friendship and help, "If you need it," he said.

In fact, I was aching for a friend, someone who didn't know all the details about my marriage already, details that my women friends had heard over and over again, leading them to finally ask me, "Why are you still staying with the guy?" to which I kept replying, "I am leaving him, but it's not easy. I have to think of the kids and I want to do the right thing." I was no longer seeing my Jungian therapist because Saren had refused to pay for any more sessions with her. "I'm not going to pay somebody who's influencing my wife to divorce me."

I felt cut off from the support I needed from my therapist Helen to work through my big decision to divorce Saren and truth was, I was scared. What if I was making a mistake by divorcing Saren? On the other hand, I knew I'd done everything I could to keep our marriage together.

During the two weeks Saren and the kids were in Greece, Paul and I began to spend entire days together with me pouring out my doubts and anxieties about getting a divorce and he being supportive and understanding. The sexual attraction was growing more intense as we spent more time together. We talked openly about how we felt, something I'd only done with my women friends and professor Joe back in New Mexico. We both decided that when the time was right, we would make love. Well into the second week, after another wonderful lunch together, Paul asked me if I wanted to go back to his apartment. "Yes, I would like that," I replied.

******

The once blazing fire in the fireplace in Paul's bedroom where we'd been making love all afternoon had become smoldering embers of red and gray. Roberta Flack's jazzy sounds from her album *Killing Me Softly* had stopped hours ago, replaced by the murmurs and sighs of two lovers exploring each other's bodies and pleasuring one another.

Paul disentangled himself from my body, propped his head up on one arm and stared down at me.

"God, you're beautiful," he said brushing his hand against my cheek. I opened my eyes and looked deeply into his that were beaming with love. Unexpectedly, tears formed at the corner of my eyes.

"Oh, no, my *cheri*. Don't cry. Don't cry," he said, bending to kiss the tears away.

"They're tears of joy, with maybe some sadness mixed in," I said, running my hands up and down his arms in gentle reassurance.

"Sadness, be gone!" he said jumping out of bed. "You stay right there and don't move your precious body! I'm going to make us something to eat. We've got to keep our strength up, right?"

I didn't think I could have moved if I'd wanted to. It was the first time in days, or was it months or maybe years that I had been completely relaxed.

For once, my mind wasn't running its obsessive thoughts about my life, the impending divorce from Saren, my failures and fears about what my new life might hold for the children and me. I felt peaceful, something else I hadn't experienced recently. Wherever this new relationship with Paul was going, he was good for me right now. He was protective, noticing when I hadn't eaten and insisting we take some time to eat. I'd lost so much weight recently that my CR group had jokingly offered to take up money to send me on a cruise. Paul had become more than a shoulder to lean on, or a good friend who listened to my troubles. He had become my lover and, in the days, and months to come, would become my most important and trusted ally in navigating the turbulent waters of my divorce.

I pulled the luxurious satin sheets tightly around my body, noticing in more detail Paul's bachelor penthouse apartment. There was a woman's robe on the door in the bathroom, women's toilette items, extra toothbrushes and feminine napkins, expensive bath oil for soaking in the bath, beautiful over-sized Egyptian cotton towels stacked alongside gleaming satin sheets in the bathroom closet, and the coup d'état, the fireplace in the bedroom ... details reflecting a sensuality born from a refinement of the senses, I thought, inviting you in the subtlest of ways to experience pleasure. I could feel the art of seduction exuding from everything in the room, surrounding me like a living essence.

"How many women do you seduce in a week or month?" I asked with a laugh, when Paul returned with a tray filled with a delicious assortment of fruit, cheeses, bread, and wine.

"I am single you know," he answered, laughing as well. "Now let's eat."
We ate like ravished street orphans from Dickens' *Oliver Twist*, talking and laughing, still lost in the afterglow of passionate lovemaking, still immersed inside the aura of the other's perceived perfection and absolute beauty.

"Do you want to spend the night here with me? Paul asked hopefully.

"No. I'd better go home. I've got to feed Oliver. Change my clothes. See if there's any messages from Saren in Greece."

When Paul brought me home, we kissed and held one another for a long time before saying goodnight. "I'll call you tomorrow," he said, lightly touching my cheek. We were falling in love, something neither of us had expected. Even though I had made my open marriage declaration to Saren some eighteen months earlier, I'd never acted on it. Even after having "your mommy and daddy are getting a divorce" talk with the children, having a lover wasn't anything I'd imagined or had sought. This was new territory for me. Paul was obviously an accomplished lover of many women, but he too seemed to be experiencing a new part of himself, an unknown territory of his heart that hadn't been touched. In fact, thinking he might be having heart problems of some kind because he was having ongoing heart palpations, he'd gone to see his doctor who assured him his heart was just fine; even asking him as perhaps only a French doctor might, "Have you recently fallen in love?"

At first, Paul's and my passionate lovemaking had surprised me because that was the one area in my marriage that had held together. For the past eighteen months I'd tortured myself by asking the same question over and over, how can I have such blissful lovemaking with a man whom I disagree with on almost every subject? Finally, I had stopped making love with Saran and moved into the bedroom with Marie or slept on the sofa when Saren was home because it was so confusing and upsetting to sleep in the same bed with him.

After Paul left, I fed Oliver, our very sweet but very dumb Shih Tzu dog. Everything was quiet, even though the apartment faced a busy street. Oliver missed the kids and followed me from room to room, jumping up beside me on the beautiful, Napoleon-style winged-arm sofa/divan where I settled after lighting a few candles instead of turning on the lights. Everything seemed so strange, as though I'd never seen any of it before. I felt as though I was a stranger in my own home. I took a shower and dressed for bed, laying there for some time, staring into the empty blackness of the bedroom, touching my hand to the empty space beside me where Saren would have been. How surreal this is. How would it feel to never lay beside Saren again as husband and wife? My, how that young Southern Belle who'd pledged fidelity at the altar of marriage in her small-town Georgia Baptist church some fifteen years ago had changed! Could I really trust this new liberated woman I'd become? Was it really too late for Saren and me? It certainly seemed so,.

During the last months before leaving Paris, Paul and I secretly continued to see each other as often as possible. Even though I disliked being deceptive with Saren, I placated myself that we were no longer sleeping together and would be divorced soon. Still, I didn't like the way sneaking around made me feel and yearned for a divorce as soon as possible so Paul and I could be open about our relationship. Hurting Saren or the children was the last thing I wanted to do.

AU REVOIR

Feminism with its new powerful sisterhood had taken residency in my heart where once only God the Father and his son Jesus Christ had been; however, just as the all-male patriarchy's version of God and Church no longer satisfied me, neither did the righteousness and blistering, alienating language and actions of women's liberation during its early days before maturing into a more authentic and carefully articulated message that more accurately represented the needs of both women and men.

In truth, I missed going to church, missed the experiences of community and the genuine spiritual uplifting I'd once received through music and fellowship, as well as the beautiful, inspiring stories of the Bible when they weren't used to incite guilt, sin or fears of eternal damnation. The church community I was part of during my growing up years had been my extended family. They were kind and except for a few rigid interpreters of what being a Christian meant, were helpful and took an interest in me as it did all its members.

I still possessed a spiritual longing for a deeper connection with something or some creative entity greater than myself. But I knew it could no longer be found inside the institution of a church; and although I had not the slightest notion of the existence of a feminine face of the Divine, God the Father/ God the Son had begun to sound like a continuation of the male patriarchy's power-over women and our lives and I wasn't interested

With these ideas around faith circulating in my head, I had the thought to go and visit Chartres again before I left France. It was curious. Why go to Chartres again? Was I looking for reassurance or a blessing from some invisible spirit of a Divine nature for an action I was about to take that would influence and change the lives of four, maybe five, people forever? All I knew was that I was feeling some kind of call to go. So, I answered the call and went. Alone.

******

On the drive to Chartres, I took my time, making mental note of the beautiful green trees at a certain mile marker, or a farmer's field of lavender or yellow mustard plants, as though trying to memorize a landscape I might never see again. I suddenly remembered the visit Saren and I had made to Italy to see the ancient ruins of Pompeii. It had been an amazing sight, with bodies of its fleeing citizens, laying like frozen statues in the streets and doorways, encased forever in the hardened ash that had fallen from the erupting volcano Mt. Vesuvius. Painted on many of the town's excavated walls were beautiful and elaborate friezes depicting the people and village life.

According to a guidebook we'd purchased, there was a Villa of Mysteries located about a mile from town that showed images of women engaged in a mysterious ritual. Intrigued, we had made our way there and stared in wonder at the exquisite friezes inside the main hall. Just as the guidebook said, the images were depictions of women undergoing some sort of ceremony or ritual. Watching over the entire event was an elegant frieze of a serene woman identified in the guidebook as Ariadne, a mortal woman and seated next to her was the Greek god Dionysus, whom she loved.

The first frieze showed a female initiate in prayer as she partook of a ritual meal. In the second frieze, the female initiate's face was fearful as she descended into an underground world where satyrs, half-human and half-beast, surrounded her. In each successive scene, the female was portrayed wearing fewer and fewer garments, indicating perhaps, so the guidebook said, that she was divesting herself of old roles or habits. In the last frieze, the initiate was being shown the image of the male phallus in a winnowing basket, indicating she was now strong enough within herself to look fully at the fertilizing and powerful symbol of the regenerative god, Dionysus. A winged goddess holding a whip in her hand stood over the initiate who was shown in a position of submission. In the final scene, the young female initiate was beautifully dressed, perhaps demonstrating, so the guidebook said, that she had undergone a profound transformation and was now ready to move into the outer world as a strong and wise heroine.

Saren and I had left the Villa of Mysteries shaking our heads, not understanding what we'd seen other than appreciating the beauty of the friezes. The concept of a woman's initiation ceremony was something we'd never heard of and had no frame of reference for, much as we'd experienced during our first visit to Chartres cathedral where we'd been introduced by guide Malcolm Andrews to the concept of a sacred feminine energy in the form of a Black Madonna that resided in the cathedral.

If there was any such thing as feminine mysteries belonging to a female divinity, it had gone missing in the faith and doctrine of my Christian upbringing as well as in the wider Western culture and history. It was hard to deny, however, that something in me, something I had no name for, had been catalyzed and re-awakened by visits to the two powerful places of Chartres and the Villa of Mysteries in Pompeii.

******

Now, for a second time here I was, standing in silence at the foot of the magnificent Rose window at Chartres cathedral. I closed my eyes, letting the rainbow-colored light streaming through the stained-glass surround and penetrate my body. Like Bernini's sculpture showing the rapture of St. Theresa in communion with God, I, too, felt an intense blissful energy wash over me as tears of gratitude began to flow down my cheeks; quite suddenly, I felt reassured and at peace with my decision to leave my marriage and divorce.

After taking in the transformational beauty of the cathedral's Rose window for a second time, I sat in silence in one of the pews for a while before leaving to look for the studio belonging to the master guild of stained-glass makers that guide Malcolm Andrews had said worked near the cathedral. I wondered if it was true that contemporary stained-glass craftsmen in the village were actual descendants of the original artisans who had constructed the cathedral's windows when it was built in the eleventh century.

As I randomly started walking down one of the streets, a Frenchman of medium height and thick mustache, wearing a coat and tie, greeted me. I told him I was searching for the studio belonging to the stained-glass makers for the cathedral. He made a slight bow, "I am the head of the guild of stained-glass makers. Would you like to see our studio? Another coincidence? I wondered as

I nodded and followed the guild master. Maybe, but I couldn't help feeling that I was being guided.

The studio was a large space with rooms, separate ateliers, nooks here and there, all filled with artist materials of every sort to accommodate stain-glass making. The guild master began by telling me how the glassmakers of today maintained Chartres' magnificent windows. "It's a difficult process, matching the old glass with the new since the secrets of alchemy originally used to construct the glass for the windows are no longer known," he said. "The first stained glass appeared in Persia towards the eleventh century in the laboratories of certain master glass artisans, among them the mathematician and philosopher Omar Khayyam, poet of the Rubayyat. You have heard of him, Madame?"

"Oui," I nodded.

"Stained glass came to the west at the same time as Gothic architecture, around the beginning of the twelfth century when many statues of Black Madonnas also came to Europe. During the two world wars, the stained-glass windows were taken down and hidden to protect them from destruction," he said, continuing the tour of his studio, with me following him, and absorbing as much as I could.

I paused in front of a large pile of discarded shards of colored glass and couldn't help staring at them.

"Would you like to have some of the shards of discarded glass used to repair the windows of the cathedral?" he asked. "Please. Take what you wish," he said pointing to the pile of multi-colored glass pieces that had attracted my attention.

"Merci," I replied, stooping down to pick up a few pieces of the glass shards, sensing there was something special about them

"Perhaps the glass pieces will bring you back to Chartres and the Black Madonna one day, Madame," the guild master said as I left the studio, thanking him again for the tour.

I fervently hoped so. I was hungry to know more, especially about the mysteries belonging to a Black Madonna and what the feminine mysteries of a women's initiation might be. Why was the Madonna, the proclaimed Mother of God, black? Were the images of a Black Madonna holding her son Jesus really based on statues of the Egyptian Goddess Isis and her son Horus brought back to Europe by the Knights Templar, as Chartres cathedral guide Malcolm Andrews had said? What was his source of this information?

Although my head was full of intriguing questions pleading for further exploration, the river of destiny had already begun to rapidly push me in another direction. I took a face tissue and carefully wrapped the glass fragments infused with the sacred energy of the cathedral's windows and tucked them deep inside a pocket of my large handbag where they would remain, along with the post card of the Black Madonna and child I'd stuffed away, both going unnoticed for years until it was their time to re-emerge.

On my drive back to Paris, I reviewed my visit and what had happened there. I considered that my life was and always had been a spiritual journey, but it was no longer one guided or held captive by dusty scriptures interpreted by men inside their cold stone artifices where the heart of Jesus' message of love had gone missing and replaced by staid doctrines of obedience, fear and guilt. God had left the building, so to speak! Now more than ever, I was convinced that the mysteries of Chartres were real. Like thousands before me, I, too, had come as a pilgrim to Chartres and willingly or not, consciously or not, my heart had been pierced by something, perhaps by the presence of a dark feminine being, a Black Madonna? It seemed like a crazy idea but then again, maybe worth investigating in the future.

******

Back in Paris after my trip to Chartres, Saren shared the unhappy news that he'd been passed over a second time for promotion to General. "I'm going to retire from the military. No need to stay on. I'm going to ask for a last assignment to Huntsville's Redstone Army Arsenal. I know people there and it'll be easy to plan my next career move."

I felt sad for him as I knew this promotion had meant everything to him and in my mind, he had worked diligently for decades and deserved it. His devotion to the military was flawless and constant; if anyone was an outstanding example of the military's excellence in leadership and respect, it was Saren.

The sad day had finally come. After three years, we were leaving Paris. Off to a new life. The family and I would meet up again in Miami after my week in Nassau with my friend Gail. All seemed to be falling into place. Of course, it did nothing of the sort, as best-laid plans often do, going in directions never imagined or desired.

SURPRISES

Destination? Nassau in the beautiful Bahamas! Two lovers aboard the flight from Paris to the Bahamas, kissing and making out like ... like Parisians. Paul and I were oblivious to everyone else and it felt like we were going to Nassau for our honeymoon.

"Don't you think it's weird that we're going to Nassau like Saren and I did for our honeymoon?" I asked Paul. It was not the last of weird synchronicities to happen reflecting my relationships with the two men who were more alike than I might ever have imagined.

On the day I was to fly from Paris to the Bahamas, I'd hugged the children in a tearful goodbye, assuring them we'd see each other in Miami in a week's time. I had taken a bus to the airport where I'd secretly met Paul as we'd arranged to fly together to the Bahamas. After a week on Nassau, according to our plan, Paul would fly with me to Miami, where he and I would stay together while I filed for divorce. Paul knew a lawyer in Miami whom he'd already contacted and hopefully, Saren and I would be able to arrive at an amenable settlement right away. Paul, who'd recently retired from his CEO job, and I could then come out as a couple, find a place to live and have the children with us as we started a new life together.

Once in Nassau, Paul and I settled into a beautiful seaside hotel. I called Gail and we arranged to meet with her and her new island boyfriend Michael for dinner. Paul and I waited outside the hotel, waving excitedly when they arrived. As Gail and I hugged, I couldn't help noticing that she was as strikingly beautiful as I had remembered, observing that Paul, too, like most men, was awed by Gail's physical beauty.

We had a sweet re-union dinner at a smart, expensive restaurant and talked long into the night. "What happened to you after we graduated from New Mexico State University?" I asked Gail, who interestingly was smoking small cigars now, which I thought was pretty sexy. "I stayed on and got my M.A. in English. Once I graduated and got the offer to teach English at the Bahamian College in Nassau, I packed up my three girls and we moved. I've been here for a number of years now."

Michael, from a wealthy English family who'd settled decades earlier in the Bahamas, was sophisticated and exceptionally mellow. He told the story of how he and Gail had met, smiling all the while, obviously happy they'd met and were together. Gail seemed happy too and I was glad for her. We would remain friends and would meet up again in the future, somewhere down the line, and have many more adventures together.

******

The week in Nassau flew by with Paul and me spending most of our time either on the beach or in our room making love, occasionally squeezing in visits with Gail and Michael. Too soon it was time to fly to Miami, something I wasn't looking forward to.

Paul had concocted a plan to "keep our relationship a secret" so that once we were in Miami, we'd check into two hotels. I would book a room at one hotel while Paul and I would actually be staying in the other one. More subterfuge, which I detested, but Paul, a former Green Beret during the Vietnam War, reveled in it. When we'd first met, he told me that he had authored a number of books, both in French and English. "My one and only novel is about a Green Beret and how he and his unit were able to survive in Vietnam," he said with pride, going on to describe the gory details of learning how to thrust his arm down a dog's throat to prepare him to get down and dirty if his survival depended on it.

What was it with men and their affinity for war and soldiering? Had I exchanged one wounded male for another who bore allegiance to war as the ultimate expression of manhood and mankind? Would my children and I be better served if I were alone? Paul often told me that he feared he was just a passing ship in the night for me, a port of temporary safety until the storm blew over and then I'd move on. I always denied it, but I did make a mental note of what he'd said. I'd had quite enough of male posturing and its resulting negative consequences. Sometimes what we want and what we get bear little resemblance to each other.

******

"I'm not a divorce lawyer," said Mark, who was Paul's friend in Miami whom we'd gone to see, "but it should be a simple procedure if your husband doesn't contest your requests for custody and a fair monthly support amount while you get set-up in your new life. Do you and Paul plan on living together?"

"Yes, we do, but we're not sure which state just yet, probably California since Marjorie has applied to law school there," Paul answered with a hint of pride.

Mark's eyebrows rose in a look of slight surprise. "Oh, you want to become a lawyer? Then you're both going to be leaving Paris and relocating to America?"

"That's the current plan. We haven't worked out all the details yet. See, Marjorie's husband Saren, doesn't know we're together. I thought it was better if he didn't know about us in case it might complicate the divorce proceedings, say, if he wanted to claim adultery, which she doesn't think he will, but I'm not so sure. He's a man and in my experience, it's not only women who can become revengeful when they're scorned."

Mark leaned back in his handsome Charles Eames leather chair. "I agree with you Paul; best to keep things as simple as possible until after our meeting with Marjorie's husband. You're not expecting him to contest the divorce though, are you?"

"No. No. Not at all. We've been talking about it for over a year and a half," I replied confidently.

"But does he know you're planning on serving him divorce papers once he arrives in Florida?" Mark asked.

"No. No, he doesn't, but he's a person of integrity and I don't expect him to fight the reality of what's been unfolding for years now in our marriage."

"Well, some people don't respond well to surprises, but I'll draw up the papers tomorrow and once you let me know his address, we'll serve him. Then based on how he responds, we'll go from there."

"How long will all this take?" Paul asked.

"It all depends. If the husband is cooperative, things can clip right along. If he puts up a fight and starts contesting everything, it can be a long process."

Paul and I exchanged worried looks.

"Don't worry! People get divorces every day," Mark said, reassuringly.

We would all remember those prophetic words as events unfolded rather more differently in the days, months and years to come.

******

Once Saren and the kids arrived in Miami to his mother's house, I immediately went to see them, hugging and planting kisses on the kids and listening to their stories about the final week of packing up to leave France.

"Where's your luggage?" Saren asked.

"Can we talk somewhere privately?" I said, avoiding his question.

"Sure," he said, a little anxiously.

Once we were alone in the bedroom, I closed the door behind us. "I've moved ahead with filing for divorce," I told him calmly, "and I've contacted a lawyer in Miami who will be serving you with divorce papers."

A look of shock spread across his face; a look soon replaced by rage. "I can't believe you're doing this," he said, trying hard to control his voice. "What are you thinking? We love another. What about the kids? I can't believe you're doing this," he repeated, pacing back and forth.

"I told you over a year and a half ago," I reminded him, "that unless we got help to work out our problems, I was going to ask for a divorce. Remember? It's been eighteen months. This isn't news."

"What? We went to that counselor, didn't we?"

"Correction. I, went to the counselor," I said, emphasizing the "I". "We only had four or five sessions, half of which you missed."

"Well, somebody in the family has to make an income and I had to travel a lot for my job, you know that!"

Yes, I am well aware of how much you had to travel for your job."

"Marjorie, you can't do this! Please don't do this!"

"Saren, we've been through this a thousand times, repeating the same things over and over and nothing ever changes. I can't take it anymore. I feel like if I stay on with you, I'll die."

236

"Didn't I let you go to all those feminist things? Didn't I? Yes, I did. Didn't I pay for that feminist therapist you saw for almost a year? Yes, I did. I don't understand what more you want from me."

"Saren, that's exactly why I wanted us to get professional help, to get some marriage counseling, so we could figure out ways to get our needs met, both of us, not just you."

The argument continued until the children began to knock on the door. "Can we please have some ice cream? Grandma Buni said we had to ask you first. Please, can we?" came their pleading voices from behind the closed door.

"Look," I said to Saren, "I'm staying at a hotel downtown. I'll leave you the hotel number. The kids can stay here with you and your mom until we get some things straightened out, okay?"

As I hugged the kids goodbye, I explained that mommy was going to stay by herself for a while and that they would be staying with daddy and grandma Buni. "I promise I'll call you first thing tomorrow morning and we'll see each other then, okay?"

As I walked past Mrs. Canto on my way to the front door, she looked at me with her usual disapproving scowl.

"Aren't you staying?" she asked sarcastically.

"No, I'm not. Saren will explain," I said, closing the door firmly behind me. I took another taxi back to "my" hotel in downtown Miami and flung myself on the double bed in the small, cramped room and sobbed until I fell asleep to be awakened by a phone call from Paul. "How'd it go?" he asked.

"It was awful, just awful!" I moaned into the phone.

"Catch a taxi and come over. You can't stay by yourself. That's why I'm here."

******

"Saren might not take too kindly to being served with divorce papers, you know," Paul warned. "The male ego is fragile at best and even more so in matters of love."

"I know. I know but even though Saren and I have our differences, he's a loving, reasonable person and even though he can be stubborn, I don't think he'll be vindictive in any way," I replied with heart-felt conviction.

Once Saren was served divorce papers, he hired a lawyer and we were summoned to a private court hearing with a judge to determine who would have temporary custody until the final details of a divorce could be worked out.

As Mark and I walked into the private hearing room near the Miami courthouse, there was a palpable feeling of unease and tension in the air. Saren had brought both children and I was nervous about that since he hadn't mentioned anything about bringing them. Once everyone was seated around the table, the proceeding began with Saren's lawyer presenting his case first, declaring, "Your honor, my client Col. Canto is suing for temporary custody of both children."

"What?" I said out loud, looking first at Saren and then at Mark in shocked surprise.

"Here are several letters, your honor, which attest to Col. Canto's good character," his lawyer continued, handing the judge letters from various people attesting to Saren's virtuous character. "I'd like to ask if it pleases your honor, to hear a statement written by the father regarding his wife and their situation before she left the children with their father in Paris to return to the states."

The judge nodded and Saren stood to read his statement in which he accused me of being a lesbian and a pot-smoker, facts which jeopardized his career; claimed I'd refused to take proper care of the children's clothes, letting them go to school with soiled uniforms, and many other negligent actions because I was too busy with my feminist meetings, and the final most devastating claim ... that when all of these things were taken together, they proved I was an unfit mother!

Stunned with disbelief at the vitriolic words coming from Saren's lips, amounting to an outright character assassination ... did he really hate me that much? I looked at my lawyer Mark whose face showed he, too, was visibly shocked. We were totally unprepared. We had nothing, no letters of good character, no nothing. I had expected an uncontested proceeding, not this! I had no idea Saren was going to sue for temporary custody of the children. Didn't he always have to travel for his jobs? Who would care for the children?

How naïve I was. After all, Saren was a military man, trained in all manner of military maneuvers and strategies to defeat an enemy; and in only a few days' time, I had become his enemy number one.

Saren's lawyer stood and began to bludgeon me with a barrage of unexpected and accusatory questions as though I were a criminal. "Is it true Mrs. Canto that you didn't cook dinner the night before you left Paris for the states, the last night that you spent with your children up until this time?"

"Did I what ... what's that got to do with anything?" I asked, my feminist consciousness in shock at such a biased assumption that the wife had to cook or she didn't love her family. I looked at Saren in disbelief as he sat across the table from me, arms crossed and wearing a look of belligerent defiance.

"Is it true that you smoked marijuana in your Paris apartment with your feminist and lesbian friends while your two children played unattended in their rooms?"

"No. I mean ... it wasn't like that ... and I'm not a lesbian and what if I was?"

"How are you going to support your children Mrs. Canto?" the lawyer interrupted me. "You're coming from Europe and don't have a job. Your husband is a Colonel in the United States Army and has a home to give the children at his new post in Huntsville, Alabama. His mother will move to Alabama from her home in Florida to take care of the children while he works during the day."

Well, damn! I'm screwed! He's got it all figured out, as usual. The divorce would be no different, it would be settled his way. I can't tell them I have a secret lover, a man who wants to marry me and give us all a home together! Even if Paul wasn't in my life, the children and I could live with my parents until I got a job and was settled. But I had made no contingency plans because I'd been too confident of a friendly parting of the ways. I hadn't reckoned on the ferocity and desire to inflict pain coming from my former best-friend, my husband.

I was absolutely devastated at the explicit accusations that I was an unfit mother, but as he would repeat numerous times during the next two-plus years, the time it took us to get divorced, "you wanted this divorce. Now you'll have to pay for it. If I suffer, so will you. I guarantee you that much." The divorce would become a competition to him; one that he didn't intend to lose whatever the cost or heartache it caused. Did he even want custody of the children or was it just a way to hurt me?

The judge announced the verdict: "Temporary custody of the two children Alex and Marie will be given to their father, Saren Canto. Mrs. Canto will be awarded $200 per month until the divorce is finalized. Mrs. Canto will be allowed visitation rights as fits with the children's schedule and to be determined by their father Saren Canto."

On hearing the judge's verdict, I jumped up from the table and ran out of the room onto the street, sobbing uncontrollably with Mark and the two children, who shouldn't have been at the hearing, running after me. I don't even remember what Mark or anyone said that calmed me down and got me back into the room to sign the court papers giving Saren temporary custody of the children.

The children were upset and crying as they left with Saren. I was crying again and Mark held onto me, helping me into his car, then driving me to the hotel where Paul and I were staying. I collapsed into a heap on the bed, both of them consoling me, while Mark told Paul what had happened at the court proceeding.

It was obvious that even though I had "raised my consciousness," I was still amazingly naïve about how things worked in a world still dominated by men and how brutal and unjust that world could be. I had fully envisioned that Saren and I would continue to be friends and raise our children in a loving and supportive environment that they deserved; that we all deserved. Still clinging to an either/or attitude, he sought no middle ground and the few good attempts at opening up and communicating we'd done while still in Paris had evaporated instantly in what had now become the battleground of our divorce, with the children being the sought-after spoils of victory.

Suddenly, I understood in the most personal and profound way why I was a feminist and why I had been so adamant and fought so hard for an equality for women. Women were powerless in most of their relationships and at many levels of society. Now, that mostly white male institution known as the legal system had just passed sentence on me, believing another man's accusation that I was an unfit mother and didn't deserve even temporary custody of my children. I was furious, humiliated, devastated and in shock, but I wasn't going to give up! The good little nice girl, the Southern Belle, would have to give way to the energy of the warrior woman if I was going to heal, grow and mature into a person who could be both a fighter when she needed to be as well as a nurturer. My children needed this to happen and so did I.

PAINFUL TRANSITIONS

"Let's go to the Great Smoky Mountains for a few days. It's beautiful there and we'll get out of the muggy heat here in middle Georgia."

After the court proceeding awarding temporary child custody to Saren, Paul had returned with me to my hometown where we rented an apartment to re-group and decide some next steps for us. Anytime we left the apartment, however, he seemed to be nervous.

"What are you so nervous about?" I asked him. "Saren lives hundreds of miles away and it's virtually impossible that we'd run into him."

"That's not it. Look, I'm Jewish and I've heard all those stories about how people in the South, especially the police, don't like Jews or black people. White people from the North who've come here have gotten arrested, locked up in jails, and killed."

"My god, Paul! That's not going to happen to you. You're not here marching or a civil rights protester. You're safe. Don't worry about it."

Paul seemed to calm down and we headed out, taking the interstate highway from north Georgia into the beautiful Great Smoky Mountains of Tennessee. Fall had come and sprinkled its breathtaking beauty everywhere, with entire mountainsides covered in swaths of rusty oranges, bright reds and yellows. It wasn't quite like riding Paul's motorcycle in Paris, hair blowing in the wind, smelling and hearing the cities' sights and sounds as we buzzed by, but there was the same sense of freedom of driving and having an open road in front of you.

For a while, neither of us noticed the Sheriff's car following behind us because its siren was off and only its red light was flashing.

"You're not going to believe this but there's a Sheriff's car behind us," I said to Paul.

"I'm going the speed limit. He can't be after us."

But the good ole Southern boy Sheriff was after us, and soon we were living a scene right out of one of the terrifying stories Paul had heard.

"Show me your driver's license, son," the fat Sheriff drawled once Paul had pulled over and let down the window.

Paul got out his driver's license, which was from New York, and with noticeably shaking hands, handed it to the Sheriff, who with his sunglasses and potbelly was easily the most recognizable stereotypical character portraying the scary-ass law men in the South.

The Sheriff glared at the driver's license, then back at Paul, then looked back again at the license as though it were an artifact from an archaeological dig, then with a big scowl on his face, thrust it back to Paul.

"Looks okay, son, but where y'all headed in such a big hurry? We don't 'preciate people coming down here and speeding on our public highways causing a safety issue, you understand?"

Paul nodded, looking straight ahead.

"I'm gonna give you a warning this time, but consider yourself lucky, ya hear?" the Sheriff drawled, handing Paul a warning ticket before sauntering his gorilla body back to his Sheriff's car.

Paul waited until the Sheriff had turned off the red rotating light and driven off in a cloud of dust, screeching tires and all.

We sat in silence for a few moments, taking in what had just happened.

"We are not going to live in the South, that's for damn sure!" was all he could manage to say.

"Never thought we would," I nodded in complete agreement, wanting to laugh but thought better of it. Always the writer, I did think, however, that *A New York Jew Meets a Good Ole Southern Boy Sheriff* might be an interesting story but I kept it to myself, remembering Paul's words about male egos being fragile.

Soon after our run-in with the law, Southern-style, in the Great Smokey Mountains, we made our cross-country road trip to California where we met up with friends from Paris who had moved to Berkeley. We drove around neighborhoods and checked out houses and prices. After the trip, Paul and I talked about living together and where that might be.

"I think I need to go back to Paris and look for work again," he said as we sat at the dining table in the small apartment in Warner Robins. "I think I retired too soon."

"Oh. Why is that?" I asked, surprised.

"I don't think I have enough retirement income to support us and possibly two children."

I'd noticed that he called his bank in Switzerland regularly during the time we'd been in America, but didn't pry or ask questions about his finances. Saren had changed all of his and my checking/saving accounts to his name only and women couldn't have credit cards in their own name, so I was more or less penniless until I got some settlement money from my divorce. I knew that wherever Paul and I settled, I would work and add to the household income. I hadn't even thought about law school since the upset at the court hearing.

We decided Paul would leave at Thanksgiving and return to Paris to resume working and find us a place to live, while I would have the kids with me over the holiday if Saren would allow.

"You can join me in Paris after Christmas. You should have your divorce by the first of the year and custody of the children returned to you. We can be a family. I think everything's working out."

I was under no illusion that I was now an enemy to Saren and that he would continue to play hardball but I had no idea just how far his desire for revenge would take him, and us. He's not the only one hurting. We were all hurting. Didn't he realize that? It was not his finest hour and to be labeled an unfit mother by him in a court of law in front of our children didn't exactly make me a warm fussy soon-to-be understanding ex-wife.

READING DORIS LESSING IN PARIS

My friend Rachael has gone to the kitchen to make me some hot tea. I've moved into her spare bedroom in the large apartment she and Abe own in the working-class district of Paris. They also own an art gallery on one of the side streets near the Notre Dame Cathedral and we became friends after I attended one of their art gallery openings.

Paul and I have broken up. We had a big fight over the children. He accused me of not letting go and being too emotional because I cry every time I talk with them on the phone. I think he's jealous. He wants all of me, doesn't want to share me with anyone, in spite of the open relationship mini-experiment we tried. He hates it if I mention anything about Saren and accuses me of still loving him. Of course, I still love him! I yell back and I'll probably always love him. We were married for fifteen years and have two children together!

I've had many opportunities over these last six months living with Paul to see how manipulative he is. If I'm honest, I'm not ready to be with anyone and definitely not interested in getting married again which is what Paul wants or, wanted. I've got a lot more grieving to do and I don't want a life without my children.

Paul was here for a brief visit earlier this afternoon and didn't want to kiss me because he was afraid he'd catch whatever I have. I don't think I have anything contagious. It was watching the disintegration of our relationship that's made me sick; that, and the reality of being thousands of miles away from my children.

I've been in bed, staring at the walls for days now, which has given me plenty of time to reflect and get out of Paul's suffocating energy pressuring me constantly to marry him and urging me to forget about whether or not I get custody of my children. I couldn't believe he was talking like that. The divorce has continued to drag on and on because Saren is contesting absolutely everything. How absurd, anyway, trying to get a divorce from someone who lives in another country.

I've been reading Doris Lessing's novel *The Four-Gated City* while laying here in bed. Friends in the CR group read Lessing's book and said I should read it. So, now I am. In the beginning of the book, Lessing's heroine Martha Quest sets out on a quest for self-knowledge, transformation and wisdom. Her quest begins when she experiences a sense of nothingness because she can't find a suitable role model for herself. Right away, like my friends in CR group, I'm hooked because I can identify with Martha when she can't find an image of herself she can make her own. Lessing writes that Martha appears to be sleepwalking in her own life, a drifter, going wherever life's events take her, always searching for meaning and clues to life outside herself.

Dear god, I think, putting the book down and giving a heavy sigh, this is exactly like me. If I'm not a wife and mother, then who am I? I think another reason I can't marry Paul is that I need time to find out who I am or what I can be besides someone's wife. That was part of the reason I left Saren.

Picking up the book again, Lessing writes that the heroine Martha has lived at the same house in London for twenty years, when she decides to move into the basement with a woman named Lynda for a month to explore regions of what Lessing calls a *non-ordinary reality*. Time spent in the basement is like a rite of passage for Martha, Lessing writes, because she now immerses herself in a territory she has only visited briefly but which has now become the center of her life. Martha realizes that this region of non-ordinary reality and the insights it offers is the goal of her quest, the four-gated city of her dreams. Together, the two women survive the ordeal of going to the uncharted regions of the mind where they serve as both teacher and guide to one another.

Was this what I was doing with Paul? I wondered as I put down the book again. Had he been the guide, like my Jungian therapist Helen, helping me to uncover the shadow side of my psyche and supporting me through the underworld journey I was on? But now, after we were out of the basement of the house, so to speak, Paul had wanted none of my insights from my experiences. He wanted to continue to be the teacher and guide, which I was beginning to see gave him power over me and our relationship; that, in fact, he didn't want a relationship of equals.

This realization brings me to tears but I force myself to return to the book again, sensing it has a clear message to give me. Reading to the end of the novel, Lessing writes that Martha leaves the house at Radlett Street with no clear idea of where she's going next, but it doesn't matter Lessing says, because Martha is taking with her a profound new trust in herself and her own process, something she's learned to value above anyone else's ideas of what she should do. Martha has learned to look to herself for guidance and direction.

I close the book and laugh, remembering how some members of our feminist group had found the ending disturbing; like a kind of mysticism on Martha's part, some said, that showed her being contented to observe rather than work or take overt action to bring about social change. Being quiet and observing was definitely not at the heart of feminist thought. I realize that regardless of what anyone else thinks, that whether Paul or anyone else approves or not, it is time for me to trust myself and value my own thoughts and process. That is being brave ... a heroine, like Lessing's character Martha Quest.

******

Merci, I say to Rachel when she returns to the bedroom with the cup of hot tea she's made. She sits on the bottom of the small bed, dressed in a peasant-styled blouse made from *molas*, pieces of cloth decorated with hand stitching using abstract designs and then sewn together, one layer on top of another, by Peruvian Indians. Rachel's art gallery features art from Indians of South America and art pieces like the *molas* are on display. It has taken her seven years to get all the necessary documents together and approved by the French authorities before she was able to open a business in Paris. I admire her persistence and tenacity to achieve her goals.

"You know, Abe and I have what you might call a sexual arrangement," she said, in her slow, mellow voice. "Pierre ... you've met Pierre ... he's been helping with the restoration of the apartment; well, he and I began sleeping together shortly after he began working for us. Abe didn't like it at first, but now he's accepted it. It was either that or divorce me and he didn't want that."

"Abe's okay with Pierre living here with you and your two girls?" I ask, somewhat incredulous at such a living arrangement, much as I'd been when learning Elaine and Sophia had moved in together and Elaine's husband Michael had left to live in a separate apartment. Pierre was a young twenty-something who liked to dress up in Rachel's dresses and high-heeled shoes in the evenings when they relaxed in front of the television and smoked pot together.

"Abe has accepted it because he's accepted me. We met in New York when I was dating actor-comedian Dick Gregory who was going on hunger strikes all the time for his various social causes. I knew I wanted kids and Abe had a good job and he was Jewish. We just sort of fell in together. That's enough of my story. I'll let you rest now," she said, getting up to go. "Listen," she said, "I know it's none of my business, and you know I like Paul because, hey, you know we Jews have to stick together but maybe the timing isn't right for you two. You've been calling your kids in America a lot; it's obvious you're worried about them. Maybe you should go back so you can see them and get your divorce. If Paul's still around, and if you want to be with him, you'll be divorced and ready to move on together."

I thought a long time about Rachel's advice, as I lay sick in bed in her spare bedroom. Maybe it was time to leave Paris, go back to America. Many of my feminist friends had already moved on, like Lisa and Elaine, and I had only seen the Bernsteins a few times since returning. I couldn't tell them I was living with Paul because I didn't want to risk their telling Saren about my living arrangement with another man. Another reason I regretted the secrecy about being with Paul since I could have used the Bernstein's friendship. But with Saren's revenge-factor knowing no limits, what would he do if he found I was living with another man? Add adultery to the unfit mother charges?

Now that Paul and I weren't a couple anymore, I knew I had to make it on my own, whether here in Paris or back in the United States. I had applied for jobs at the US Embassy and UNESCO, but the security clearance necessary to start work at either place could take up to six-months. Although I'd looked at apartments to rent, I didn't have all the necessary money for the security deposits. I had no money except the $200 a month the Judge had ordered Saren to pay, and since all our bank accounts were still frozen, leaving me with no access to any of our money, and no credit cards, I was stuck financially.

And even if I did find a job in Paris, how likely was it that Saren would let me have custody of the children?

A phone call from mother helped to convince me it was time to return to America. "Saren's in the hospital," she said, surprised that I hadn't heard the news. "They found him on the floor in the bathroom in a pool of blood and rushed him to the emergency room where he got blood transfusions. He had a bleeding ulcer and it burst."

"Is he okay? What about the children?"

"Saren's mother said that the doctors told her he'd be okay, but would have to stay in the hospital a few days. She's been living with them since that court hearing, keeping the kids while Saren works, so I guess they're okay. I really haven't talked with them much."

After we hung up, I tried calling Saren's number in Alabama, but no one answered. When we finally talked a few days later, he said that he and the children were fine. I told him I was thinking I needed to come back to America.

"You don't need to come back to America on my account. I don't need you anymore and the children are doing just fine with my mother watching them. Enjoy your life in France," he said and hung up.

YOU USED TO BE A NICE GIRL

"What's happened to you, Marjorie? You used to be a nice Christian girl. Everybody looked up to you. Now, you've become selfish and self-centered. You don't even care what happens to your children," mother said to me late one spring afternoon while we sat in the backyard of the Georgia home where I'd grown up and to which I'd temporarily returned after leaving Paul and Paris for a second time.

"You should go back to Saren and stay married if only for the sake of the children. That's what I did for you and your brother," she continued in an agitated voice.

"But mother," I protested, "Saren doesn't want me back and so that's never gonna happen, and sorry, but no one asked you to sacrifice your life for me and Jack and stay in a marriage if it made you unhappy. That was your choice."

"Don't you talk to your mother like that! You're only interested in what you want and I'm ashamed of you," she said, grabbing her ice tea and stalking into the house, leaving me again to make whatever I would of her critical assessment of me.

Mothers got a green thumb, I'll give her that, I said out loud, trying to brush off her hurtful words by turning my attention to the beauty of late springtime in the South and her yard filled with blooming azalea bushes lush with pink blossoms and rose bushes lining the fence, begging to have their sensual smells inhaled, and a few beds of fragrant, purple-hued iris. Such beauty, I sighed, looking around the same back yard that bordered the First Baptist Church where I'd done so much growing up, the same back yard where I'd twirled and danced as a young girl, gazing up at the blazing starry night, imagining myself singing in front of an admiring audience, one that didn't include critics like my mother.

She's probably right, though, I sighed again. I'm not a good Christian girl anymore because I'm not a girl and I'm not a Christian. But she's wrong about my kids. I love them with all my heart but I couldn't stay in a dysfunctional marriage for their sake; sacrificing my life wouldn't have insured their happiness. It was never my desire to create a new life that didn't include my children. I felt some comfort in knowing that in a few weeks I'd be moving to Huntsville where the kids had been living with their dad since the temporary custody hearing and I'd be able to see them more often.

Sipping on my sugary ice tea and sinking into the beauty and solitude of the backyard of my childhood, I mulled over another disturbing relationship. What had happened to Paul and me and our relationship that had been so good at first?

When I'd returned to Paris to live with Paul, it didn't take long for some major differences to emerge. Understandable in one way. After all, it was a most unusual circumstance we found ourselves in.

******

I should have paid more attention from day one of my return to Paris at Christmastime last year that a grievous miscalculation on my part had been made, one that all boiled down to the absolute absurdity that Paul and I would be *living in the same apartment where Saren and I had spent our last two years in France!* It was Paul's surprise for me. Surprise? It was beyond any synchronistic happening I could ever have imagined; something I felt certain that Swiss psychologist Carl Jung who first introduced the concept of synchronicity, describing it as "circumstances that appear meaningfully related yet lack a causal connection," might also have done some head-shaking.

Honeymooning in Nassau, as Paul and I had referred to our time there, and Nassau being the same place Saren and I had honeymooned, seemed like an interesting coincidence, but returning to live with Paul in the same Paris apartment where Saren and I had lived? How could Paul possibly have considered it to be a place where we could live, especially me, with memories still fresh from my former life there with Saren and the children engulfing me on a daily basis?

The obvious question to Paul: Why did you buy this apartment? Why THIS apartment out of all the apartments in Paris?

"Look, darling," he explained, "when I returned to Paris and started looking for a place to buy, a friend told me about a great apartment that had just come on the market in the 7th arrondissement. I called the realtor who told me how great it was. But of course, the first thing I wanted to know was why, if the apartment was so great, it hadn't sold. He told me it had been empty for months because the owner who lived in Spain had died and the estate had been in limbo for a time."

"Oh, my god, Paul!"

"I thought you'd be happy," he said.

"Well, it's not that ... I mean, living in the same apartment at 37 Avenue de Breteuil? When did you realize it was my and Saren's old apartment?"

"Not until I got in this neighborhood. I was surprised too!"

Paris the second time around. Once again, I was living on the Left Bank in the 7th arrondissement of Paris, only not with my husband but with my lover.

Initially, it was very weird to be living there with Paul and not Saren and the kids. But Paul had changed everything so completely that the look and feel of it was totally different. The Saren-Marjorie-Canto family's vibe had been wiped away, as though it had never been, which in a way helped me to be able to live there with Paul. Turns out, living in the same apartment as I'd lived in with my soon-to-be ex-husband, was the least of Paul's and my problems.

Since we'd never actually lived together except for the few months in Georgia, there was a lot of getting used to the other's daily living habits. Paul was up at the crack of dawn, sending out job resumes to businesses throughout Europe, writing another children's book, and organizing his many other interests, and all before 8 o'clock in the morning. For the first time in my Super Woman charged life, I felt lazy, and he hinted that maybe I was.

In spite of our different daily rhythms, we did some wonderful things together. We talked about what it would mean to have a spiritual component in our lives and went to the Transcendental Meditation Society where we learned how to meditate using a special mantra the teacher gave us. We talked long and openly about living together, getting married, and what that might mean, especially his becoming a father to my two children; and, although he wanted to marry me as soon as I was divorced, I wasn't so sure, but we even talked about that. That was one big difference between Paul and Saren; Paul and I were able to talk about things and how we felt ... at least in the beginning.

Another subject we discussed at some length was whether we wanted to have an open-relationship, and we agreed we wanted to try it. Paul had been a bachelor in Paris during his fifteen years of living and working there as an ex-pat and had a number of ex-girlfriends, including a few whom he was dating when we had gotten together. He called an old girlfriend and made arrangements to see her. I, having been married, actually was still married I reminded myself, didn't really know any men that I might consider seeing, even as a friend, much less as a possible lover.

At first it felt surreal to be thinking about anyone I knew in Paris who might be a potential lover, especially when I began ticking off names of the men I knew.

There was Harry the professional clarinet player with the Paris Symphony but I'd heard he'd gone back to America. Too bad, because he was single and attractive and would have been a great person to have an open relationship with. Oh, my god! I can't believe I'm even thinking like this. Maybe I'm not ready for this. No. You can do this. You can.

What about Chris, the head of the music department at the American School of Paris whom I'd become friends with while working on creating the children's musical play? No. No. No. His ex-wife was in my old CR group and so that wouldn't work besides, I wasn't attracted to Chris in that way.

So, who else was there? I racked my brain. Finally, I remembered the kid's Physical Ed teacher Marco from Pershing Hall School who had taken a strong liking to both Alex and Marie. He and my good friend Lisa had even started a part-time business to take kids on outings, because they both liked kids. Marco was a handsome, single, late-twenty something Italian, originally from New York.

I'll call him, if he still lives in Paris.

"Hello Marco," I said after dialing his phone number about half a dozen times and then hanging up before he could answer; eventually forcing myself to stay on the line, while praying that he wouldn't answer, then praying that he would. When I let the phone ring long enough for him to pick up, I gave him as few details as possible, simply telling him *the kids aren't with me*, and *I've been in America for the past six months*. Details could wait. For now, I just wanted to set up a meeting to have coffee and see what this open relationship thing that I had once so confidently presented to Saren, might be, if anything.

Marco came by the apartment when Paul wasn't there. I didn't even mention Paul. Marco knew the address, having come by often to pick up the kids for an outing. We went out to a nearby cafe, ordered an espresso and began to make awkward, small talk.

"So, how are the kids?"

Such a simple question, but every time I started to answer, I choked up and could feel myself starting to cry.

"Oh, my god! Are Alex and Marie okay? I mean, I hope everything's okay. Is everything okay?"

"I'm getting a divorce Marco; the kids are living with their dad in the states. As far as I know, I mean, I talk to the kids as often as I can, and they seem to be okay. They miss their mommy..." that was as far as I got before the tears gushed. I grabbed my purse from the table, left Marco sitting in the café, and rushed out the door. This just wasn't going to work for me on any level.

"Hey, hey. Wait up!" Marco yelled, running to catch up with me and taking my arm.

"I know this little park nearby where I used to take Alex and Marie to play sometimes. It's close. Can we go there for a while?" I nodded, becoming more and more aware that I had almost no control over my emotions regarding my grief over the loss of my kids and our family. Tears could come at any moment. Not the way I had planned for my meeting with Marco to go.

We found the park, with a large swath of green grass, and sat down on one of the black iron benches. We sat in silence, watching as cars sped by and people walked past on the sidewalk, watching as though we were in no hurry to go anywhere, or do anything. Finally, having gained a semblance of composure, I reached out and touched Marco's hand, giving it a squeeze.

"Thanks," I said.

"For what?"

"Just for being here with me ... for not asking any questions ... for being my friend ... the childrens' friend."

"Of course," he said, adding one of his funny quips that he seemed to draw from an in-exhaustible personal encyclopedia of funny things to say. I laughed out loud, staring at Marco who was really quite handsome, and certainly had a great sense of humor. It felt so good to laugh.

I think Marco is good for me, I thought, relaxing a little, and besides, he was always genuinely interested in the kids and still seems to care about them. With Paul, it was becoming increasingly obvious that he preferred kids in the abstract, only seeing his own son once a year at most; preferring instead to write and publish kid's books featuring a fictional French boy and girl whom he called "my children." He designed a lovely necklace with their likenesses and gave it to me as a present. "These are my kids," he said.

"What happened, I mean with you and your husband, if you don't think I'm being too personal?" Marco asked.

"Saren and I were just too different," I answered slowly, aware of how impossible it was to explain how a relationship can be one thing for a long period of time and then can seemingly change overnight to something else. "We loved each other but we have such different values about so many things, important things, like how to raise the kids. He wanted to send Alex off to a military boarding school. I fought to keep that from happening but if Alex's therapist hadn't intervened and told him that it would be a poor idea to send him away, Saren would have sent him to military school."

"Oh, Alex wouldn't like that."

"I know, but that's the kind of thing I'm talking about." I said, exhaling a big sigh, realizing again the futility of trying to explain to anyone why and how a relationship that's seems to be okay until one day it isn't.

The afternoon light was fading and we watched in silence as the twilight began to spread its fingers of pink and gold light across the city. "I'd better go now," I said, even though there were no kids to get home to and Paul was out on a "date" with an old girl friend named Francesco.

Marco leaned over and kissed me lightly on the neck. I turned my head and he kissed me gently on the lips. "Can I see you again," he asked as we walked back to my apartment, well, technically, Paul's apartment.

"I'd like that very much," I answered, as we hugged and lightly kissed goodnight. I could use a good friend, I thought as I opened the apartment and went inside.

******

Later that evening, after Paul had gotten home from his evening out with his old girlfriend, we lay in bed discussing our "dates."

"What was it like, being with Francesco again?" I asked, trying to sound interested but casual.

"It was good, really good…like nothing had changed between us."

"Did you make love?" I blurted out, terrified to hear the answer.

"We did."

"Is sex better with her or with me?"

"What?"

"Did-you-like-having-sex-with-her-better-than-you-like-having-sex-with-me?" I repeated slowly, emphasizing each word.

"I don't know if we should go into these kinds of details, I mean, what was it like with Marco?"

"Well, he and I kissed but we didn't have sex!" I yelled.

"Okay. Okay. Calm down. Come here. Please," he urged, opening his arms to embrace me. I fell into his arms, needing re-assurance. "I thought we'd agreed on having an open relationship, me seeing other people, you seeing other people, and that it was okay with you."

"We did and it is okay. But ... well, you're absolutely right though, we can't give details about time we spend with anyone else. And, it can't interfere with our relationship which is our primary focus, ok?"

"Right," he said, stroking my hair and then my breasts. I stiffened and pulled away. "I can't make love with you after you've just made love with someone else only a few hours ago."

"You're right. Yes. Okay. We're just finding our way here, *cheri*, that's all. Nothing's wrong with us. Actually, Francesco and I talked about a threesome, if that would ever interest you."

"What? Oh, my god! Well, I'll have to think about it. Maybe. I don't know. I'm more inclined for a threesome with me, you and another guy, but I don't know. I can't think anymore. Let's just go to sleep. I'm exhausted,"

I said, turning away from Paul and pulling the satin bed sheets over my body, satin sheets that had once been sensual parts of our lover's nest but were now just reminders of a time when things between us were much simpler.

WELCOME BACK TO THE LAND OF COTTON

My amazing life in Paris was dead and gone ... only a memory now and fading fast as waves of culture shock and personal loss swept over me as I made a less than grand re-entry into America; more specifically, the Deep South, to the Land of Cotton, the very Heart of Dixie itself, Alabama. Had I by some act of fate hit the re-play button called *My Life*, causing me to circle back in time and move in, once again, with my cousin Betty and her husband Hank, like I'd done almost twenty-years ago when I'd first met Saren? Would there be a different outcome in this re-play? Was I getting a second chance to start a new life? Was I being given a chance to do better, be better, smarter, kinder, wiser? I doubted it.

I felt nothing like the heroine Martha Quest whom I'd admired in Doris Lessing's novel *The Four Gated City* ... no, I felt more like a survivor of a prison camp, limping along and in need of a great deal of repair; a tin man or scare crow with no wizard of Oz to fix her up.

Was I going through some kind of women's initiation thing like the one depicted on the friezes at the Villa of Mysteries in Pompeii? If so, then I guessed I was at the frieze where the Goddess was holding a whip over the initiate, and instead of beating her maybe, just maybe, she would say something encouraging, like: "Times up girlie! Time to quit feeling sorry for yourself and get your act together! Remember how powerful you are, young woman!" Maybe she *was* saying those things to me.

But life had shifted now and it seemed to be focused more on my learning humility and acceptance for the parts of life that I saw as crappy. It was humbling to have no access to any financial assets and having to ask relatives if I could live with them until I could find work; humbling to implore my husband, time and again, for money to buy a car, a used car, so I didn't have to borrow my cousin's car to drive to work; humbling to beg and cajole said husband to see our children for a few hours a week. Perhaps just as humbling? I was only able to find work as a secretary, a job that in my eyes was another example of women being in service to the patriarchy, my personal version of hell-on-earth, not because a secretarial job was below me, but because it meant having to cater to some white man in the front office; which in fact, was my exact situation when I was hired to be an executive secretary to the director of one of the largest military contractors in Huntsville. Now I was punching a clock five days a week, typing, answering phones and warding off unwanted flirtations from boring, fat, married white men and, insult to injury, making and bringing them coffee every morning! I exaggerate. I only had to bring coffee to my boss who was a nice, divorced white guy who did ask me out on a date and when I nicely refused, he was a gentleman about it.

Writing a new narrative while living inside the old one, trying to hold yourself steady while straddling between the two stories, is no easy task. I thought wryly of a popular feminist poster at the time of Israeli Prime Minister Golda Meir with a caption that read, "But can she type?" Sometimes, I imagined Golda and me sitting next to one another in a clerical pool, composed of all women, of course, typing at our typewriters, page after page of boring documents about missiles, their procurement and distribution. How's it going? I'd ask Golda as we sat together in the typing pool. Oh, I think it will all work out if we give it time, she'd answer me. She didn't seem to mind being a secretary as much as I did. I think it was because she knew she didn't need to type to be Prime Minister. What did I know for sure? Maybe all the feminist ideas about equality were just an illusion, some curiosity that kept me and other women entertained while men continued ruling the world. Judging from my current situation, working as a secretary was a damn good thing. It was deemed "appropriate" women's work and would soon be paying my rent, making it possible to move into an apartment of my own where I could bring the kids.

Over lunch that I'd brought from home and ate at my desk, I'd muse over questions like "What had happened to my life?" and "Had I mysteriously gone to sleep and woken up in somebody else's life?" I wondered if it was a possibility that I had actually emerged from doing time in an underworld or a non-ordinary reality that writer Doris Lessing said was a necessary experience to gain self-knowledge, and if so, I sure as heck had walked through an incorrectly marked doorway! Obviously, I'd thought the sign read, this way to the *Elysian Fields*, but instead written in fine print at the bottom, it must have said, *this way to hell on earth*! Another exaggeration, but honestly, moving from Paris to Alabama did feel like a kind of hell.

What was living like in Alabama in the late 1970s as a single, divorced (soon to be), freedom loving, sexually uninhibited (well, maybe only slightly sexually inhibited), feminist and ex-Southern Belle? Pretty much a description of hell! The Deep South was not friendly to any of those "fancy" ideas, as anything was called in the South that threatened to shake up the status quo, "fancy" things like feminism or integration and people of color wanting to sit anywhere they pleased. "Not on my watch," was what Alabama's governor George Wallace had made perfectly clear on the day he stood in the doorway of the University of Alabama and blocked two African American students from entering.... meaning: we like the way things are down here in the Land of Cotton so don't mess with 'um.

Daily, sometimes several times a day, I'd push the chair back from my office desk and the Holy Grail, the typewriter, and make my way to the ladies' bathroom, lock myself inside a stall, and flush the toilet over and over to drown out my sobbing. Then, after multiple splashes of cold water to the face, I'd dry my eyes, put on some more lipstick and head back to the desk to type and answer the phone. I was quickly learning first hand that out in the "real work-a-day world" a woman had few rights. I was also quickly learning first hand that a woman did need someone who would defend her if she wanted to have an easier time out in the "real world" where white men ruled and had dominance in all domains. It wasn't enough for a woman to be smart and accomplished, and it definitely wasn't "fair" or equal.

I may have emulated Joan of Arc in France but I was in the Deep South now and it was clear I would need to become a Steel Magnolia if I was going to survive and have any chance of thriving. *Steel Magnolia* was a popular phrase used to describe a Southern woman who exemplified both traditional femininity as well as an uncommon fortitude, which translated meant she could come across as being sweet as pie but would kill you in a heartbeat if you got in her way. Summoning strength and determination I must have inherited from some brave Steel Magnolias who had gone before me, knowing they would never have given up on something they'd dedicated themselves to accomplishing, I determined I would become a Steel Magnolia.

If I was going to become a Steel Magnolia, I was going to have to steel myself, which the dictionary defined as *"to steel one's self: to gain great strength and toughness or hardness."* So, I set about steeling myself. I steeled myself while working as a secretary; steeled myself while waiting for a divorce that seemed to never come; steeled myself to endure only seeing my children whenever Saren would allow; steeled myself against the misogyny and racism pulsating around me like a living organism reading to eat me alive; and steeled myself to fill out more law school applications even though I didn't have much hope of getting into law school because my LSAT scores were miserably low, I was a woman and few women were being admitted into law school, but I steeled myself and filled them out anyway.

I was beginning to understand that the best way to create change in the warped system of inequalities and prejudices wasn't necessarily to join another feminist group in Huntsville. Instead, I realized I would have to become the change I wanted to see. I would have to be the feminist no one liked; the one who spoke her mind like Mrs. Commanding General in New Mexico or Elaine back in our Paris Feminist group. Most importantly, I'd have to make myself better in whatever ways I could, step by slow step. In my present shabby state, I didn't have much to work with but I had to stay strong for my children; had to become that Steel Magnolia because I knew in my heart that one day we'd be living together again and I couldn't give up on that happening.

******

One of the many culture shocks that hit me the hardest when I returned to Alabama in the late seventies was the absolute unhidden racism and misogynistic attitudes towards women that still prevailed and were daily fare on television and in newspapers. I had long ago realized that my education in the South had been a narrowly focused, sexist, racist one, and I'd worked hard to change my perspectives. In the process of learning a broader, more inclusive perspective on these subjects, it had led me to see that children do need to "be carefully taught" as they're growing up, just as the lyrics from the song in *South Pacific* said.

But, what were we teaching our children? I had grown to believe through my own education in studying to become a teacher, through reading, research and observation, that children needed a very different kind of education than was being provided both in public and private schools. I was so passionate about what a good education for children needed to include, that before leaving Paris, together with a teacher from the children's school at Pershing Hall, we'd written a book called, *Discovering Myself: Lessons on Thinking and Feeling* which was a compilation of daily lesson plans designed for teachers to teach children such things as equality of the sexes, how to help children to recognize and express their feelings, and ways for them to explore their creativity through art and music, all with the intention to become more balanced and happy human beings while being aware of the needs of others.

Now, back in Alabama, whenever I watched television at the end of a long day at work, I began to keep track of various children's programs and how the roles of women and girls were being presented. I also began tracking numerous adult television programs to see how they treated relevant feminist issues such as sexism, gender and race. I began to fill a folder with these notes, clippings from local newspaper articles, documenting what local and national groups were doing and saying about women's roles, sexism, and children's issues.

Burning with a fiery urgency to help in the liberation of women and children from destructive stereotypes, I set off one day after work, folder of evidence tucked under my arm, foreshadowing my lawyer-self, I imagined hopefully, and headed to the local PBS television station where I planned to present my case to the program director for better local programming addressing these issues in a more balanced and equitable way. Driving my recent purchase of a used VW bug up the mountain overlooking Huntsville where all the television stations were located, I turned into the driveway belonging to PBS, which I would later discover was actually the driveway to the ABC television affiliate station.

Remembering my training in Southern Belle and Beauty Queen skills on how to make yourself appealing, I'd decided to go all out in trying to make myself look good. No jeans and black blouses. Nope! I was back in the South now and a women needing to be pretty was still a value that I decided to co-op for my own ends. *Sassy in silk but smart* was the look I was after. Wearing a beautiful purple silk blouse and paisley design silk skirt I'd bought in Paris, stylish shoes and gold jewelry, I acted every bit the role of someone who knows who she is and what she wants, my own imagined version of the heroine Martha Quest. It must be working, I thought, as the receptionist with a thick southern drawl like the one I'd worked hard for years to eliminate, immediately showed me into the Program Director's office. "Have a seat and Mr. Smith'll be right with y'all, okay?"

So far so good, I thought, pressing down my short skirt and re-positioning myself in the chair so my underwear didn't show. Oh, my god! Did I put on any underwear? Like my not-favorite Southern Belle heroine Scarlett O'Hara had so poignantly said after Rhett Butler told her to go to hell, "I'll think about that tomorrow." Nothing I could do about it now except keep my legs crossed! God! Women have to worry about so many things, don't they?

The moment Mr. Smith appeared in the doorway, I launched full on into my passionate presentation regarding the need for better local programming addressing women's and children's issues in a more balanced and equitable way. "My question is, Mr. Smith," I continued in my adrenalin-pumped, non-southern drawl voice but most certainly channeling my own recently re-discovered Steel Magnolia persona, "are these programs dumbing down kids or are they challenging them in positive, self-affirming ways through art, music and self-awareness processes and learning situations?"

About halfway through my impassioned testimony on behalf of women and children, I happened to glance at some of the plaques displayed on the wall. No way! This is an ABC affiliate network, not PBS? What the...? By now, it was too late, same as the no underwear situation. Besides, I reassured myself, the major networks also needed to straighten themselves up and get current with the way they presented women and children on the airways.

Buz, as Mr. Smith asked me to call him, must have caught some of the heated Steel Magnolia passion I was beaming out, because before I could catch my second breath and continue, he had called in the station manager, a gentleman named Mr. Dempsey. What followed was an act of destiny aimed at causing me to choke on all my prior condemnations of Southern men as being mostly variations of *Gone With the Wind's* Rhett Butler or even worse, Ashley

Wilkes. Right on the spot, the two Southern men of generous proportions offered me a job as co-anchor on a daily morning television talk show!

"But gentlemen," I stammered in pure amazement, praying that I was indeed wearing underwear because I felt sure I was going to wet myself, "I don't have any experience in front of the camera. I brought all this in," I said, holding up my stuffed folder of evidence, "to give to someone who already works here."

"You can learn everything you need to know in two weeks or less," the two men agreed, nodding to each other and dismissing my protests as nothing to be concerned about.

"What? I don't think ... I don't know ... this is all so sudden. Well, if you say so ... but I don't know, I mean ... this is most unexpected," I said, struggling to comprehend what they were saying, hardly daring to breathe, thinking I was surely going to faint. Oh, my god! How Southern Belle would that be? All we needed to complete this fantasy scene was someone to walk through the door with some mint julups! "When would you want me to start, I mean, if I did accept such a position, which I'm not sure I can?"

"As soon as possible."

Some fifteen minutes later, with feet only slightly touching the ground, I left the television station, clutching my evidence folder of notes and clippings in one hand and a piece of paper in the other with a date written down to report to work for my new job as co-anchor of a morning television talk show program on the ABC affiliate channel in Huntsville, Alabama! Well, kiss my Southern Belle butt, I said out loud, and with shaking hands, put the key in the ignition of my yellow, $1,000 Volkswagen the kids had named Herbie, pressed my shaking foot on the gas pedal and, still in a complete state of shock, let Herbie the magic car drive me back to my dark apartment with its dirty brown shag carpet and hand-me-down furnishings, all the while repeating, "I'm going to work in television! I'm going to work in television!"

Funny the things you can find in hell when you've more or less given up and least expect it.

THE STEEL MAGNOLIA
MEETS BILLY BOB

As it began to sink in that I actually *didn't* have any television experience, I started to sweat a little, well, quite a lot. It wasn't like I could call somebody up and ask, "Can you tell me how to be a co-anchor on television?" There weren't any books like *Television Hosting for Idiots!* I began to think I might have dug myself a spot in a graveyard for losers by accepting the television job. Maybe this was a test of humility, one that was showing me I should start coloring *inside* the lines of acceptable behavior for women and turn the job down. After hours of obsessive back and forth thinking, I decided that anything, even humiliating myself in front of possibly hundreds or maybe thousands of people would be better than remaining a secretary with a military defense contractor. After all, giving one's energy and talent building a military defense system for making war was the very thing I had criticized my husband for doing. Surely, I reasoned, staying on as secretary with a military contractor and not taking the TV job would make me a hypocrite. Bit of a stretch, but to take on a job that you know nothing about and one where lots of people would be witness to all your possible mistakes was daunting, or maybe just plain crazy. Meantime, I nervously gave my two weeks' notice at my secretarial job and received the blessings of my contractor boss who sent flowers.

******

"Come on in Miss Beene and meet your co-host, Billy Bob," Buz said, inviting me into his office on my first day of work at the television station.

Since I had never watched the morning show that I would be co-hosting with Billy Bob, I had no idea what he looked like. There, sitting on the edge of Buz's desk, like a rooster on his perch, sat Billy Bob decked out in cowboy attire with alligator boots and a cowboy hat to finish off the look.

Barely able to contain my shock, I walked over and we shook hands while he gave me the up and down once-over look.

I didn't know whether to laugh or cry. My co-host was a "thank-god-I'm-a-country-boy," guitar-pickin' Alabama-born-and-bred, red neck!

"First week you'll be observing your co-host, Billy Bob," Buz said as I sat motionless in the chair with the mounted deer head hanging directly above me. It was a Daniel-in-the-lion's-den moment of knowing that unlike Daniel this wasn't going to end well for me.

From the moment Buz introduced us, guitar-pickin' Billy Bob hated my guts! For over a decade he'd been filling up the early morning television airways in the northern part of Alabama and southern Tennessee with his two-hour show featuring his circle of cronies and other good-ole Southern, guitar-pickin' boys!

Billy Bob was outraged that the television suits were treating him without the dignity he deserved. Hiring a woman who was one of those feminist weirdos to do the show with him? He, Billy Bob, who'd been the big name at the station for over a decade? "How could y'all do this to me?" he'd asked, having stormed into the manager Mr. Dempsey's office after Buz had broken the news to him.

It was no surprise, then, that in less than a week's time on the set observing Billy Bob, we were all sitting together again in Mr. Dempsey's office. With cigarette ashes dropping on white shirts and bad ties, the big bosses carefully and forcefully outlined the reasons to Billy Bob for their strange and otherwise unfathomable action. "Ain't nobody watching your show anymore, Billy Bob! The advertisers are dropping like flies and don't want to sponsor you no more. You're old news. Done. Worn out. Nobody likes your music and guitar-pickin' anymore. Bottom line? The show ain't making us money. You either do the show with Miss Beene here or you got the highway."

Nobody ever said those good-ole boys aren't tough sons of bitches, right? I didn't know what to say as I watched the scene unfold, so I sat still and said nothing, knowing I was watching a facsimile of the war of the titans, Southern-style.

After that second meeting, Billy Bob tried to make my life hell. He didn't tell me anything about the show's set-up and ignored me as much as possible. It was the engineers, producers, camera people and numerous others on the set and at the station who got me up to speed and running. Billy Bob and I both got to choose the guests whom we would interview ... fifty/fifty. We weren't two days into the new show with me as his co-host when our differences exploded.

I had invited the sole woman on the Huntsville police force to come and demonstrate self-defense techniques for women. Before I could relish the thrill I felt that such great information to help women was being sent out on the airways, Billy Bob jumped in. "I don't reckon a woman would be needin' any of that self-defense stuff if she didn't dress in those mini-skirts girls are wearing these days. A girl's asking' for it if she dresses like a prostitute!" My policewoman guest and I ... mind you, the cameras are rolling since it was a live show ... were so shocked, we weren't able to speak. When I snapped to, my almost forgotten warrior woman, now having taken on the persona of a Southern Steel Magnolia, kicked into high gear and verbally set into my Alabama red neck co-host Billy Bob with a vengeance.

"Nobody says anything about men when they wear those ridiculous tight-assed polyester pants suits and strut down the street like peacocks," I said, emphasizing the "cocks" in peacocks. "Nobody accuses them of wanting some, do they? No, they do not! Women should be able to wear anything they want without the threat of rape or verbal abuse from pistol-toting, ignorant male chauvinist pigs! And furthermore, I think you owe the police officer and myself an apology!"

"Cut to commercial. Cut to commercial!" the show's director yelled. Then, more yelling on the set, which had by now become a scene of total chaos. It was a call-in show for the first hour of the two-hour show, and suddenly the phone lines lit up like a Christmas tree! During the extra-long commercial break, we got enough control of ourselves to finish the show.

The moment the show ended, the director called out over the studio set, "Billy Bob and Miss Beene, you're both wanted in the Manager's office."

I knew they were going to fire me, but I didn't care. Billy Bob deserved all he'd gotten from me. I would take back nothing! I deliberately threw my shoulders back as I marched towards Mr. Dempsey's office, biting my lip, determined not to cry. Dammit, I thought, I can't cry. No crying. No crying. I repeated all the way to his office on first floor, plopping down on his large, fake-leather chair, like a schoolgirl who's been sent to the principal's office and knows she's in trouble.

Once we were all seated in Mr. Dempsey's office, I began to squirm thinking that my life had annoyingly begun to resemble that of Alice in Wonder Land when she'd remarked that her adventures down the rabbit hole were "getting curiouser and curiouser."

"Curiouser and curiouser" indeed! Without a prelude or any warning, the bosses exclaimed, wearing what could only be described as ear-to-ear Cheshire cat grins, "We loved the show!"

Billy Bob and I both did a double take, chiming in unison, "You loved the show?" Before Jerry Springer and his ilk were spawned and dirtying up the airways, ole Billy Bob and I had pre-shadowed their kind of journalism and its soon-to-be rapid rise to popularity and success. Nothing to be proud of in my mind but it apparently had appealed to some in the viewing audience.

"All those phone lines lighting up mean people are watching the show. If people are watching, then advertisers will place ads and money will come rolling in! Just keep it up and don't kill one another! Also, Miss Beene, just to remind you, we're in the South. So, watch your language."

Daily for almost four weeks, the good-ole Alabama boy Billy Bob and I battled it out, fussing and fuming and yelling at one another over topics ranging from what women should or shouldn't wear, whether women were capable enough to work outside the home and if they did, what about the children they left home to fend for themselves and who should be cooking the meals anyway?

One Friday morning after we'd finished a particularly combative show during which I'd challenged one of Billy Bob's racist remarks, he yanked off his mike, and stormed off the set, boot heels clicking like he was getting ready to rope and ride in a rodeo. "That's it for me. I'm gonna go see Dempsey right now and give him a choice. Either you or me has gotta go and I think you know who he's gonna choose. So, better pack your things sweetheart, cause your time is up!"

The phone was ringing when I walked into my tiny, peanut-size office. It was the manager's secretary Ellen, the lovely young woman with the honey-filled Southern drawl. "Mr. Dempsey wants to see y'all right away in his office."

Well, I guess I never imagined I'd make it this long, I thought as I made the dead-woman-walking march to Dempsey's office.

He motioned for me to be seated in the chair I hated most, the one directly underneath the mounted deer head.

"Billy Bob came to see me this morning."

"Yes, I know."

"He wants me to boot you off the show. Says he's been doing the show for over ten years and doesn't want a woman on there who's gonna tell him what to do or how to think."

"Yes, I know."

"Well, Buz and I have come to a decision."

Here it comes, I thought, holding my breath. I'm going to get the boot. Back I go to the secretary job or maybe worse the typing pool with Golda Meir.

"We want you to take over the show. Probably give it a new name. You can come up with one that works. We'll get you a new set and a new producer. You can plan it all and have anybody on you want, just as long as it's a good show and people watch it. The ratings have increased since you've been on. People are calling in and people are talking. They like all the arguing the two of you do, but Billy Bob don't want you on, so we had to let him go."

"You did what?" I exclaimed in disbelief.

"Look, we need a change around here," Mr. Dempsey was saying, "like I said when we hired you. People like to see some new faces and hear some new things once in a while. Keeps them interested and tuned in. Good television. Good ratings. Are you up for it?"

"I ... I, well, I ... yes. Absolutely. Yes. Yes. I can do it. Yes."

"Good. We'll set you up in a new office. Well, actually, it'll be Billy Bob's old office. Anyway, it's bigger and it'll give you a place to talk to the guests before the show and to make all the arrangements for people you want on."

"Okay. Great. Great. Beginning next Monday? Great."

When I left Mr. Dempsey's office, as one might imagine, you could have knocked me over with a feather! What a surprise! It was unbelievable! Just when you think you've got someone pegged and know what they're gonna do, they go and do the opposite. These good ole Southern boys were whipping my butt when it came to thinking I knew what made them tick or what they would say or do next.

Later, after work, I went to a local bar with a few friends from the television station. Billy Bob was there and drunk as a skunk. As soon as he saw me, he staggered over and started yelling, "I'm gonna get even with you, you little bitch. You stole my show, ruined my television career and my life."

I felt bad for Billy Bob and didn't know what to say since no one could have been more shocked at the outcome than myself. After a few minutes of his bombastic remarks, I thought it best if I left, so I said goodbye to my friends while Billy Bob raged on.

******

Would I miss Billy Bob? Would anyone miss Billy Bob? I didn't know but having a co-anchor, even someone as outrageously and culturally offensive as Billy Bob, meant there was another person to share the two-hour's worth of screen time. Now, it was all on me. There was a lot of pressure when doing live studio shows because if you made a mistake or something got screwed up, there was no way to stop the camera rolling, go back and film a re-take. Doing a live show meant whatever happened, happened and that's what the audience would see.

As anyone knows who's taken a risk, when you're about to go into a new situation where you're in charge and you know next to nothing, you have to improvise until you can figure out what's going on. You're like a deer in headlights but instead of freezing up you have to learn to push fear aside and move quickly and with confidence, maybe pull a few rabbits out of that magician's hat you wore last Halloween when you dressed up like a magician and knew you weren't a magician but you acted like one.

Calling on all my faculties, I tried to remember any remotely similar experiences from my past. I knew from my acting experience in Little Theater productions and musical performances that when you're on stage, it's not enough to know your lines and music perfectly because for the whole thing to come together, you've got to respond and interact with the other actors there with you as though it were your first time, like a virgin, so to speak; and you have to act every time like it's your first time. Being fresh and present in every moment was the only way to build a creative tension between all the players, and once that happened, the audience could feel it and participate in it. Without that tension between the players and the audience, the words or music would become stale, flat ... like listening to a child repeating her multiplication tables.

In fact, there were many similarities between acting live on stage and performing on television, which turned out to be a bonus for me in getting my television hostess legs. On stage same as on live television, there couldn't be any "dead" time, meaning not a single moment when there wasn't some action happening or someone wasn't talking.

Talking on camera. Is it easy? It looks easy but it takes a while to make it look easy. I quickly learned that for me to talk on camera with ease and without freezing up, and most importantly, to help the people I interviewed not to freeze up, was to ask questions and then completely immerse myself in their answers; to listen so intently and fervently that they felt my interest was genuine and that whatever they were saying I found it to be absolutely amazing! People relaxed and opened up; often, after the show, they'd thank me. "I can't believe I was so relaxed and did that much talking."

Where did that bit of savvy communication/listening skill come from? Directly out of the Southern Belle's playbook; i.e., listen in rapt attention at what the person likes to talk about, most especially if it's a man; then answer with the greatest interest and astonishment at their answers; play to his strengths or weaknesses; and never let on that you're smarter. I would never have thought there was anything I wanted to take from the Southern Belle's playbook but being back in the South again, and finding those same insipid behaviors and platitudes still being valued in women, I was learning how to re-interpret them in a way that worked for me; learning how to give them my own spin, proving that in the end, there were a few good things to be found in the Southern Belle's playbook once you figured out how to adapt them to your own sensibilities.

The biggest difficulty? ...how to break for commercial when guests were talking. Since childhood I'd had it drilled into my head that *it's rude to interrupt other people when they're talking.* But I found a role model in Barbara

Walters who was quite good at interrupting people when interviewing them even during her early days as a journalist. She may even have perfected that style of interviewing.

******

Just as the station manager had promised, I was free to plan every show's content and the people who would appear.

I renamed the show, "Good Morning Huntsville," re-designed the set and chose new furniture. The show's producer had a teenage son who hung around the engineer's booth a lot. One day he asked me, "Why don't you get some cool music for the introduction to the show and at the end when the credits are rolling?"

"What do you suggest?"

"Fleetwood Mac's got a new album," he said. I'd never heard of Fleetwood Mac because I'd been living in France for the last 4½ years and knew no popular singers. He played their album for me and I loved it, finally choosing two favorites, *Rhiannon* and *I Don't Want to Know* to play during the rolling credits.

Now, we had some cool music! We did away with the telephone call-in part of the show; and best of all, the entire re-do was a team effort and I felt the support of everyone. It was like all the best times of genuine team effort by the Paris feminist groups when we'd worked together to create a successful event.

My first solo show without Billy Bob was perhaps one of my best. There were four guests: a clown from Ringling Brothers Circus currently performing in Huntsville; a talented actor who was starring in the latest Little Theater production; a handsome cowboy who was traveling and performing at rodeos with his fast-drawing six-shooter; and a Zen Master from San Francisco who was visiting the local Zendo and giving Buddhist teachings ... someone I would meet again in the future. It was the kind of diversity that was to be my trademark. Everything went smoothly and I was walking on cloud nine, a place I'd almost forgotten existed.

Especially rewarding for me over time was the number of women from all walks of life, from artists, homemakers, psychologists, teachers, to doctors, who appeared on the show to share their ideas of ways to help women empower themselves.

THE BUTTERFLY EFFECT

Nine months into the new job at the television station and things were going well. One day Mr. Dempsey the station manager approached me with a big grin on his face.

"Get ready for the big interview," he said excitedly.

"Who is it?" I asked, thinking nothing could be more wonderful than the recent interview I'd done with television show *Star Trek's* Lt. Uhura, Nichelle Nicols who was in town visiting the Marshall Space Flight Center to learn more about their astronaut program.

"Governor George Wallace is coming to Huntsville and is making himself available for interviews. Try not to insult him, okay? You'll have ten minutes."

Everybody knew who Governor George Wallace was. When elected governor of Alabama in 1963, he had delivered his infamous inaugural speech, declaring "Segregation now, segregation tomorrow, segregation forever!" That same year he had stood in the doorway of the University of Alabama, refusing to let two black students into the building to attend school, even though segregation had been declared illegal. Federal Marshalls were ordered in and Wallace backed down, but his racial message was clear and had been broadcast for the world to see.

I wasn't sure I could do an interview with him and stay professional which meant not insulting him. "What the hell, George? What's with your crazy-mad racism? Get over yourself!" But I'd been warned to keep it cordial and anyway, confrontational interviews with your guests weren't a thing yet.

Security around Wallace was tight ever since he'd been shot and crippled by an attempted assassin's bullet in 1972, which left him restricted to a wheel chair. He would be accompanied to the television station by a squad of county sheriff's cars and would be escorted into the studio through the downstairs entryway to accommodate his wheel chair and for added safety measures.

I positioned myself at the back entrance to greet Wallace; fully aware that my worst interviews were with politicians because they always ignored questions and simply used the *free* airtime to recite their political views. I expected nothing less from Governor Wallace, but had dutifully prepared questions, and since it was going to be a taped interview for playback at a later time, that took a little pressure off.

It's probably not going to be fit to air, I told myself as I nervously paced back and forth by the entrance door waiting for the Governor's arrival; but it's my job and I've got to be professional. I can ask one good question and he'll go off, spouting his racist philosophy and then it'll be over. Okay, I can do this.

Everything was already set up in the studio to record the interview. Once Governor Wallace had wheeled his wheelchair onto the studio set, the producer pinned the mike on his suit lapel, we did the sound test, and after asking the Governor if he was ready, the cameras started rolling and the interview began.

"Welcome Governor Wallace. We're happy to have you visit us here in Huntsville today. Can you tell us a little about the purpose of your visit?" I asked in a cordial tone, then sat back and waited for the man to talk. Quite unexpectedly, Wallace turned out to be a man of amazing charisma; a "big" presence even though seated in a wheelchair, a position that might have been perceived as diminutive. Like a Baptist minister on fire for the Lord, he spoke with authority and passion, gesturing boldly from his seated position. I had expected a "lesser" man, not because he was in a wheelchair but because of his small-minded, racist views. I watched, however, as his words and presence seemed to draw people to him for seemingly no apparent reason other than they wanted to sit in his aura and drink in some of his juju that made him seem larger than life. The ten minutes flew by and the interview was over. No confrontation. No arguing. Just simple information being delivered on the upcoming event he'd be attending in Huntsville.

After saying a moderately sincere "thank you Governor Wallace for the interview and goodbye," I returned to my office where I sat thinking that the Governor hadn't been the complete jerk I'd thought he would be. Was it because of his juju?

Years later I learned that George Wallace did an amazing thing. He recanted his prejudicial attitude towards blacks and actually apologized. "I was wrong to stand in the doorway of the University of Alabama and block the black students from entering and I'm sorry for that," he'd told the press. Then he did a second amazing thing. He went to black civil rights activists and church leaders and told them he didn't want to be remembered as a racist and asked them for forgiveness!

******

After two years of fighting a relentless battle over custody and everything else, Saren had finally agreed to a divorce because he'd gotten a new civilian job in Washington, D.C. and had to move immediately. The settlement gave permanent custody of Marie to me and Alex to his father.

"A girl might need her mother more than a son does, so you can have custody of Marie," he'd said, as though the children were pawns on a chess board instead of little human beings who had feelings and needs. It was an unfair agreement financially as well. "We can keep going here if you want to pursue getting more of your savings or an alimony payment, but I don't know how much longer you're prepared to continue this thing," my lawyer had advised.

"I don't want alimony," I told him. "Let's just get this thing over. It's gone on too long as it is."

"Done," he agreed. "I'll get those papers over to your soon to be ex-husband to sign before he changes his mind again."

******

As the weight and drama of the divorce began to lift, calling to an end an exhausting two years of back-and-forth haggling, I had slowly begun to piece my life back together to become the person I had long imagined I might be again: caring, interested in matters of spirit, loving mother, dedicated to social justice and change, and a Steel Magnolia woman who liked pleasurable things and did not suffer fools!

It was a bittersweet comeback from the land of the dead, however, because as I literally began to feel better about myself, I remained brokenhearted that Saren and I had ended our commitment to one another amidst such pettiness and vindictiveness. The dark ending to such a magnificent beginning cast a long shadow over our lives, especially the children who suffered most from such a hurtful parting of their parents.

Our relationship reflected a deeper wounding, however, than arguments over war and peace, or what rules to obey or challenge. Weren't we, like everyone else, in various stages of recovery from Western civilization? Weren't we all in recovery from an outdated and destructive cultural paradigm that pitted men and women against one another in order to control the narrative that benefited the few on top; an outdated cultural narrative that pitted one race or one religion against another; that promoted and reveled in top-down or power-over-others style of leadership and of living together? Hadn't we all knowingly and un-knowingly cooperated with the patriarchal model of men on top, usually white men, for so long that many of us had forgotten who we were and, in our forgetfulness, had brought death and destruction to the very thing that had given us life and sustained us: Mother Earth and by extension, the feminine aspect in all of us?

As hurtful as the ending of my marriage was, it reflected the deep love I had once shared with another person; a bond that nevertheless had to be broken in order for us to become the individuals we were meant to be, each choosing a path that was more suited to the pursuit of our soul's destiny or as psychologist James Hillman called it, one's Soul Code.

******

During this time, I was still burdened with a lingering desire to make my mother proud of me, but that effort also came to a shattering halt in my aunt's kitchen not long after my father's death. Mother was up from Georgia visiting the family and to put flowers on my dad's grave in Huntsville where many family members are buried. We were sharing a lovely Southern dinner of fried chicken, mashed potatoes, green beans, gravy and biscuits. Mom had made one of her spectacular caramel cakes, which she was so rightly famous for. As we sat around the dinner table, enjoying the feast, the conversation turned to the success I was having with my television show and how people were talking about it, saying good things.

Mother listened for a few moments; poking at the food on her plate before speaking. "Well, I sure don't know what all the fuss is about. The show's not such a big deal and probably won't ever be. Marjorie certainly isn't making all that much money either."

Everyone around the table became silent, dumbfounded by the unexpected cruelty of her remarks. It was like a replay of her response years earlier after I'd won the town's *Miss Warner Robins Beauty Contest* and would be going on as a competitor in the *Miss Georgia Beauty Pageant*, when she'd told my sponsor that she was surprised I'd won.

The caramel cake was brought out and presented as an omen of goodwill, one might say, but it was too late. I did learn a very valuable lesson that day, however; I learned that I would probably never be able to please my mother and that nothing I would ever do in my life would be good enough to win her approval. I finally got it! With that deep and painful recognition, I was set free from thinking I had to do things to please her or gain her approval. Instead of a great piece of caramel cake that day, she'd given me my freedom, the very best gift of all. It was my Martha Quest moment, the time when I, like the heroine from Doris Lessing's novel was released from her doubts and need for approval. It was the moment when a butterfly's wings fluttering in Alabama caused a tsunami in Paris, or perhaps it was the other way around.

******

The wild woman, dope-smoking, sexually flamboyant person Saren had accused me of being during the hearing in the Florida Judge's courtroom had finally become a reality. I'd made a lot of friends in Huntsville and was enjoying my social networking, the marijuana-smoking parties and the new sexual independence that many of us exercised during the 70s. I had a delicious fling with a black man from the television station, admittedly to shock all the white suits, and with a woman who worked for a local radio station, as well as many others whom I was attracted to. With music of Elton John, Pink Floyd, the Eagles, Jackson Browne or Fleetwood Mac blaring in the background while marijuana joints were being passed around, we laughed and talked and sang and ate and had a lot of sex. And it was fun! I was smiling again, almost as much as I was crying.

Shortly after my divorce was finally granted, I had come home from work one day and was absentmindedly leafing through the mail. There it was. A letter from Golden Gate Law School in San Francisco, one of several law schools where I'd applied. With shaking hands, I tore open the envelope.

"Marie. Marie. Come down here!" I yelled a few moments later at my daughter who was upstairs in her room doing homework.

"What is it mom?" she asked, peering down the stairs.

"I've just been accepted into law school. Your mother's going to be a lawyer. Your dope-smoking, sexually perverted, unfit feminist mother's going to be a lawyer!"

******

I felt terribly conflicted the next day when I went to work. In spite of my love for the television job, I would be giving notice to leave. Having my own television show had given me a purpose and a venue for my creativity and it had also provided an avenue for other women's voices to be heard. The opportunity had shown up in my life during a time when I felt I was a big failure. When I walked into Mr. Dempsey's office holding my acceptance letter to law school, just as I'd held up that original folder of clippings and notes the first time we'd met, I sat down in the chair underneath the mounted deer head. But today, I didn't mind the disgusting deer head. In fact, I didn't even notice it, or maybe I waved. Who knows?

"Here, I just got this," I said with a mixture of timidity and ecstasy, handing him my acceptance letter to read like one might hand something to a parent hoping for their approval. To my utter amazement, he was excited for me. "Go be a lawyer," he said. "You'll make a good one, and then come on back to Alabama. We could use a few good lawyers." He also encouraged me to apply for unemployment insurance while I was looking for part-time work and going to law school. "I'll approve all the paperwork." Amazed again at the kindness from such an unexpected source, I left the television station; walking on air like I'd done the day I was hired.

Driving home after work on my last day, I threw open my apartment door and yelled upstairs to my daughter, "Get packing, Marie! We're moving to California!"

Later that evening, as we sat on the patio eating dinner, I began to cry. Marie, who was now almost 12 years old, put her plate down and walked over to give me a hug. "It's gonna be okay mom."

"But what about your brother? He's not gonna be with us in California," I sobbed.

"Maybe he will one day," she said, trying to reassure me.

I looked at my young and very wise daughter who would soon start her moon time and realized how much she had grown during the two-years since our leaving Paris.

"You are so grown up now," I said, hugging her tightly. "And soon you'll start your moon time. Have I told you about that?"

"Yes, mom. About a hundred times," she sighed. "I know I'll bleed once a month and it's a blessing not a curse ... okay?"

We both laughed. It was wonderful to have my daughter living with me again, sharing our laughter and happiness. Soon we'd be heading out to a new life ... one that within a few years' time would see her brother joining us, not in California but in the Land of Enchantment where we would embark on another new chapter of our lives as a family ... and how life in another fifteen years would bring us all together in Hawaii, coming full circle to where we'd begun as a family on another small island in the South Pacific, where stars had guided our future journeys and beauty walked before us.

ACKNOWLEDGMENTS

How to acknowledge the many shoulders of those I have stood upon during this journey of writing a memoir of my early life? Too many to name individually so please know that I hold you in my heart when I speak of the following groups.

To my ancestors who walked the hills and forest lands of Ireland and Scotland and through our blood connection, bequeathed to me the art, magic and necessity of storytelling. I salute those ancestors whose arms rocked the babies and sang the lullabies that shaped their souls; to the ancestors that hoed and planted the gardens and fields that fed the hungry mouths of kith and kin; to my ancient women kin who knew the importance of giving praise to the Earth, who built fires to celebrate the turning of the seasons, who danced and sang together; to those that sat hearth-side and wove the stories so's everyone had a magic garment to wear as they passed over into another time and place.

To my Southern family in the Deep South who mostly never understood how it was that such a nice Christian girl could become a wild woman but who nevertheless gave me a place to lay my head, food to eat and supported me through difficult cycles of my life with love and utmost caring. Thank you. I am so grateful.

To my own children who signed up for this journey a long time ago. To them I owe my life, my heart and my everlasting love.

To all the teachers and mentors along the way ... to both those who sought to defeat me and to those who gave me succor, instilled courage and heaped me with enough love to go to the stars and back.

To the amazing men, friends and lovers, who have loved me and whom I've loved back. Thank you for all the lessons you taught me, especially to the men whose shining character and intellect showed me both a strength and a new understanding of what it means to be a male hero.

And, where would I be without all the amazing women who've graced my life? You taught me everything I know. To those feminists in Paris who first showed me so much about myself and gave me strength to open my eyes to what a woman's journey is inside the patriarchy and what "sisterhood is powerful" means. Thank you.

To all the women who've been in my writing classes and retreats over the past decade. You taught me what it means to open up your heart on the page and fearlessly share your deepest truths. You taught me through the bravery of telling your stories how unique each of us are and through the expression of your creativity in words and art-making, left us all in awe. All of you blessed me with a deeper understanding of the phrase "we are all one."

To all my non-human teachers, allies and friends: Chartres cathedral, the Black Madonna, all the flowers and gardens past and present, to the crystals, stones, rocks and drums that have shared their stories and opened my heart to the invisible realms, and to all my furry friends and companions through the years, I am grateful.

With Aloha!

A special thanks to Suzanne Canja & Dawn Prince for financially supporting me while I wrote my first memoir draft many years ago and took it to my first ever writing conference at the Ritz Carlton on Maui!

**And to Denise Weaver Ross, who has helped me midwife this my third book. In gratitude to you Denise for your patience & talent.*

1. Baby Marjorie with her parents
2. Marjorie at 4 years old
3. Being crowned *Miss Warner Robins*
4. Beauty walk as *Miss Warner Robins*
5. Wedding Under the Sabers
6. Author's children Kwajalein Island

7. Marshalese Maid, Jai, with author's son
8. Marjorie and children in Alabama
9. Marjorie graduating from
   New Mexico State University
10. Children at White Sands National
    Monument
11. Marjorie and children in Paris

ABOUT THE AUTHOR

Marjorie is an author, writing coach and writing teacher. She has been teaching memoir and creative writing classes for over a decade and has held annual writing retreats at such venues as Ghost Ranch, Abiquiu and Mabel Dodge Luhan Inn in Taos, NM.

She holds a BS degree in English from New Mexico State University, an MA degree in Whole Systems Design from Antioch, Seattle and a PhD/ABD in Women's Studies from Union Institute & University, Ohio.

Throughout her varied career she has made it a priority to focus on helping women come into full awareness of who they are by re-connecting with the essential women's ways of knowing the world through their bodies, minds and spirit, as well as through their creative powers of art and writing.

She presently makes her home on the island of Maui with her two lovely furry cats and is busy at work on writing her second memoir: "Hopi Odyssey" that describes her experiences as a teacher at the All-Indian High School in New Mexico and her many spiritual experiences with the Hopi Indians of Arizona.

Connect with her at WritersAdventure.com.

www.ingramcontent.com/pod-product-compliance
Lightning Source LLC
Chambersburg PA
CBHW020435130626
46549CB00001B/153